Psychodynamic Therapy

Psychodynamic Therapy

Conceptual and Empirical Foundations

STEVEN K. HUPRICH

Routledge
Taylor & Francis Group
NEW YORK AND LONDON

Published 2009 by Routledge
605 Third Avenue, New York, NY 10017
4 Park Square, Milton Park, Abingdon, Oxon OX14 4RN

Routledge is an imprint of the Taylor & Francis Group, an informa business

Library of Congress Cataloging-in-Publication Data

Huprich, Steven Ken, 1966-
Pyschodynamic therapy : conceptual and empirical foundations / Steven Huprich.
p. ; cm.
Includes bibliographical references and index.
ISBN 978-0-8058-6400-7 (hardbound : alk. paper) -- ISBN 978-0-8058-6401-4 (pbk. : alk. paper)
1. Psychodynamic psychotherapy. 2. Psychoanalysis. I. Title.
[DNLM: 1. Psychoanalytic Theory. 2. Mental Disorders--therapy. 3. Psychoanalytic Therapy--methods. WM 460 H958p 2008]

RC489.P72H87 2008
616.89'14--dc22 2008016083

ISBN 13: 978-0-8058-6401-4 (pbk)

Contents

Preface

One of the best experiences of my professional development was my training and experiences on my predoctoral internship at the State University of New York (SUNY) Health Science Center in Syracuse (now called Upstate Medical University). A major drawing point of the internship was the program's emphasis on psychodynamic training and the empirical support for psychoanalytic ideas and theory. The program's training director, Dr. Roger Greenberg, and his colleague, Dr. Seymour Fisher, had recently published an updated edition of their book, *Freud Scientifically Reappraised: Testing the Theories and Therapy* (Greenberg & Fisher, 1996).* My doctoral program had limited opportunities for exposure and training in psychodynamic theory and therapy, so the opportunity to train in Syracuse was very exciting.

My year-long instruction did not leave me disappointed. All of my supervisors and instructors had considerable experience and interest in psychodynamic psychotherapy and a strong respect for a broad and diverse orientation to psychoanalytic and psychodynamic theory. They also were highly invested in a scientific understanding of clinical psychology, which made for an intellectually stimulating work environment. One of the many influential instructors was Dr. Dennis Bogin, a local psychologist who taught and supervised at the internship, along with maintaining a successful private practice. Dr. Bogin was highly skilled in working with patients, especially those with long-standing character pathology. He could quickly formulate an understanding of their defensive structure, object relations, ego functioning, and the corresponding impairment in drive expression. For relatively inexperienced professionals, such as us interns, we were amazed with the

* The first volume is titled *The Scientific Credibility of Freud's Theories and Therapy* (Columbia University Press, New York, 1985).

precision with which he assessed and understood these patients and offered invaluable guidance in treating patients successfully.

From this experience, I found myself even more interested in the application of psychoanalytic and psychodynamic theory to clinical work. Over the past 9 years, I have maintained a clinical practice, along with supervising many doctoral students in their therapy and assessments of patients. My students, their patients, and my own patients have taught me much as they shared their inner-life experiences and the challenges they faced in their lives' journeys or in their experience of working with patients. Countless books, articles, and chapters, as well as fruitful consultation with psychoanalytic colleagues in Ann Arbor, Michigan, have all shaped my firm conviction that psychoanalytic and psychodynamic theory, broadly conceptualized, has more to offer clinicians and patients than the numerous other theories and approaches to psychotherapy that exist today. In fact, as I highlight in this book, psychoanalytic and psychodynamic ideas are found in many other theoretical and therapeutic models and offer a unified explanation for the mechanisms underlying much psychopathology and corresponding therapeutic change. Contrary to what is flagrantly misconstrued and taught as relic and historical artifact, Sigmund Freud's ideas and their evolution offer a comprehensive, very useful framework from which clinical psychology and psychiatry can benefit. As these ideas have been applied for over a century to improve the lives of real people, clinical science and practice can and will benefit from ongoing attention to this paradigm. *Time Magazine* (November 29, 1993) had a picture of Freud on its cover and asked the question, "Is Freud really dead?" The answer to that question is a resounding "no."

The opportunity to write this book was rather serendipitous. During a phone call to former Lawrence Erlbaum and Associates editor Steven Rutter, I was asked if I knew of anyone with interests in psychodynamic theory. I indicated that I did, and Steve presented the opportunity to write this textbook. He indicated that his market research led him to identify a real need for a book on psychodynamic therapy that (1) demonstrates that psychodynamic ideas are very much alive and utilized in clinical work today; (2) highlights how there is strong empirical support for psychodynamic theory and therapy; and (3) exemplifies how psychodynamic therapy is related to other approaches to psychotherapy. Without hesitation, Steve offered me the opportunity to write the book, and it did not take any work on his part to my agreeing to undertake the task. Once Erlbaum Publishers was sold to Taylor & Francis, I had the opportunity to work with George Zimmar, who was helpful and supportive of the task I had begun earlier and could now finish with him.

In preparation for writing this book, there are numerous people who have been helpful and influential: Harvey Falit, MD, and the Michigan Psychoanalytic Institute; John Porcerelli, PhD; James Hansell; PhD; V. Barry Dauphin, PhD; Robert Cohen, PhD; Michael Shulman, PhD; Joshua Ehrlich, PhD; Julie Jaffee Nagel, PhD; J. Stuart Ablon, PhD; Jack and Kerry Kelly Novick, PhDs; Richard Summers, MD and the Residency Education Subcommittee of the University and Medical Education Committee of the American Psychoanalytic Association; Mark Solms, PhD; and John Knapp, PhD and Eastern Michigan University's Faculty Research Fellowship Award for Spring–Summer 2007. I also am appreciative of the American Psychoanalytic Association's Reading List that was prepared by Robin Renders, PhD, and Lisa Mellman, MD, which proved to be a useful reference tool. One of my research assistants at Eastern Michigan, Ann Wilson, deserves a lot of credit, too, for her enthusiastic and prompt attention to my requests for copying and obtaining articles and book chapters.

Finally, I want to recognize the unwavering and remarkable love and support provided by the love of my life—my wife, Donna. Although she occasionally joked about my having the summer "off from work" while I was writing this book, she offered me her genuine support, encouragement, and praise for the task of writing a book such as this throughout a 4-month period. I truly am grateful to have a wonderful wife and life situation that has allowed me to do something that I love as much as this.

1

Introduction

Patients enter psychotherapy for a host of reasons, and, with few exceptions, almost all who seek treatment do so because they cannot find a way to solve their psychological problems. In other words, they are blocked from knowing or understanding something about themselves in a different way from that which they currently do. They come to treatment believing that such knowledge or insight would allow them to be more satisfied or to live in a more gratifying or satisfying way.

It also is not uncommon to hear many patients say, "I know that I should not feel this way," or "This obviously is bad for me," yet they are unable to make the kinds of changes that ultimately would reduce their suffering and increase their sense of well-being. Other individuals may not be aware that what they are thinking, feeling, or experiencing or what is motivating them is problematic. For instance, the man who is successful yet is despised by his coworkers may refuse to consider the possibility that his needs for control and his perfectionism are what alienate him from them. He may well believe that his lifelong work ethic, attention to detail, and "Midwestern values" that were instilled in him and his siblings account for his success and that it is others who need to adapt to him, not vice versa. But, as he becomes more depressed over the lack of friends in his life, he may attempt to ingratiate himself to others by taking them out to lunch or buying them a drink after work, which only increases their sense that he is trying to control or manipulate how they feel. He may have the same attitude in his social life, which he may find dissatisfying for much of the same reasons.

In virtually all patients, it also is the case that there is an element of interpersonal relatedness that becomes part of the focus of treatment. Ask any therapist, and she or he will likely state that it is difficult, if not impossible, to separate how a person's reasons for being in psychotherapy are not related in some way to the person's interpersonal relationships. Interpersonal relatedness evokes emotional states, ideas, wishes, fantasies, desires, and impulses to act (or not act) toward another person or group of people. Psychological difficulties do not occur in isolation, although the suffering that many patients experience makes it seem as if they are alone, as if they cannot be understood, or that their unhappiness may be representative of a more severe problem. Additionally, if their problems are brought more to the surface, many patients fear that they would be disliked, disapproved of, shunned, humiliated, or rejected rather than helped with their pain. For instance, if a married man's fantasies of being sexually involved with another man were to be made known, they may lead to feelings of disgust and a possible separation or divorce from his wife. Thus, even in those problems that seem most private or hard to experience, how the problem interfaces with other people in the patient's life takes on salience and meaning.

Good therapists know that effective therapy is based on a theory of personality and psychopathology that has substantial explanatory power and applicability to people's lives. Without theory driving the applied action of therapy, treatment often proceeds in a haphazard way. In this situation, therapy can be ineffective and potentially harmful to the patient. Now over 100 years old, psychoanalytic and psychodynamic theories have stood the test of time. They have considerable explanatory power and applicability, even in a climate in which brief and (empirically supported) treatments are preferred. It is the focus of this text to review psychoanalytic and psychodynamic theories and their application to various kinds of psychotherapy.

So, to begin to understand psychoanalytic and psychodynamic therapy and the theory it is based on, it might be helpful to examine some case studies and to review the major tenets of psychoanalytic theory to see their therapeutic applications, after which I discuss them in the context of psychodynamic theory, hoping to draw attention to what has become a very effective and highly relevant approach to clinical work.

The Case of Mr. Shelby

Mr. Shelby was a 19-year-old high school dropout who worked for his family's restaurant. He was referred by his parents, with whom he lived, because they believed he needed help with the severe bouts of panic that had come upon him about 8 months earlier for no apparent reason. Though he was legally an adult and responsible for his own treatment, he came to see the psychologist only with his parents and at their insistence. In the first session, the therapist learned from his parents that Mr. Shelby was rather quiet as a child, one who seemed to keep to himself often. His interactions with his family were generally good, and even as he entered into his teenage years he tended to favor playing with cousins who were in preschool or just entering the primary grades. Mr. Shelby had few friends in school, though as he aged, the friends he made had interests in computer games. These games had aggressive and violent themes, in which characters were killed; however, they could be "resurrected" through a spell cast upon them by another character in the game. As a child, Mr. Shelby was not particularly violent, although on one occasion when he was 12 he became so angry with his parents that he broke a lamp. Neither his parents nor he could recall why he became so upset, yet he was punished, which all remembered as having a strong effect on curtailing his behavior. At the time therapy began, Mr. Shelby showed very little affect, except for some disdain toward his parents, particularly his loquacious and domineering mother, who had made him come to see a psychologist.

Mr. Shelby stated that he dropped out of high school when he was 17 because he did not like it. Later, it was learned that Mr. Shelby was becoming very anxious at school and did not want to be there for fear of how he might behave (e.g., getting anxious, red in the face). His parents conceded to his wish, and shortly thereafter Mr. Shelby began working at the restaurant, initially clearing tables but then starting to work as a waiter. His parents stated that he did well with customers, despite some initial anxiety.

About 1 year before, Mr. Shelby's favorite uncle had died suddenly. He attended the funeral but said he did not cry. Two months after the uncle's death, Mr. Shelby was leaving his home to go to work when he became very anxious. He felt faint and had many symptoms of panic disorder. Upon getting into his car, he felt nauseated, vomited, and felt unable to go to work. These symptoms happened several times and generalized once to when he was going to a movie with a friend. Over the past few months, the symptoms had subsided somewhat, but Mr. Shelby continued to have anxious feelings and was highly concerned about leaving the house.

The Case of Ms. Murdock

Ms. Murdock was a highly successful 43-year-old businesswoman who came to therapy after suddenly breaking up with her long-term male partner (David) of 6 years. Ms. Murdock was rather sad, lacked energy, and could not seem to get over David's sudden departure from their home. Several years prior, she had been married to another man, Nathan, for about 3 years. The marriage ended after they seemed to "grow apart." Again, this relationship was hard for her to get over. She described Nathan as needing much support and reassurance, particularly when others did not appreciate his hard work. David was unlike Nathan in that he was outgoing and free-spirited and liked to be the "life of the party." Particularly upsetting in her relationship with David was his capricious spending and gambling. Ms. Murdock reported that David spent thousands of dollars on goods and products that he wanted and had lost about $2500 in gambling over the past 6 years.

Ms. Murdock had a hard time identifying what went wrong with David. She did not appreciate his spending habits but did not think it affected how she felt toward him. More often, she speculated that she must have done something to annoy him and worried what this might be. At times, her ruminations about the separation woke her up in the middle of the night, leading to notable sleep deprivation.

Ms. Murdock had a strong network of friends and a mother who was generally supportive and understanding. Her father, however, had grown increasingly negative and bitter toward her, which stood in contrast to the almost idealized role that he had toward her as a child. Their relationship had changed at the time Ms. Murdock entered high school when her father had lost his job due to a layoff. He was unable to find meaningful employment after that and had become sullen, isolated, and negative toward his family.

Basic Psychodynamic Ideas

Psychoanalytic and psychodynamic theory has been and is primed to address the very issues that lead patients to seek treatment. In one of the most comprehensive and well-researched review papers on the legacy of Sigmund Freud, Westen (1998, pp. 334–335) highlighted five major postulates that define contemporary psychodynamic theory, which are easy to see in the cases presented herein:

1. Much of mental life—including thoughts, feelings, and motives—is unconscious, which means that people can behave in ways or can develop symptoms that are inexplicable to themselves.
2. Mental processes, including affective and motivational processes, operate in parallel so that, toward the same person or situation, individuals can have conflicting feelings that motivate them in opposing ways and often lead to compromise solutions.
3. Stable personality patterns begin to form in childhood, and childhood experiences play an important role in personality development, particularly in shaping the ways people form later social relationships.
4. Mental representations of the self, others, and relationships guide people's interactions with others and influence the way they become psychologically symptomatic.
5. Personality development involves not only learning to regulate sexual and aggressive feelings but also moving from an immature, socially dependent state to a mature, interdependent state.

Mr. Shelby and Ms. Murdock each experienced distress, for which they had little realization of why it occurred and how to manage it (point 1). The origin of their symptoms resided in that part of their minds that was not accessible to them, namely, the unconscious mind. Not only were the symptoms unconscious, but so were many other aspects of each patient's life. Mr. Shelby could not account for why he enjoyed playing violent video games so much. Yet it seemed to be associated with ways he managed his angry and aggressive feelings. In Ms. Murdock's case, she was not aware of the extent to which she had become involved with partners who were highly self-focused and for whom their own self-interests were essentially supported at her expense. She also was not aware of the way her frustration with them ultimately was directed toward herself, leading to feelings of guilt and consequential depression.

Both patients had adopted a compromise solution (or compromise formation as it is called in psychoanalytic terminology) for managing their distress (point 2). Mr. Shelby developed severe panic symptoms, which were associated with two opposing feelings: (1) frustration toward his parents for pushing him to become more independent; and (2) fear of losing them someday. His conflicted feelings of hate and fear of loss led him to experience anxiety and panic that led him to physically expel the conflict from his body. In this way, he was able to avoid facing the conflict directly. Ms. Murdock had been successful at blocking out of awareness her angry feelings toward her selfish partners by acting as if things were all right. When angry feelings began to surface, she asked herself what she might have been doing that led to problems in the relationship. And when each partner eventually left because of their own self-focused needs that could not be met by Ms. Murdock's patient and kind support, Ms. Murdock became very depressed and self-critical.

Both cases also show how personality patterns developed in early life continued to exist in adulthood (point 3). Mr. Shelby was a rather quiet and introverted child. Except for the time he broke a lamp, he caused very few problems for his parents. As he grew older, he continued to identify mostly with younger children, who were dependent on adult figures to care for them and to protect them from the troubles and challenges of life's experiences. This was a safer world, which in early childhood is characterized by naiveté about the dangers that exist and in which magical solutions still seem possible. Indeed, as Mr. Shelby became a young man, he continued to return to the electronic world, where dangers lurk but protection and care are available. It came as no surprise that he had no interest in leaving his parents' home and had few, if any, ideas about what his future would look like.

Ms. Murdock shared a mutually strong attachment with her father as a child. She was idealized and received much love and support from an attentive and adoring father. Like Mr. Shelby, she appeared to have a normal development and reasonable success in school, yet when her father experienced a traumatic job loss and an inability to be a good caregiver his attention to her waned. She was puzzled by his evolving distance but seemed to have few negative feelings toward him, instead feeling occasional guilt and bewilderment at his absence. Thus, when men to whom she was close as an adult left her, she responded with similar disbelief and confusion.

Closely related to these longstanding personality patterns is point 4, which describes the mental representations and templates individuals develop of others. Such templates, or object relations as they are described in psychodynamic theory, involve thoughts, feelings, and desires that are developed about oneself, others, and relationships. Mr. Shelby had very little to say about himself; he identified no strengths or weaknesses, could not describe many long-term goals, and only desired more time on the computer to play video games and (somewhat parenthetically) to be free of disabling panic. Others had greater definition or representation in his mental life, although such definitions were not always realistic. His mother, in particular, was represented as a powerful and oppressive woman, who forced therapy on him, as well as the idea of finishing high school, moving out someday, and becoming more independent. His father was seen as less oppressive and at times almost treated him as a peer. Yet when his father introduced the idea of becoming more independent Mr. Shelby became quite hostile. In his interactions with both parents, Mr. Shelby had a very poorly developed sense of himself as a capable, distinctive individual who had a lifetime in front of him to make it what he pleased. With little there to draw upon, Mr. Shelby's reactions to his parents' reasonable concerns took on a sense of danger and fear, and his parents were viewed as much more forceful and less compassionate than they really were.

As already described, Ms. Murdock's representations of herself were that of a dutiful, responsible woman who could please a man to whom she was attached. She felt special and important to men in her life, and when they disappointed her she was devastated and self-critical. As she had formed an early, idealized relationship of her father and his love toward her, Ms. Murdock could not analyze the faults or weaknesses in her father, who was a real person devastated by a job loss and permanent disability who had inexplicably disappointed her. Consequently, the same was true of her partners, whom she held in high regard despite their frustrating qualities. Her experience of them and herself was held prisoner to her childhood representations of each.

Point 5 describes the important developmental tasks of mastering sexual and aggressive impulses, as well as learning how to move from dependence to interdependence. In the case examples, it is clear that Mr. Shelby was at a much earlier (in analytic terms, primitive) level of development. He did not seem like a typical 19-year-old. He had very little interest in sexual relationships, mentioning only one woman in whom he had some interest. He did not date, nor was he at all comfortable talking about sexual feelings or desires. His aggressive feelings and impulses were contained in the fantasy world of an electronic medium. This was well documented one day when he described having a stressful day at work with some of the employees.

When he came home, he went to the computer for several hours and "blew up" many characters. When his therapist made the connection between these two events, his response was that he "felt better." Mr. Shelby showed little awareness of the connection between these events, only indicating (when asked) that he very strongly disliked these coworkers. In terms of his dependency needs, it already has been noted that Mr. Shelby was highly dependent on his parents for having his basic physical and safety needs met. He came to recognize his parents' frustrations with their business and identified with them without analyzing a situation from his own perspective. So if his father was angry at an employee, Mr. Shelby became angry at the employee. However, Mr. Shelby's only solution to how his father (and he) might feel better was to fire the individual immediately. In no way did Mr. Shelby see that his shared experiences of the employee, which might well differ from his father's view or add to his father's understanding of the problem employee, might be helpful to his father in deciding what his next step should be. For instance, might further training help resolve the problem?

Ms. Murdock, being more developmentally advanced, had less severe problems than Mr. Shelby. While being able to seek out and maintain sexual relationships for an extended period, she experienced some difficulties in recognizing her aggressive feelings toward the men in her life, instead directing them toward herself. Consequently, this led her to experience relationships in a more dependent way, in that her sense of satisfaction in the relationship was dependent upon her partner's reactions to her. Instead of viewing the relationship as that of two adults who shared a mutual interdependence on each other for love, support, and care, Ms. Murdock unconsciously took on more responsibility in maintaining the stability of the relationship, putting her in more of a dependent relationship to her partner, and enabling her partner to be less responsible for maintaining interdependence that could lead to mutual satisfaction.

In the chapters that follow, I provide an introduction to the fundamental concepts and ideas of psychoanalytic theory and psychotherapy and show how these have evolved over the past 100 years. I then discuss the empirical support for psychoanalytic ideas and psychotherapy. I call particular attention to the research literature that has evolved in cognitive neuroscience and how findings in this area of discipline support many of the ideas Freud had about the psychic operations of the mind. I then close with two chapters about psychodynamic and psychoanalytic diagnosis and assessment and then provide a case study that is conceptualized from a psychodynamic perspective. It is my hope that this text will demonstrate the clinical utility and empirical support for psychoanalytic and psychodynamic theory. Contrary to the numerous supporters of empirically validated treatments who have disdain for psychoanalytic and psychodynamic treatment, psychodynamic and psychoanalytic theory and therapy are useful and scientifically supported approaches for working with patients who seek relief from their conflicts and suffering. While writing (and completing) this text has been very gratifying, the most gratification I can imagine is for readers to find themselves energized and excited about these ideas, their scientific merit, and clinical relevance. In this way, students of psychoanalytic theory and mental health professionals will find themselves in a position to advance this method for many years to come.

As a final comment, I want to define some terminology that I use in this text. The terms *psychoanalytic* and *psychodynamic* mean different things to different people. In general, *psychoanalytic* ideas are associated with Freud and modern-day ego psychology. Thus, ideas about drives, impulses, defenses, and conflict are the focus of attention. *Psychodynamic* ideas, by contrast, refer to ideas about the psychic representations of the self and others and the predominant way emotions and desires are played out interpersonally. While some prefer to separate these ideas because of strong preferences about the relevance of one set of ideas over the other, I often do not separate these terms in the text. Psychodynamic ideas evolved from, and are strongly rooted in, psychoanalytic theory. It is not my intention, nor is it really possible, to dissect the terms and to associate certain ideas with just one theory. Theory has evolved over time, and one theory incorporates many of the ideas and concepts from its predecessor, but with some differences. Therefore, with apologies to those who are only "psychoanalytic" or "psychodynamic," I combine these terms where and when it seems appropriate and attempt to highlight important differences throughout. This approach, I believe, makes for a more unified and coherent story about the evolution and empirical support of what Freud began some 100 years ago.

Section I

Theoretical Underpinnings

2

Basic Principles of Psychoanalytic and Psychodynamic Theory

Although psychoanalytic theory and its implication for treatment have evolved substantially over time (Frank, 2000; Kernberg, 1993; Marcus, 1999; Pine, 1998; Rangell, 1981; Wallerstein, 1989, 2002), certain principles remain as guiding elements as part of any discussion of psychoanalytic or psychodynamic psychotherapy. As noted in Chapter 1, these are summarized by Westen (1998, pp. 334–335):

1. Much of mental life—including thoughts, feelings, and motives—is unconscious, which means that people can behave in ways or develop symptoms that are inexplicable to themselves.
2. Mental processes, including affective and motivational processes, operate in parallel so that, toward the same person or situation, individuals can have conflicting feelings that motivate them in opposing ways and often lead to compromise solutions.
3. Stable personality patterns begin to form in childhood, and childhood experiences play an important role in personality development, particularly in shaping the ways people form later social relationships.
4. Mental representations of the self, others, and relationships guide people's interactions with others and influence the ways they become psychologically symptomatic.
5. Personality development involves not only learning to regulate sexual and aggressive feelings but also moving from an immature, socially dependent state to a mature, interdependent state.

It is perhaps these five principles that best distinguish psychodynamic and psychoanalytic psychotherapy from other forms of treatment that are commonly practiced today, which focus mainly on conscious cognitions, behavior change, and symptom reduction. Psychotherapy process also is part of psychoanalytic and psychodynamic theory, unlike many of the common therapies espoused to be empirically superior. Issues of how the patient responds to the therapist, how the therapist responds to the patient, how and when a person resists a particular topic of investigation, and how all these processes change in the course of the session are part of understanding and conducting sound psychodynamic and psychoanalytic treatment.

In this chapter, I present an overview of the basic principles of psychoanalytic theory. These principles reflect the basic ideas of Sigmund Freud and his early followers, although in the next chapter I highlight the evolution of Freudian theory into what is now a more interpersonally oriented focus, away from the biological drives and instincts that Freud articulated early on.

A Brief Background and History on the Career and Culture of Freud

To understand psychoanalytic theory, it is important to recognize the background and context in which Freud developed his ideas. Many individuals are surprised to learn that Freud was a physician and that his medical training was in neurology. Prior to his writings on the mind and psychoanalysis, Freud was involved in anatomical research. His first study was with eels and trying to understand their reproductive capacities, which proved to be elusive given their "intersexuality" (Solms, 2002, p. 19). Later, his work on the histology of nerve cells was instrumental in identifying what is commonly referred to as the neuron. He also was involved in identifying cranial nerve pathways and was particularly recognized for his contributions to the understanding of cerebral palsy, which provided him with "international fame" (ibid., p. 30) at an early point in his career.

As a neurologist, Freud observed many clinical phenomena, including hysteria, neurasthenia, and what are now known as somatization disorders (e.g., conversion disorder). Because there were no known physiological deficits for many of these disorders, Freud's interest turned more toward methodologies that allowed him to better understand the clinical phenomena he observed and methods of treatment. Such disorders were common in Freud's era. In those days, human rationality and ascendance above the animal world was part of the zeitgeist of the religious and philosophical communities. Human reason and intellect had led to the development of machinery and modes of transportation that outperformed human and animal work. Victorian values and virtues were pervasive throughout Europe, which countered any discussion of one's impulses, urges, and resemblance to the animal world.

A contemporary of Freud's, Charles Darwin, developed the theory of evolution, which focused on living organisms' adaptation to their environment and conditions in order to survive. Those creatures that adapted passed on their genetic blueprint to their offspring, which further enhanced survival and performance. As a physician and scientist, Freud was struck by the logic of Darwin's ideas and the natural association between physiological adaptation and survival. He recognized that survival of the organism was one of the strongest forces throughout the animal world, thus placing sexuality at the level of a primal instinct. As humans evolved, the mind took on more evolutionary significance. Analytical reasoning and mastering the instincts of one's animal ancestry allowed for improved adaptation. Yet the very forces that promoted survival also were the ones that Freud eventually recognized as playing a significant role in human suffering: That is, within one's body were physiological processes that promoted the survival of the species through sexual activity, a central nervous system that was organized at its most basic level for survival via a fight-or-flight (and at higher levels for mastery of instincts and impulses for the promotion of analytic reasoning and thought), and the storehouse of acquired rules and guidelines for appropriate behavior within one's culture. It was the latter that, when interacting with the more basic instinctual forces and impulses, led to distressing symptoms.

Freud's interests moved more toward clinical work as his career advanced. Within the culture he lived, he saw many patients who had exaggerated emotional and physical reactions that were described as "hysteric." He also had the opportunity to treat patients who had experienced a loss of physical functioning for which there was no biological cause. The most notable case of this was that of a "glove anesthesia" in which a man had lost use of his hand from the wrist down. As no known biological condition could cause such symptoms, Freud pondered what it was about the brain that led to such symptoms and conditions. As with this patient and hysterics, he came to see that the repression of one's sexual urges and impulses led to these symptoms. Uncovering the ideas associated with these impulses led to the reduction and elimination of symptoms. This meant that the symptoms Freud was observing were diseases of the mind. Within the biological scaffolding of the brain were the sources of these diseases, and as the mind was freed of these disturbing and unsettling thoughts and ideas, the patient returned to a more adaptive way of functioning. In other words, *ideas and thoughts* not consciously available to awareness to the patient were fundamentally related to the suffering the patient experienced. Freud sought to identify those mechanisms within the brain and its processes that accounted for these symptoms.

As Freud continued his neuroanatomical studies, his ideas about the mind began to take shape. He was aware that cocaine could alleviate neuralgia and depressive symptoms. Thus, having used cocaine himself for research purposes, Freud noted its ability to heighten his sensory and perceptual experiences toward achieving greater clarity. Freud's studies of cocaine led him to conclude that biological substances must underlie most forms of psychological arousal (Freud, 1905). Because of this growing interest in the mind and its association with biochemical mechanisms, Freud chose to work with French neurologist Jean-Martin Charcot and later with the Viennese internist Josef Breuer. Both men developed a technique of hypnosis, in which a patient could be enticed into an altered state of consciousness. In this state, those unsettling thoughts and impulses associated with more sexual and biological urges would be spoken, eventually leading to relief of the disabling symptoms once the reason for the symptoms was understood. Freud found the ideas of Charcot and Breuer very stimulating and important in understanding the psychological processes that led to the manifest symptoms that were observed. And perhaps more important, he found that patients actually improved from this approach.

Initially, Freud actively utilized hypnosis for treating his patients. However, his passion for this approach quickly fell out of favor as the technique failed to produce successful results, sometimes even evoking memories or ideas that were not based in the real experience of the patient. It was Breuer's work with a patient, Bertha Pappenheim, that shaped much of Freud's subsequent thinking. During his hypnotic work with Pappenheim, Breuer found that by allowing Pappenheim to speak freely without censoring her or interfering with what she had to say, she began to speak of ideas she had that had not yet been verbalized. In allowing her to speak in this manner, Breuer laid the groundwork for what would become the technique of free association—that is, allowing the patient to speak freely about whatever comes to mind in the moment. Thus, the hypnotic cure evolved into a talking cure. Freud consequently modified his hypnotic technique. He had patients lie on a couch to foster a more relaxed state. By asking patients to then speak freely about what comes to mind, Freud introduced the psychoanalytic technique of free association.

The Early Topographical Model

Freud (1900, 1915b) began to develop a model of the mind (the *psyche*) that accounted for what he had been observing in his practice of neurology. He described a *conscious* part of the mind, which experienced immediate awareness of events in the outer world and inner world. There was a *preconscious mind*, which consisted of knowledge and experience that could be brought to awareness with little effort or energy. Finally, there was the *unconscious* mind, which was the storehouse of the ideas, wishes, memories, impulses, and desires that were implicated in the symptomatology that was observed. Freud thought that the unconscious mind was the largest part of the psyche. By activating upsetting and untapped components of the brain's activity through a free association process, suffering could be relieved and symptoms eliminated or reduced. Thus, no longer did the conscious mind have to ward off what was unconsciously too dangerous. Freud (1923a) later expanded his idea of the unconscious when he developed the structural model of the mind (see p. 19). He did so after observing that patients used various strategies to defend themselves against upsetting unconscious material. These strategies, or defenses, were not known to patients; rather, they were observed by Freud himself. Because patients did not know that their defensive strategies were warding off unconscious material, Freud thought that the conflict causing the symptoms and the defensive strategies were operating at the unconscious level. Thus, a model of the mind formed in which conflict was occurring at an unconscious level in which instinctual impulses, wishes, and urges were seeking to be expressed but thwarted by a defense of some kind.

Westen (1998, p. 336) stated, "The most important proposition that has distinguished psychoanalysis from other theoretical systems since its inception is its postulation of unconscious mental processes." Shevrin and Dickman (1980, p. 432) were so bold to suggest that "no psychological model that seeks to explain how human beings know, learn, or behave can ignore the concept of unconscious psychological processes." Indeed, underlying all forms of treatment within the psychoanalytic and psychodynamic traditions is the assumption of the unconscious. However, what exactly is meant by unconscious has been expanded and debated in psychoanalytic circles. Freud's idea of what was unconscious included mainly the instinctual urges, impulses, and wishes. Others, however, suggested that the unconscious houses affects, defenses, motivations, object/person representations, schemas, and fantasies (Arlow, 1969; Bucci, 1997, 2000; Eagle, 1987; McClelland, Koestner, & Weinberger, 1989; Sandler, 1976; Sandler & Rosenblatt, 1962; Sandler & Sandler, 1984, 1988, 1994; Schafer, 1968; Westen, 1999). These components, along with many other automatic processes involved in processing information, are now considered to be part of "nonconscious" mind, which is greatly expanded from Freud's original ideas. In fact, upon reviewing the cognitive and psychoanalytic literature on nonconscious/unconscious processes, Westen (1999, p. 1095) concluded that "we should speak of unconscious processes" instead of using the term *the unconscious*. (See Chapter 8 for a greater discussion of this issue).

Just as the unconscious has undergone a reworking, so, too, has the concept of the preconscious. Arlow and Brenner (1964) and Gill (1963) argued that the term *preconscious* should be abandoned because of its ambiguity. A specific example of this may be found in Sandler and Sandler (1994), who noted that Freud used the term *preconscious* in different ways. Besides saying that the preconscious is "mental content that is readily accessible to consciousness" (ibid., p. 283), Freud said that the preconscious uses a form of thought known as "secondary process," which involves more rational and higher levels of thinking that are not based on the pervasive desire to reduce an urge or impulse. Freud also suggested that the preconscious engages in a censorship of material that is to be expressed and that its contents are not accessible. This censorship occurs after a different censorship had occurred between the unconscious and conscious mind. Sandler and Sandler (1984, 1988, 1994) suggested that the term *present unconscious* be used in place of preconscious, in that the present unconscious operates within that part of the mind that is conscious and its content can be accessed. It also has a stabilizing function through which material from the inner world and outer world may pass, making upsetting thoughts, ideas, or impulses more acceptable. As for the traditional use of the word *unconscious*, Sandler and Sandler (1984, 1988, 1994) suggested that the term *past unconscious* be used to represent the parts of the mind that house and store wishes and fantasies that must be passed into the present unconscious prior to their conscious awareness and expression. Clearly, there are differing positions on the nature of the preconscious as originally explicated by Freud.

The Structural Model and Drive Theory

As noted previously, Freud reworked the topographical model of the mind into one that involved the description of psychic structures. These structures seemed to better account for what he observed in patients and included the id, ego, and superego. The *id* was considered to be the repository of instinctual urges, impulses, and desires. The id mainly resides in the unconscious, though such impulses can and do become conscious. It operates under what is called *primary process thought*, which is irrational and associational. The id is *pleasure seeking*, which looks for an object by which to gratify its desires. As adaptation and survival were strong motivating factors in the human organism, Freud (1923a) postulated that sexuality, called the *libido*, was stored here. Mitchell and Black (1995, pp. 13–14) noted, "There was not a singular beginning of sexuality, in either a sudden awakening or a specific trauma.... Sexuality has many, many tributaries (Freud called them 'component instincts'). It does not begin as being experienced at the genital level, but in a diffuse sensuality, located in many different body parts, stimulated through the many different activities in the first year of life." Freud (1920) also described a second major drive, *aggression*, which was associated with the newly formulated death instinct. This drive is housed in the id and expresses itself in different ways, such as self-destructiveness. The creation of the death instinct came out of Freud's original ideas that self-preservation and its corresponding aggressive activity were a basic instinctual drive that was located in the ego. However, he gave up the idea of aggression being a basic drive that was associated with the death instinct—an instinct that was considered to be of the same caliber of libido. Very little subsequently was written about the death instinct, and few therapists today believe it to exist, though many adhere to the idea that aggression is a fundamental drive.

The *superego* is that part of the mind that has taken in, or *introjected*, those rules and principles of socially appropriate behavior. It, too, works under unconscious influence, though its content can become conscious. The superego serves as the moral compass for the individual, and when its influence becomes too strong at the unconscious level, symptoms emerge. Typically, these symptoms come to represent what Freud described as a neurotic conflict, in which the desires of the id unconsciously conflict with the prohibitions of the superego.

The *ego* is that part of the mind in which consciousness occurs. It interfaces with the outer world and operates under *secondary process thinking*, which is governed by rule-based, rational, cause-and-effect thinking and reasoning. Its grounding in the world around it led Freud to say that the ego is governed by the *reality principle*. The ability to accurately attend to and perceive reality is a crucial function of the ego; severe ego deficits, such as psychoses, are indicative of significant maladaptation. For Freud, psychosis was a product of the unsuccessful management of primary process thinking and its corresponding drives and impulses.[1] Optimal functioning occurs when the impulses of the id and the constraints of the superego work together to discharge the impulse in a socially acceptable way that is governed by secondary process thinking.

Of course, there has been an evolution of Freud's ideas about the id, ego, and superego, which is discussed in the next chapter. In the context of psychoanalytic and psychodynamic conceptualization and treatment, these basic ideas nonetheless remain very important. For instance, many patients seek treatment for depression. It is not uncommon to learn that their depression is associated with a loss of something important to them, usually an interpersonal relationship. They cannot seem to resolve their grief, despite wanting to do so. Treatment often leads to the identification of unconscious anger toward the person who is now gone, which has become directed toward oneself, in the particular form of, "How could I harbor such angry feelings toward someone I cared so much about?" Once the identification of feelings of anger become identified and appropriately directed, the depression often remits. Of course, not all patients who experience depression have a course of treatment that proceeds along these lines, though Freud's (1917a) classic description of "melancholia" does fit what many clinicians observe as part of their treatment of depressed patients.

As demonstrated already, inherent within the structural model is the idea of conflict. Because sexual impulses and fantasy occur within the id and mostly at the unconscious level, along with the corresponding rules of what is socially appropriate behavior and socially acceptable to discuss, the mind becomes conflicted when impulses clash with constrictions on behavior. Freud suggested that such conflict led to anxiety and the development of the *psychoneuroses*, which included such phenomena as hysterical and obsessional psychoneuroses (Freud, 1896a, 1896b, 1898). To manage these conflicting feelings, the mind—in particular, the ego—employs a *repressive* mechanism that defends oneself against conscious awareness of this anxiety. Symptoms develop when the defensive process of repression is not fully successful. In some cases, the desire gets directed toward an alternative person or situation for its fulfillment, which produces a compromised solution. Thus, a *compromise formation* is created, which is a behavioral expression of the way persons channel instinctual urges into their discharge and eventual internal satisfaction. An example of this may be seen in the following situation. A patient came to therapy because he was concerned about how much time he spent looking at Internet pornography. As the therapy progressed, the patient discussed ways he felt ignored and misunderstood by his wife. Although he did not consciously acknowledge feelings of disappointment, frustration, and anger toward her cold demeanor, it became more evident in the course of therapy that his unrequited desire for support, love, and sexual pleasure were being fulfilled by the images and brief video images he watched on the Internet. Hence, his behavior was a compromise formation that was an attempt to help him "solve" his problem.

As it turned out, Freud actually saw a number of patients who had experienced sexual trauma, which helped him develop his theory of sexual conflict underlying many of the psychoneuroses. Initially, Freud thought that all psychoneuroses were related to sexual seduction of the patient (as a child) by an adult, which was the case in many instances. However, Freud came to see that many patients' neuroses were rooted in their own unwanted fantasies and ideas about their own sexuality, thereby leading him to posit a theory of *infantile sexuality,* which resonated so much with his ideas about the importance of adaptation and survival that were basic to living organisms (Freud, 1906).

Freud believed sexual desires were experienced in their rudimentary forms in infancy. In the course of infancy and early childhood, these early desires were experienced with specific body regions, known as *erogenous zones*. Such regions quickly become associated with sources of frustration, pleasure, and gratification. Freud speculated that a body region (known as its *source*) created an awareness of a need for some behavior related to biological gratification (its *aim*) and became attached to some external object or person by which satisfaction occurs (its *object*). The source and aim are inherently the nature of the drive; objects, by contrast, are discovered and are "created" by the individual out of experience of drive satisfaction and frustration (Greenberg & Mitchell, 1983, p. 44).

As development proceeds, Freud observed that children progress through various phases—*psychosexual stages of development*—in which certain erogenous zones become the focus of much activity. Corresponding with these stages is the development of the psyche and its components. These stages are labeled as *oral, anal, phallic, latent,* and *genital*. Should excessive levels of frustration or gratification occur with the aim or object that gratifies during one of the stages, the experiences become stored in the unconscious mind. Freud believed that "every human activity can be traced ultimately to the demands of drive, although a full explanation of behavior requires that we include an analysis of the forces which oppose its pressures" (Greenberg & Mitchell, 1983, p. 44).

Later, however, Freud (1923a) made some significant changes to the structural model that had implications for the nature of the ego and how the drives were understood throughout psychosexual development. He suggested that the libido, which was object seeking, became narcissistic—that is, seeking its own gratification. In other words, since all aims (behaviors) reduce a drive through the individual's interaction with an object, and since the ego seeks to balance its instinctual desires with the constraints of reality and limits set by the superego, the ego must find an acceptable outlet for the drive that is considered pleasing, acceptable, and satisfying. Consequently, the individual does not operate with the intention of drive reduction but by the intent to receive narcissistic gratification. Such ideas implied that a separate psychic process or space must exist by which individuals evaluate their experiences with the object world and the gratification they receive. While not using the word *self* to describe that psychic space, Freud's introduction of this idea led to major theoretical revisions by object-relations and self-psychology theorists.

Oedipal and Electra Complexes

Nowhere in Freud's theory is there arguably any greater controversy than his concept of the Oedipal and Electra complexes. For Freud, residues of oral stage conflicts may be observed in fixations with oral activity, such as smoking or excessive eating. These behaviors are expressions of sexualized conflict during the oral stage of development. Anal stage conflicts may be observed with preoccupation with neatness and order or with strong desires to make things messy or chaotic. Such tendencies may lead to phobic avoidance of certain objects that symbolically represent sexual objects (e.g., a snake as a phallus) or experiences or to the need to dominate and control. In the phallic stage, however, a more complicated (and controversial) series of events occurs. Briefly, it is during the age of 5 to 6 that young children come to the awareness that they are sexual beings, possessing a penis or vagina, and that these parts of themselves are associated with pleasure. They also come to the basic understanding that sexual pleasure is experienced in the context of a relationship with the opposite sex, such as is observed between the mother and father. With this realization, the first love object, namely, the opposite-sex parent, becomes highly desired. However, this thought is dangerous, as it leads to fears of castration in young boys by their father, who is more powerful and associated with the mother. Freud understood these fears to be universal, given the way societies denounced incestuous relationships. Thus, drawing upon Sophocles's character of Oedipus, the *Oedipus complex* was described to account for castration fears that young boys have toward their fathers.

Freud sought to understand the same dynamics in young girls; here, he believed that young girls viewed their clitoris as inferior to the male penis. As a result of this disappointment, they sought to possess the father's penis, which would eventually lead them to have a baby of their own to care for. The penis became equated with a baby, which allowed the girl to feel as if she could make up for her shortcomings in not having the penis. These dynamics crated the *Electra complex*. For both girls and boys, to overcome their Electra and Oedipal complexes they had to repress their sexual desire for the opposite-sex parent and to identify with the same-sex parent, who continued to provide guidelines for social behavior in a civilized society, which led to the further development of the superego.

Fisher and Greenberg (1996, p. 118) stated that the Oedipal (and Electra) triangle of mother-father-child represents "a crucial configuration packed with consequences for every aspect of the child's development" in that it was linked to tensions surrounding issues of love and competition. Nevertheless, it is easy to recognize that Freud's ideas were strongly influenced by the cultural and family dynamics of the times, which included a strong paternal influence and a passive maternal figure. In our present culture, these ideas are recognized by many as being sexist and demeaning toward women. As is discussed in the next chapter, expanded and revised versions of the Oedipal formulation have been put forth that present a more balanced perspective on sexual development for both women and men.

Treatment: Making the Unconscious Conscious and the Obstacles Therein

As noted earlier, Freud's earliest clinical interests in the mind led him to eagerly study the technique of hypnosis. In this form of treatment, Freud believed that Charcot and Breuer were able to access parts of the mind that were not available in conscious awareness, yet held the key to understanding the many symptoms a patient had. Freud found that the technique was not always successful—not everyone could be hypnotized—and that patients recalled memories that were fantasies and not experienced sexual traumas. That fantasies held such a powerful place in many patients' minds affected Freud profoundly, leading him to postulate that sexual conflicts are central to psychopathology. But how to access these memories became puzzling, given the limitations of hypnosis. As noted earlier, this was accomplished by using the method of *free association*, which was similar to hypnotism. Patients would come into the office and lie down in a comfortable, relaxed position. Freud would sit behind the patient and encourage the patient to say whatever it was that came to mind. Although patients were not induced into an altered state of consciousness as in hypnotism, Freud believed that patients in a reclined position would be more in a relaxed state of mind, thereby fostering the associative process. He also encouraged patients to be observers of their own thoughts and report them to him. This was an important element of the technique. Patients were to co-observe with Freud the associative process that was unfolding and to share their reactions to it. As will be seen later, this self-observing capacity is an important component not only of psychoanalysis but also of psychoanalytic and psychodynamic psychotherapies.

While free association was used as the central technique, it was also observed that patients resisted certain kinds of associations, became inhibited in engaging in the process, or found themselves unable to say anything. Without a guiding presence and direction, the free association process seemed aimless or futile. Freud understood that he had to explain—or offer an *interpretation* of—what the associations could mean. Though one may consider interpretations to be highly subjective, they were produced by Freud after very careful observation and consideration of the material the patient presented in conjunction with the nature of Freud's theory as it was developed at the time. Solms (2002) and others have commented that one of Freud's greatest talents was his ability to make careful, attentive observations that led to well-articulated speculation about what the associations meant.[2] That Freud was able to attend so closely to his patients' associations, to integrate them into his working theoretical ideas, and to subsequently rework his theory was truly one of his greatest skills as a clinician.

Freud's interpretations were based on the content of the material presented by the patient. He found common themes to emerge as patients spoke of specific kinds of conflicts, particularly around psychosexual stages of development. For instance, concerns about being cared for and fears of becoming separated and autonomous were common themes in patients with oral stage conflicts. Language about order and control was common in patients with anal stage conflicts, whereas issues surrounding feelings of jealousy and competition represented phallic stage conflicts.

Freud believed that these concerns, and the words patients selected to share them, were symbolic representations of deeply personal, language-transcendent experiences of the patients. Such thinking naturally led him to take a great interest in the experience of dreams. Just like the words used to describe associations to one's experiences represented more primitive concerns and conflicts, so, too, did dreams contain material that had a surface meaning and a deeper, hidden meaning. Thus, a dream about being attacked by a snake crawling on one's body and not being able to control it was considered at a deeper level for its phallic implications and fears about a phallic object attacking oneself. The obvious content of the dream is considered its *manifest content.* In this case, it is the snake and the person's body that are manifest content. The content representative of the nature of the conflict is the *latent content.* In this case, it is the fear of sexual contact by a penis and being overcome by what it might do.

As noted earlier, patients often found themselves unable or unwilling to speak about certain material or to engage in the free association process. Freud quickly recognized that *resistance* was a fundamental part of what happened in treatment. While initially viewing resistance as an obstacle, he soon came to believe that it served an adaptive purpose: to protect the individual from information that was too painful to experience at the conscious level. It was these manifestations of resistance to content that, in part, led Freud to identify and work with patients on their *mechanisms of defense.* Many times, this resistance came in the form of *repression*, a process of blocking one's own awareness of the upsetting material. Freud also identified other defenses such as *projection* (attributing onto another person those unacceptable ideas, feelings, and wishes that the patient cannot accept as being within himself or herself) and *displacement* (transferring one's drive, impulse, or affect from one object onto another one), though it was his daughter, Anna Freud (1936), who came to offer some of the most elaborate descriptions of the defense mechanisms.

In developing his therapeutic technique, Freud recognized that the ways patients responded to him were ways they tended to describe relating to their parents and caregivers. He suggested that patients transferred onto him their past feelings, desires, and subsequent interpersonal behaviors, a process he aptly described as *transference.* Like resistance, Freud initially saw this as an obstacle to the treatment but quickly recognized that it was a very powerful part of the treatment process. He understood that an important part of the treatment involved the development of a transference neurosis, in which patients felt highly conflicted toward the analyst, much like they felt toward their own parents. Transference neurosis was thus observed when patients recognized that they were feeling very angry and conflicted toward the analyst, even though they knew rationally that nothing had happened to warrant such a response. McWilliams (2004, p. 15) described the therapeutic power of transference very succinctly: "… When the atmosphere of the patient's childhood emerges in treatment, with the analyst and experiencing the analyst as having the emotional power of a parent, the patient becomes keenly aware of long-forgotten (repressed) feelings toward parental figures, can express what was inexpressive in childhood, and can, with the analyst's help, craft new solutions to old conflict." In other words, the relational element of Freud's technique was what held much power in the process of freeing a person from his or her conflicts. While remaining very grounded in instinct theory, Freud saw the nature of the relationship with the analyst as a fundamental part of treatment.

Freud also found that at times patients would say things that were highly evocative or that led him to identify feelings of conflict of discomfort within himself. He identified this as *countertransference* and recognized its potential for adversely affecting treatment. Countertransference could take on many forms, such as going out of one's way to be especially accommodating to a patient who evokes feelings of empathy, sympathy, and a need for protection. It also could manifest itself as starting a patient's session late, feeling dread or boredom when the patient enters the room, or responding in more direct and confrontational ways to someone toward whom anger is felt.

All of these observations and experiences led Freud to develop a true talking-cure: *psychoanalysis*. This process required patients to come for treatment five to six times per week for approximately 1-hour intervals. Patients would lie on the couch while the analyst would sit behind them. So that transference could develop, the analyst was to be like a mirror in which patients' expressed feelings, wishes, and impulses could be reflected back to them, thus making what was unconscious more conscious. The analyst was to refrain from personal comments, instead directing patients toward their own thoughts and ideas. This stance was considered to be one of *neutrality*. Similarly—and related to the principle of neutrality—the analyst was not to reveal things about himself or herself that could interfere with the transference process or hinder the analyst from being neutral. This stance was considered to be one of *anonymity*. Finally, the analyst was to refrain from the temptation to gratify patients' transference-based desires and wishes, such as offering words of comfort or advice. This stance was considered to be one of *abstinence*. Interestingly enough, Gabbard (1999) and others noted that Freud did not hold to these principles very tightly. He was known to share his opinions and ideas with patients about nontreatment issues, would become upset with patients when they resisted, offered them food and beverages, and even introduced them to his family. Gabbard wrote, "Freud actually was not as austere in his writings on technique as he is sometimes portrayed. In his advice on technique, he tended to oscillate between endorsing flexibility and tact, on the one hand, and more authoritarian directives, on the other" (p. 94). Even more interesting, McWilliams (2004, p. 11) noted that in a letter to Carl Jung, Freud "made a serious comment—with which anyone who has experienced a transformative personal psychotherapy can resonate—that analytic treatment is essentially a cure through love (McGuire, 1974, pp. 8–9)." Hence, psychoanalysis was created as a means by which to help individuals become free of their suffering and improve their life quality.

Psychoanalysis in Disrepute and Disrepair

Although the next chapters discuss the evolution of psychoanalytic and psychodynamic theories as well as research supporting psychoanalytic ideas and therapy, it is very important to discuss up front the positive and negative perceptions and realities of psychoanalytic theory and therapy. Such a task is necessary if one wants to critically evaluate the clinical utility and empirical foundations of these ideas in a day and age where the established narratives about the theories associated with Sigmund Freud have clouded (and in some cases blinded) the minds of many from being more objective and balanced in their analytic thinking on these issues.

From a very practical, "layperson" perspective, psychodynamic or psychoanalytic therapy—not to mention psychoanalysis—are expensive propositions in money, time, and energy. The American health-care industry tends to have limited benefits for psychological treatment, especially those that seek to address unconscious conflicts and difficulties that can take many months to years to fully uncover. Managed care, a fixed number of sessions, and high copays make psychodynamic treatment practically unavailable to some people. A more egregious comment I have heard is that psychoanalysis is available only to the wealthy and for those "neurotic housewives with nothing better to do." While the latter comment is a misrepresentation of reality, the former does capture something that is indeed true—treatment that lasts 3 or more years costs thousands of dollars. Health-care benefits, regrettably, often dictate patients' participation in analytic and dynamic treatment. Nevertheless, it remains true that some individuals seek out analytic or dynamic treatment.

McWilliams (2004, p. 11) wrote that many people only "know the psychoanalytic tradition from its caricatures represented by untalented practitioners attracted to its status, or from nonanalysts identifying with their fantasy of a perfectly sterile medical technique, (and) define it as the procedure in which the therapist says little beyond the occasional accusation that the patient is 'resisting.'" As I address throughout this text, such ideas are indeed "caricatures" and not representative of standard analytic and dynamic practice. More concerning are the ideas provided by Robert Bornstein (2001) in a paper titled "The Impending Death of Psychoanalysis." He described the "seven deadly sins of psychoanalysis" that are contributing to its demise in scientific psychology and clinical practice. First, he noted that psychoanalysts are "insular," acting only with each other, particularly those of their own theoretical preference. Second, he noted that certain constructs in psychoanalytic theory are inaccurate based on the empirical studies that have been performed on them. These include constructs such as "penis envy" and "castration anxiety." Third, he noted that many in the psychoanalytic community are indifferent to alternative points of view, refusing to accept external evidence to the contrary. (In fact, as part of the reactions to this paper, Bornstein, 2002b, described how some analysts' criticisms of his ideas were factually inaccurate and based on premises that were known not to be true). Fourth, because the psychoanalytic community is insular and indifferent, "psychoanalysis has become irrelevant in contemporary psychology" (Bornstein, 2001, p. 9). Fifth, Bornstein (2001) believed that many psychoanalytic writings and therapies are done with much inefficiency. Sixth, he noted that many of the key concepts lack precise operational definitions, which makes understanding their presumed mechanisms more difficult. From a scientific perspective, this renders a theory untestable and consequently difficult to expand. Finally, Bornstein wrote, "Psychoanalysts can be arrogant … interacting only with each other … becom[ing] increasingly certain of the correctness of their ideas" (ibid., p. 11).

In a follow-up paper, Bornstein (2005) offered additional ideas to further support his position. He suggested that psychoanalysis and theory fell into decline around the mid-1950s. This occurred as positivistic thinking took hold of American psychology. Positivism is embedded in an empirical framework of operationalization and controlled experimentation, something that psychoanalysts shunned during this time period. Bornstein suggested that postmodern ideas about the construction of both internal and external reality affected psychoanalysis in a particularly adverse way. Because of its insularity and reticence to engage with the scientific community, "new ideas" were constructed in the sciences that actually reflect older, psychoanalytic ideas. Bornstein suggested that it is extremely difficult to change this "truth" back to the original ideas from whence it came because the construction of narrative truth is so powerful. Thus, it has been the case with psychoanalysis and psychoanalytic theory that its ideas still exist today, but in a new format (discussed in a following section).

It could be suggested that because Bornstein is not trained as an analyst, he does not have the background necessary to level such criticisms. However, his concerns are shared by many psychoanalysts. Frank (2000) revisited the criticisms of psychoanalysis put forth several years earlier by Rangell (1974, 1988). Frank (2000) noted how Rangell (1988) described psychoanalysis as fragmented and failing to achieve parsimony and cited Rangell (pp. 317–318: "It has been my increasing experience and conviction ... that the science of psychoanalysis has been undergoing not an advance, but a declining spiral." Frank concluded that an integrated conceptualization of personality and psychopathology from the psychoanalytic framework is needed: "The elephant exists; we just must learn how to represent it" (p. 179).

More empirical data provide some sobering information about the status of psychoanalysis in scientific psychology. Robins, Gosling, and Craik (1999) surveyed keywords related to psychoanalysis in many of the leading psychology journals. They found that less than 2% of the published articles contained these words and that there were no citations in any of these journals from the four major psychoanalytic journals. They also found that less than 1% of doctoral dissertations published in the 30 years preceding their article contained keywords related to psychoanalytic theory. In a survey of undergraduate psychology textbooks, Bornstein (1988) found that psychoanalysis is described in negative terms. In graduate programs, there are few faculty or programs that identify themselves as psychoanalytic. (However, in an informal survey I did on Web sites of clinical psychology doctoral programs, there are more opportunities for psychoanalytic and psychodynamic training in PsyD programs compared with PhD programs).

A major criticism of psychoanalytic theory is that its ideas are untestable. This idea is false and has been proven incorrect by many (e.g., Bornstein & Masling, 1998a, 1998b, 2002; Fisher & Greenberg, 1996; Kandel, 1999; Masling & Bornstein, 1993, 1994, 1996). Bornstein (2002b) responded specifically to this position as it was articulated in a somewhat ironic, perhaps "self-destructive" comment by psychoanalyst Jon Mills (2002, p. 556), who wrote, "Empiricism becomes a fundamentally bankrupt criterion when applied to psychoanalytic concepts that by definition that cannot be directly observed or measures." Rather astutely, Bornstein (2002b) noted that every subfield of psychology studies nonobservable or measurable constructs, such as memory and motivation and added that "the same is true of physics (gravity), chemistry (molecular bonding), and biology (natural selection). Each field has developed innovative methods for operationally defining those 'unobservable' constructs that form the foundation of their discipline, often using indirect strategies to measures and quantify those constructs (e.g., by assessing the effect of an unobservable construct on other, observable variables)" (p. 584).

The outlook just presented does not appear favorable for psychoanalytic theory and psychoanalysis. However, there are many reasons to be optimistic. This originates, in part, from the research literature in which psychoanalytic ideas have regained new status and attention, but with slightly different language. For instance, Bornstein (2005) constructed a list of concepts that are commonly understood in cognitive psychological science today that have their specific origin in traditional, psychoanalytic ideas. These ideas are presented in Table 2.1. Although some may believe Freudian ideas are dead, the ideas he originally described about the workings of the human psyche have resurrected themselves in numerous domains of cognitive psychology. To regain their status and appropriate place in clinical psychology and psychiatry, however, psychoanalytic ideas and concepts must be appropriately credited and highlighted as such by those who do research in this field. As additional research is conducted in these domains, the psychoanalytic and psychodynamic origins of the concepts can be highlighted further.

Besides the list provided by Bornstein (2005), there are many other ideas in which psychoanalysis and its core concepts have been

TABLE 2.1 Revisions and Reinventions of Psychoanalytic Concepts

Psychoanalytic Concept	Revision or Reinvention
Unconscious memory (1900)	Implicit memory (Schacter, 1987)
Primary process thought (1900)	Spreading activation (Collins & Loftus, 1975)
Object representation (1905)	Person schema (Neisser, 1976)
Repression (1910)	Cognitive avoidance (Beck, 1976)
Preconscious processing (1915)	Preattentive processing (Treisman, 1969)
Parapraxis (1916)	Retrieval error (Tulving, 1983)
Abreaction (1916)	Redintegration (Bower & Glass, 1976)
Repetition compulsion (1920)	Nuclear script (Tomkins, 1979)
Ego (1923)	Central executive (Baddeley, 1992)
Ego defense (1926)	Defensive attribution (Lerner & Miller, 1978)

Note: The years beside the psychoanalytic concept refer to the year in which Freud first described the concept question.

Source: Bornstein, R. F., 2005, *Psychoanalytic Psychology, 22,* p. 327 (with permission from the American Psychological Association).

"rediscovered" and "packaged" in a different form. I provide three examples of this. First, there is dialectical behavior therapy (DBT; Linehan, 1993), which is a cognitive-behavioral, therapeutic approach for patients diagnosed with borderline personality disorder. DBT targets borderline patients' use of splitting and other maladaptive coping mechanisms, their poorly developed sense of self and relatedness to others, and the inability to manage and regulate distressing emotions. The language used to describe these behaviors and mechanisms—and the skills needed to become more healthy—are conceptually the same as those provided by many prominent psychoanalysts (Adler, 1985; Grinker, Werble, & Drye, 1968; Kernberg, 1975) and include things such as immature defenses, poorly developed object relations, and poor frustration tolerance.

Second, there is a rather new type of behavior therapy known as acceptance and commitment therapy (ACT; Hayes, Follette, & Linehan, 2004; Hayes & Strosahl, 2004) which is based on relational frame theory. According to the website http://www.contextualpsychology.org/act focuses on the language that patients use: "Through metaphor, paradox, and experiential exercises clients learn how to make healthy contact with thoughts, feelings, memories, and physical sensations that have been feared and avoided. Clients gain the skills to recontextualize and accept these private events, develop greater clarity about personal values, and commit to needed behavior change." This approach rests on the idea that patients should not avoid or work to remove unwanted thoughts, feelings, and so forth. Rather, they should approach them with a sense of acceptance and curiosity in how they have shaped their own personal history. It is not a big leap to recognize the similarity of this approach to psychoanalysis and psychoanalytic psychotherapy.

The third example comes from a review I provided of the second edition of the text by Aaron Beck, Freeman, Davis, and Associates (2004), *Cognitive Therapy for Personality Disorders.* In my review, I noted how many of the ideas discussed in the text are similar to ideas from psychodynamic psychotherapy (Huprich, 2004). For instance, Beck et al. noted how schemas developed early in life in a relational context provide cognitive templates by which to interpret the world. There are many parallels here to the concept of object relations. Beck et al. also discussed how schemas affect cognitive, affective, and behavioral patterns that are played out with the therapist and that these patterns are also prominent in the work of the therapist. These ideas seem very similar to the concepts of transference and countertransference. Finally, Beck et al. described the process of bringing unknown cognitions and schemas to conscious awareness: "Once the underlying beliefs are made accessible (conscious), the patient can then apply realistic, logical reasoning to modify them" (p. 80). These ideas seem very similar to the task of expressive, or insight-oriented, psychotherapy, which has been the focus of clinical work ever since the time of Freud.

Also as a way to advance psychoanalytic theory, Bornstein (2005) suggested that epidemiological studies of personality development and meta-analytic studies of psychoanalytic ideas should be conducted. This idea is not just a fantasy. A whole series of edited texts by Bornstein and Joseph Masling (Bornstein & Masling, 1998a, 1998b, 2002; Masling & Bornstein, 1993, 1994) was published by the American Psychological Association that review and discuss empirical verification of psychodynamic ideas in the areas of the unconscious, the therapy hour, gender and gender roles, psychopathology, object relations, and developmental psychology. Interesting texts also exist that review and integrate cognitive psychology research with psychoanalytic theory (Bucci, 1997; Shevrin, Bond, Brakel, Hertel, & Williams, 1996). Similarly, recent review papers on object relations

(Huprich & Greenberg, 2003; Stricker & Healey, 1990) and defenses (Cramer, 2000) have been published and are gaining increasing attention. Thus, the kinds of studies suggested by Bornstein (2005) are strongly backed in the literature and make valuable contributions to clinical science.

Bornstein (2005) suggested that clinicians and researchers become better advocates of psychoanalytic ideas via education of their fellow colleagues and their respective trainees and students. More so, becoming more active in the media and public forum would be a welcome addition to this spirit of advocacy. Bornstein suggested that, were nonpsychoanalytic researchers to more readily discuss the historical origins of the ideas presented by psychoanalytic theory, and were psychoanalytic researchers more likely to discuss and advocate the psychoanalytic origins of these ideas, psychoanalytic ideas will assume a more powerful role in empirical science.

From a diagnostic perspective, a monumental achievement in the advancement of psychoanalytic and psychodynamic theories has been the production of the *Psychodynamic Diagnostic Manual* (*PDM*; *PDM* Task Force, 2006), which was a collaborative effort of the American Psychoanalytic Association, International Psychoanalytic Association, Division 39 of the American Psychological Association, American Academy of Psychoanalysis and Dynamic Psychiatry, and the National Membership Committee on Psychoanalysis in Clinical Social Work. The *PDM* is designed to provide a more comprehensive assessment of the individual than current diagnostic manuals and considers itself a complement to the existing *Diagnostic and Statistical Manual of Mental Disorders* and the *International Classification of Diseases*. (More will be said about the *PDM* in Chapter 9).

Summary

This chapter has reviewed the basic principles of human mental functioning proposed by Sigmund Freud and his technique of psychoanalysis. It also has discussed the disrepair that has taken hold of psychoanalysis and psychoanalytic theory. While some of Freud's original ideas have fallen by the wayside, many have remained as fundamental tenets of psychoanalytic or psychodynamic practice. In the next chapter, I discuss how classic Freudian ideas have given way to a more commonly accepted and practiced relational perspective, de-emphasizing drives and focusing more on the nature of the therapeutic relationship and the patient's perception of the therapist and meaningful others.

Notes

1. In less severe forms of psychopathology, such as the neuroses, patients' reality testing is intact, and it is the undue influence of the superego that contributes to the production of symptoms leading to distress or dysfunction.
2. This skill was so well developed, in fact, that Solms (2002, p. 26) noted how Freud became well known for his ability to detect brain lesions very accurately, based just on the observations he made of the patient's life, such that "the pathological anatomist had nothing to add to Freud's clinical formulations in the autopsy report."

3

The Evolution of Theory I

Drive, Ego, Object, and Self[1]

Psychoanalytic theory has evolved since Freud. Some of his ideas are no longer central within psychoanalytic and psychodynamic theory, while many others have become further elaborated and understood. Although it cannot be stated at this point that psychoanalytic and psychodynamic ideas are unified both in theory and practice, some important principles remain central to those who practice from these perspectives. This chapter describes many of the major developments in psychoanalytic and psychodynamic theory, including theoretical expansions within the past 20 to 30 years. In short, this chapter demonstrates that the emphasis on drives has been shifted toward an emphasis on relationships and the development of one's sense of self. It is within these frameworks that most modern psychoanalytically and psychodynamically oriented practitioners operate today.

An Expanded View of the Psychosexual Stages

Sigmund Freud's ideas on psychosexual development were rooted in the assumption that bodily erogenous zones and the experiences of pleasure created from drive gratification affected the individual's personality development and created a relatively permanent psychological template through which the mind operates. Oral, anal, and phallic stages thus became associated with character traits such as dependency, perfectionism, and sexual promiscuity, respectively (e.g., Freud, 1917b, 1923b). Further, all psychopathology was regarded as being traced back to the unresolved conflicts of these stages.

While psychosexual development is clearly an important underpinning of personality and psychopathology, the ideas contained within the theory may be better understood today as more a theory of development per se. Libidinal derivatives remain present within the theory, but the emphasis now has shifted toward cognitive, emotional, relational, and defense development. These ideas are presented in Table 3.1 and are articulated sequentially herein.

The Oral Stage

Huprich and Keaschuk (2006) noted that the oral stage is of importance in at least three ways. First, it provides the framework with which very young children begin to develop a sense of relatedness to the world, thereby allowing them to establish a basic sense of trust. Second, it is the time in life when self and other begin to become differentiated, thereby setting down the psychic template on which experience may be evaluated as originating from within or without. Third, as self–other differentiation occurs, babies develop a sense of the inner world of drives, fantasies, impulses, affects, and wishes. This includes such things as being able to recognize their bodies and their caregivers and to experience positive feelings toward their caregivers.

Psychodynamic theorists believe that the oral stage provides the framework by which young children become aware of their inner experience and begin to receive attention and direction from others. In this phase of life, which lasts roughly from birth to 18–24 months, the world begins to be understood as a safe, trustworthy place but simultaneously as dangerous and frustrating. As perception develops, sensory experience (as it was first described by Freud) is organized by the ego into a world of people and objects, which are capable of soothing, comforting, and amusement. This includes things such as the mother's voice and a teddy bear. Oral stimulation and gratification serve as basic filters for experience. Throughout this stage, the ongoing development of object and person representation permits the young human to draw upon memory traces of people, things, and experiences. McClelland, Koestner, and Weinberg (1989) noted that this period consists of preverbal, affective experience, whereby young children "implicitly" learn rules of behavior that shape their burgeoning sense of self and other. The experience of the outer world and the representation of others occur without the function of language. Hence, conscious retrieval of experiences from this period is extremely difficult, though implicit sensory, affective, and motor

TABLE 3.1 Basic Themes in Development

Psychosexual Stage	Predominant Issues and Themes	Important Outcomes
Oral (0 months to 18 months)	Beginning to separate inner and outer world Predominant absorption in the inner world Establishing trust with the caregiver Being dependent upon a caregiver Gratifying physiological and relational needs quickly; expressing frustration when needs are not met Emphasis on oral eroticism Language and motor activity development	Basic trust in the caregiver and environment Use of language to begin to express needs Expectation of caregiving from parent Ability to act on impulses with parental care, oversight, and protection Beginning recognition of ambivalence toward others
Anal[a] (18 month to 3 years)	Further differentiation of self and other Cognitive distinctions between self and other Taking in rule-governed behavior Developing internalized controls of behavior Emphasis on behavior and independence Emphasis on control, orderliness, regulation Emphasis on anal eroticism Guilt and distress when acting outside of internalized controls	Developing sense of autonomy and mastery Growing sense of distinction between what is from within and what is not Growing sense of self-regulation Capacity to use volition without guilt Ability to act cooperatively Growing sense of ambivalence toward others Beginning to recognize the intentions of others
Phallic (3 years to 5 years)	Triadic relationship of mother–father–child Recognition of one's sex and sexual differences Recognition of sex roles and values Desire for opposite-sex parent Competition, shared desires, jealousy Fears over harm and loss because of desire Guilt over one's sexual impulses and wishes Emphasis on genital eroticism	Repression of sexualized and aggressive feelings toward parents Recognition of competition, jealousy, and shared desires that minimizes potential for loss and harm Growing recognition of complexity of others' thoughts, feelings, wishes, and desires

(*Continued*)

TABLE 3.1 (Continued)

Psychosexual Stage	Predominant Issues and Themes	Important Outcomes
Latent (5 years to puberty)	De-emphasis on sexual interest Tendency to play with same sex Further refinement of self and other representations Further development of empathy Further development of analytic reasoning	Repression or redirection of interests toward other activities Expanded ability to use various types of reasoning Good mastery of impulses and drives Further consolidation of sex-role identification Further consolidation of mastering skills, activities Broadened social contact, social interest Quality of relationships matures; other represented in more holistic ways
Genital (Puberty to young adulthood)	Onset of menses in girls and expression of secondary sex characteristics in both sexes Interest in sexual activities, relationships Psychological separation from parents Developing sense of self-identity	Ability to both love and work successfully Ability to manage conflicts that evoke earlier psychosexual themes Acceptance of societal standards and capacity to operate within these parameters

[a]Some have made reference to a urethral stage of psychosexual development. See Meissner (2000) for further discussion of this issue. This table was developed with reference to Blatt, Wein, Chevron, and Quinlan (1979), Brenner (1973), Compton (1995), and Meissner (2000).

Source: From Huprich, S. K. & Keaschuk, R., In F. Andrasik (Ed.), *Comprehensive Handbook of Personality and Psychopathology: Volume II: Adult Psychopathology* (M. Hersen & J. Thomas, Series Editors), New York: John Wiley & Sons, 2006. (With permission.)

experiences provide a way by which young children respond to new experiences and new people. Not surprisingly, overgratification of, or unfulfilled, oral needs may lead to later problems with dependency as well as to problems with depressed mood if loss of the caregiver's love and support occurs.

The Anal Stage

The second stage, the anal stage, is known for its emphasis on control, orderliness, regulation, separation, and independence. This stage occurs roughly from 18–24 months to 36 months and derives its name from children's increased awareness of anal functions, their ability to control or regulate these functions, and their interactions with parents or caregivers to master this bodily function. Conflict is felt and experienced when bodily impulses and tensions and appropriate means of relieving them do not comfortably coexist. More broadly, however, is the importance of increasing self-awareness and the deliberate exercising of their desire to act on their inner wishes, states, and needs. Conflicts with the caregiver occur regularly, as willful and curious children seek to learn about the world and their parents' or caregivers' sets rules, guidelines, and even prohibitions about what they may or may not do. Within this time period, language is rapidly acquired, motor skills quickly develop, and an interest in doing things for oneself occurs. This often leads to conflict between protective and caring parents and willful and curious children. For many parents, this period is described as the "the terrible twos," though many parents would add that the next year of life—"the terrible threes"—also is part of this developmental period. And while self and other representations become more defined and articulated, there is an ongoing internal struggle to understand and accept ambivalence toward others and life's experience. This can be observed, for instance, in children's insistence on having a snack or toy when it is not appropriate to do so (e.g., having an extra cookie or taking a toy from a sibling who is playing with it).

Inherent in this stage is the growing ability of children to associate and judge their actions as right versus wrong or good versus bad. Stated differently, as the superego develops during this stage, children come to evaluate their experience in moral terms. This evaluation may originate from a direct pronouncement from the parent (e.g., saying, "No, do not hit your sister") or from an identification process with the caregiver (i.e., acting and being like the caregiver who is admired and respected). Ideally, children near the end of this stage (roughly around 2 1/2 to 3 years old) come to act on their desires and intentions without guilt while at the same time have a rudimentary sense of what is right and wrong and a belief that caregivers can and will provide them with guidance and instruction.

The Phallic Stage

The phallic stage, which lasts roughly from 3 to 5 years of age, presents the child with new awareness and psychological challenges. Recognition of one's own sex and difference from the other sex becomes a preoccupying theme. Early in this stage, children experience desires for love and care from both parents. As cultural, societal, and parental values are introjected and internalized, they play a predominant role in shaping children's sense of their core gender identity, gender role identity, and sexual partner orientation. Children become more aware of their needs and wishes to have a relationship with their opposite-sex parents, but they also become aware that same-sex parents share their affections for opposite-sex parents.[2] Consequently, feelings of competition and jealousy become predominant in the psychic life of the child. The child may feel guilt for having pleasurable or aggressive feelings toward the parents if the emphasis of the past has been on order and control (i.e., a strong superego presence). Conversely, if children's impulses express themselves forcefully and with relatively lower levels of restraint, children may pursue what they want and may become highly aggressive or oppositional toward their parents or others when their wishes or desires cannot be fulfilled. Since children are ultimately frustrated in achieving the kind of relationship they desire with the opposite-sex parent, angry, hostile, or competitive affect may come to characterize the object relations of children and their same-sex parent. To the extent that this frustration is successfully repressed and other relationships later come to take the place of the parental relationship is the extent to which jealousy, competition, and desire comprise the inner life of the person as an adult. Not surprisingly, narcissistic and antisocial tendencies may be observed in adulthood when the aforementioned feelings are not resolved.

While these major themes remain of interest to those who practice psychoanalytically or psychodynamically, Freud's original ideas about gender identity and sexual orientation are not accepted in their entirety by many. For example, some analysts prefer to think of the first genital stage as occurring between 2 and 6 years of age (Parens, Pollok, Stern, & Kramer, 1977). Others criticize Freud's emphasis on the primacy of the male gender identity in both male and female sexual development, though they are understandable within the culture in which Freud lived. Some have suggested that Freud actually repressed a deeper universal fear: the dread and denial of the encompassing powers of the mother's vagina (Chasseguet-Smirgel, 1988). Others advocated a more balanced perspective of the influence of the male and female phallus and children's development of their sexuality and gender within the context of their relationship with both their mother and father. At the same time, others have advocated for a substantially new understanding of female sexuality (Kulish & Holtzman, 2008) and what is now known as the first genital phase, which is composed of Oedipal features. This view has replaced the traditional view that espoused Oedipal and Electra phenomena—the latter term is used now only by Jungians. Fast (1984) suggested that each sex envies what the other has: Boys envy their mother's capacity to bear and nurture children, while girls envy the power and advantages of a penis. Benjamin (1992), too, has suggested that masculinity and femininity come to be understood in both sexes as a balance between the tension for assertion (which is more reinforced as a quality of males) and interpersonal relatedness (which is more reinforced as a feminine quality). Bisexual longings and desires are considered to be a universal phenomenon by many psychoanalytic and psychodynamic writers (e.g., Benjamin, 1988, 1995; Butler, 1995; Elise, 1997, 1998; Fast, 1984, 1990; Hansell, 1998; Kernberg, 1991; McDougall, 1995; Stoller, 1972; Winnicott, 1971). Indeed, the development of gender identity and sexual orientation are "complex psychological and social constructions, not at all a simple extension of either our anatomically based reproductive capacities or our brain physiology" (Mitchell & Black, 1995, p. 224). In fact, a significant literature with diverging perspectives has emerged on those factors that shape the eventual development of a homosexual or heterosexual orientation (Isay, 1986; Parens et al., 1977; Roughton, 2002; Socarides, 2002; Socarides & Volkan, 1991).[3]

Latency

Latency, the fourth psychosexual stage, is a relatively docile stage. Lasting approximately from age 5 through the onset of puberty, the child enters into primarily same-sex relationships, engaging regularly in play and other shared activities. Cognitive and intellectual abilities quickly expand, and thinking moves to formal operational and abstract levels in the analytic and moral domains (Kohlberg, 1981; Piaget, 1990). By this point, impulses and desires as well as how to appropriately have them met are enacted, and greater awareness of the thoughts, needs, and desires of others occurs. Social interest and investment in relationships also should occur, as should mutually gratifying peer and family relationships.

The Genital Stage

The final period of psychosexual development, the genital stage, begins with the onset of puberty. Secondary sexual characteristics begin to develop, and hormonal and physiological processes prepare the young person for physical reproduction. Consequently, interest in sexual relationships reappears, and latent sexual interest now is expressed. At this time, like in any other time, conflicts from past stages may shape or influence behavior. For instance, strong needs to control may lead the individual to press for definition and greater control of the interpersonal dynamics of a new relationship.

Thus, a more modern understanding of psychosexual stages is that they are a theory of personality development. Cognitive capacities, the increasing ability to master impulses, affects, and desires, and the interaction of children with important people in their life become the foci of personality development. In other words, the activities of the ego, the way interpersonal relationships come to be understood, and individuals' sense of agency and effectiveness are of prime importance.

Ego Psychology

Freud observed in his psychoanalytic work with patients that they tended to avoid particular topics, issues, or material. He quickly deduced that this material consisted of psychic conflict that was ripe for analytic exploration and understanding. Yet patients' defensive processes served a protective function in preventing them from examining these elements within themselves. Later in his career, Freud began to discuss more frequently the necessity of understanding defenses—an important property of the ego. It was Freud's daughter, Anna, who came to elaborate on these processes more completely, which contributed to a shift that occurred in psychoanalytic theory to understanding the functions of the ego. Her book *The Ego and Mechanisms of Defense* (Freud, 1936) quickly led analytic practitioners to move beyond understanding id derivatives of psychopathology into a more here-and-now understanding of what it was that kept patients from exploring conflicted material. In this work she described nine commonly used defense mechanisms: regression, displacement, reaction formation, isolation of affect, undoing, introjection, identification, turning against the self, reversal, and sublimation. Other defenses that have been described include repression, projection, projective identification, splitting, somatization, conversion, devaluation, intellectualization, and rationalization. These are described in Table 3.2 (although other defenses have been described that are not reported here). In addition, it should be noted that patterns of defenses often are observed to occur together, such as is found in various personality (or character) types. For instance, projection, devaluing, and idealizing are common defenses found among individuals with a narcissistic personality.

Heinz Hartmann

The one individual who is often associated with being the "founding father" of ego psychology (Mitchell & Black, 1995, p. 34) is Heinz Hartmann. Hartmann was an astute student of psychoanalytic theory and was particularly influenced by Anna Freud's ideas about the importance of understanding defense mechanisms. He also was strongly influenced by Charles Darwin's ideas about adaptation and how evolution led to organisms' increased ability to adapt. For Hartmann, it did not make sense that the human psyche was inherently conflicted without any natural abilities that were interfered with by internal conflict. This seemed to be logically implausible in the context of evolutionary theory. While Freud saw the ego developing

TABLE 3.2 Mechanisms of Defense and Examples

Mechanism	Example
Conversion	This defense is most commonly observed in patients with a histrionic personality and is the symbolic representation of psychological pain via a physical condition. For example, a woman experiences great difficulty in walking and resorts to a wheelchair after her husband dies. Her physical symptom represents her fears and sense of danger she would consciously experience were she to have to "stand on her own two feet" to care for her family.
Devaluing	This defense occurs often in conjunction with idealization and is observed when a person unconsciously experiences a threat from another person and subsequently minimizes or refutes the actions or accomplishments of another. For example, a student unconsciously is envious and jealous of the accomplishments of another student and begins to make disparaging comments toward and about the other student.
Displacement	This occurs unconsciously when feelings associated toward one person or source are directed toward another. For example, this defense is inherent in the idea of transference or may be seen when an angry woman treats her spouse with contempt when he requests something from her, which masks her unconscious frustration toward her father who had made requests of her that she did not believe she could fulfill.
Idealization	This defense occurs unconsciously when an individual attributes very favorable properties or qualities to another person without considering the person's negative qualities or attributes. This defense allows a person to protect himself or herself from the disappointment that would be felt in recognizing the person is just as human and real as he or she is. For instance, a patient engages in psychotherapy and attributes great power and brilliance to the therapist, despite instances in the therapy where the therapist has misunderstood the patient or not empathically identified with the issues the patient presents.
Identification	This occurs when an individual takes on physical or psychological qualities of a person to compensate for his or her own feelings of inadequacy or other unacceptable urges. For example, a young man believes he is unattractive but starts to dress in ways that are like a rock star so that he can be sexually attractive to others. In situations in which a person has been held against her will, the victim may start to harbor the same feelings as her perpetrator as a way to avoid her own angry and distressing feelings of being detained.

Intellectualization	This is an explanation a person makes for an upsetting or troubling situation in which affect is not addressed. For example, an individual attributes his poor performance on an exam to his lack of studying, despite the fact that the entire class did poorly on the exam and that his study habits are the best in the class. This explanation averts his feelings of anger and hostility toward the teacher who made an unfair exam.
Introjection	This defense occurs when a person internalizes aspects of a meaningful person who is no longer present or available (i.e., object loss). It also can occur when someone internalizes some element of a bad or hostile object as a way by which the person believes he or she can have more control over that person. For example, a man begins to wear the same kind of clothes that his father did after his father passed away. Or, an individual gives much credence to the criticism of a coworker and works hard to make changes to prove to the coworker that she had the wrong impression of her. She also subsequently talks negatively about the coworker as a means of unconsciously punishing her for making such comments.
Isolation of Affect	This defense occurs with intellectualization and allows the person to acknowledge affect, but only in a detached, nonemotive way. For example, an individual who performs badly on the exam acknowledges that he has hostility toward the instructor who made the exam in a matter-of-fact, unelaborated manner.
Projection	This occurs when an individual unconsciously attributes an unacceptable idea or feeling within himself or herself onto another person, in which such feelings are readily identified and dealt with. For example, an individual feels angry and guilty about his inability to relate to others yet openly voices his disdain for the mistreatment he has perceived from all the people he knows.
Projective Identification	This defense occurs in three steps and is often observed in the therapy process. First, the individual unconsciously experiences an unwanted thought or feeling and projects it onto another person, such as the therapist. Second, the therapist or other person experiences or identifies with this unwanted thought or feeling. Third, the therapist or other person begins to respond to the individual in ways consistent with this projected material. Ideally, a therapist recognizes this process before the third step and is able to use the experience to address the patient's defensive processes. As an example not related to a therapy process, projective identification can be dramatically observed in sexual homicide perpetrators. The individual begins to experience sexual and dependency feelings toward another person and begins to express his sexual feelings. The victim may comply out of fear or be forced to comply. When the perpetrator has completed his sexual act, he sees in his victim his own neediness or dependency, which is abhorrent to him. Subsequently, he kills the victim to eradicate in himself the feelings that are so strongly detested.

(*Continued*)

TABLE 3.2 (Continued)

Mechanism	Example
Rationalization	This defense occurs when an individual posits an explanation for a situation that allows the person to avoid or approach the situation with less conflict than what was experienced before the explanation. The explanation can vary in terms of its rational plausibility. For example, a faculty member is denied tenure by her department because the department believes that she has not been a good mentor to students. This belief allows the members of the department to avoid their own feelings of inadequacy as mentors and to express their jealousy toward her in a way that is more acceptable.
Reaction Formation	This occurs when an individual unconsciously disavows an idea or impulse by doing the opposite. For example, an individual becomes a minister and strongly opposes pornography and wars, which mask his own unconscious sexual urges and murderous impulses toward those who psychologically hurt him.
Regression	This defense may be seen in behaviors or in psychological functioning and permits the individual to return to an earlier, more child-like way of functioning that permits unwanted feelings or desires to be expressed. For instance, a woman who becomes depressed remains in bed all day and is brought food by her husband, as a way by which to obtain support and care that is not openly expressed. As another example, a patient who has experienced a trauma begins to have irrational fears and paranoia about being traumatized again.
Repression	This is a commonly used defense in which unwanted or unacceptable thoughts, wishes, or ideas are unconsciously blocked from awareness. For example, an individual may be very frustrated at a friend but will not allow himself to consider that such feelings exist.
Somatization	This occurs when an individual unconsciously transfers psychologically uncomfortable experiences to a body part or region, which subsequently feels pain. For example, an individual is angry at his employer for perceived mistreatment and develops wrist and elbow pain, which mask the impulse to physically lash out.

Splitting	This defense is commonly observed in individuals with borderline personality disorder or other severe personality pathology. Splitting occurs when individuals are not able to integrate both pleasing and frustrating aspects of either themselves or others, such that the self or other person is experienced as pervasively pleasing or frustrating. For example, a woman becomes enraged with her boyfriend of six months when he cannot spend the evening with her due to a work commitment. Despite their relationship history, she experiences him as uncaring, cruel, and rejecting.
Sublimation	This defense occurs when an individual is able to redirect an impulse or desire from something that would be socially unacceptable to something more acceptable and adaptive. For instance, a person who has aggressive feelings toward a coworker and acts out physically toward him would lead to considerable problems; however, by engaging in physical exercise, she may be able to discharge her frustration and tension in a more adaptive way.
Undoing	This defense involves magical ideation in which a person engages in a symbolic action that keeps other thoughts or ideas out of awareness. For example, an individual compulsively checks locks on the house multiple times when leaving, which masks feelings of fear, intrusion, or being violated.

after birth and acquiring its adaptive skills through the necessary use of secondary process thinking (in contrast to the default mechanism of primary process thinking), Hartmann (1939/1958) believed that at birth there must be part of the psyche that functions independent of conflict so that children can quickly adapt to their surroundings. He consequently argued that perception, comprehension, thinking, language, and thought all are *ego functions* that are *innate, autonomous,* and *conflict-free*: They exist at birth and operate independently from the prominent id impulses. This view of the psyche, and human nature for that matter, was significantly different from Freud's. However, this does not mean the ego is unaffected by conflict—these processes can become impaired because of the conflict and maladaptive use of defenses (e.g., sexual and aggressive desires intrude into thought and perception). While Freud saw sublimation—transforming socially unacceptable impulses into behaviors that are more acceptable—as a necessity for the individual to adapt to a civilized culture, Hartmann believed that sexual and aggressive drives could be removed by the ego, such that sublimation was no longer necessary because the sublimated activity was valued for its own sake. Hartmann described this process as *neutralization* and said that the behaviors took on secondary autonomy (independence from their drive). For example, an individual who enjoys tasting and sampling various wines may be viewed in Freudian terms as having strong oral needs that become sublimated in adulthood. From an ego psychology perspective, the wine tasting has lost an attachment to oral libidinal needs and, instead, is associated with the pleasure of mastery over an area of interest and other potential gains, such as the interpersonal pleasures of sharing the interest with a friend.

In observing the development of ego psychology, both Marcus (1999) and Wallerstein (2002) noted how ego psychology in the tradition of Hartmann and Anna Freud became the fundamental driving paradigm in American psychoanalytic circles for decades, despite the development of object relations theory in some of the British schools. In an expansion of the role of the ego and defenses, Waelder (1936) wrote about how the id, ego, and superego contributed to psychopathology and psychological symptoms, noting that therapeutic intervention must address how each of these elements were involved in the formation and maintenance of the symptoms. Eissler's (1953) paper on clinical work "served for at least two decades as the benchmark against which the analytic technique of those trained in American ego psychology would be measured" (Wallerstein, 2002, p. 140). Simply stated, Eissler suggested that free association and the interpretation of transference were the core components of treatment and that it was the work of the analyst alone that led to a reduction in the patient's symptoms and conflicts. Wallerstein (2002) noted how psychoanalytically oriented therapy was derived from this position, with expressive therapies being described as approximating the work of psychoanalysis and supportive therapies being the most deviant. Expressive therapies sought to uncover intrapsychic conflicts, whereas supportive therapies were aimed at strengthening the ego's ability to identify, manage, and overcome inner conflict and turmoil. All of these approaches—psychoanalysis proper, expressive therapies, and supportive therapies—rest on the idea that the patient's ego must participate at two levels. One of these is the experiencing ego, which experiences affects and feelings and reenacts old affects and feelings (such as is observed in transference). The other is the observing ego, which takes on the role of an outside observer who comments on and understands experiences and processes that are going on within oneself. Although the idea of this split in the ego was first introduced by Sterba (1934) and was expanded upon by Eissler, they remain today as important components of patients and their behavior in the context of treatment.

Jacob Arlow and Charles Brenner

One very important development and theoretical transformation during this time period was the articulation of *compromise formations* (Arlow & Brenner, 1964; Brenner, 1982). Expanding upon Freud's ideas, Arlow and Brenner (1964) suggested that the compromise formation should be understood within a tripartite format; that is, id, ego, and superego all are involved in the development and maintenance of the formation of symptoms. Stated simply, instead of just dwelling on the drive (id), therapeutic intervention should look at the dynamic interplay of ego functions and superego constraints to best understand how the patient's symptoms and problems were manifest. In a seminal text, *The Mind in Conflict*, Brenner (1982) suggested that there are no specific defense mechanisms. Rather, there are four important forces involved that produce the symptoms and problems observed in neurotic patients: (1) the push of drive expression; (2) the pressures of the superego to act (or not act as the case may be); (3) the ego's defensive need to regulate these forces for maximal adaptation to the environment; and (4) the ego's intent to minimize dysphoric emotional states, such as anxiety and depression.

As an example of a compromise formation, consider the patient described in chapter 2 who reverted to the Internet to obtain sexual gratification. In the course of treatment, it became clear that his wife was not providing much support or encouragement for him and was highly critical of most of his activities around the home. The patient turned to the Internet as a means by which to look at and to interact with images of women who were friendly, engaging, and seductive. While the patient was clearly distressed about the amount of time he spent looking at these images, he seemed rather motivated to look at them, despite conscious protests about his behavior. It is obvious that the patient's sexual and emotional urges were not being met at home (pull of the drive [1]) and that his superego consciously opposed his activities. However, at a more unconscious level, his superego also permitted him to engage in such behavior because he rightfully deserved to be treated more appropriately and deserved sexual gratification and enjoyment [2]. More so, his behaviors represented an aggressive element in which he could symbolically get back at his unavailable wife by being more intimate with another woman. In terms of the ego's adaptation to environmental contingencies [3], engaging in Internet activities in an office in his private business provided him a way to obtain sexual gratification and support from others such that he would be protected from being "discovered" by his wife or by others who might condemn his "affair." And in terms of protecting himself from dysphoric affect [4], it is quite obvious that his sexual gratification and arousal masked anxiety he would feel around his critical wife, as well as potential depression he may feel from the loss of love and support he experienced from her.

Margaret Mahler

Greenberg and Mitchell (1983, p. 272) described Margaret Mahler as "the most influential follower of Hartmann's strategy of expanding the drive model to encompass new dimensions of psychological development." Mahler was a pediatrician before she was an analyst and took special interest in the first few years of life, when children begin to make distinctions between the inner world and outer world, self and others, and the stability and trustworthiness of others and oneself. For Mahler, resolving the Oedipal period was not the most fundamental achievement of development; rather, the *separation and individuation* of children from their mother was paramount.

Mahler thought of separation and individuation as a milestone in the psychological birth of the child (Mahler, Pine, & Bergman, 1975). Infants enter the world in a stage of *autism*, which occurs during the first few weeks of life. Here infants seem impervious to the world around them. They are oriented internally and are unresponsive to much of the stimulation of the external world.[4] Knowing that the sensory organs are not fully developed in this time period, Mahler saw this time period as having evolved to help protect children from external threats or pressures as they are orienting to the new world. In the *symbiotic phase* (starting around 3–4 weeks), children begin to show increased sensitivity and responsiveness to the outer world. Experience begins to be organized at this stage as pleasurable or painful, and an awareness of their mother begins; however, this experience is symbiotic. Infants do not realize their mother is separate from them.

In the third phase, *differentiation*, a series of events starts to unfold. Beginning at the fourth or fifth month, children enter into a subphase known as *hatching*. They are more alert and oriented to the world surrounding them. Children begin to recognize their mother as separate, and they seek her out. Other objects start to take on recognition. There is a beginning awareness of internal and external perception. In the next subphase, *practicing*, children are about 10 months old. They begin developing locomotion through crawling and eventually walking. Their mother still remains an important source of emotional comfort. Once upright, children have officially experienced *psychological birth*, as they have an expanded orientation and mastery of their body and ability to interact with it.

The final subphase is called *rapprochement*, which occurs around 15–18 months. Here children begin to recognize that they are small people in a very large environment and are in need of their mother for help and comfort. No longer is there the sense of omnipotence that came with walking and early exploration. With expanded cognitive and perceptual abilities, children see that their mother is not immediately available and must be sought out. Around 18–24 months, a rapprochement crisis ensues in which children recognize their need for mother while at the same time very much want greater independence. Intense neediness and dependency (coupled with being clinging and feeling frustrated) alternates with willful attempts at separation and subsequent fighting. There is intense splitting here, where experiences of mother are considered as "all good" or "all bad." Likewise, mothers' responses to their children become very important. As mothers attempt to understand their children's frustration yet allow for separation, children must come to learn that the frustrating mothers, upon whom they are so dependent, are also the loving mothers, who allow them to pursue their separation and individuation. Mothers can be very attuned to children's changing needs at this stage. Alternatively, they may overtly encourage clinging behaviors and dependency or direct their child toward independence too quickly. Thus, a child later may become dependent or obstinately independent and assertive. Mahler believed that mothers' responses to children during this time period would have a tremendous influence on how they come to internalize their sense of self as being separate from others, yet interdependent with others, and that others will be sensitive to their needs. Once this has happened, children have achieved *libidinal constancy* and will be on their way toward functioning independently without the ongoing requirement of the presence of their mother. Patients with borderline personality disorder often exhibit the behavior of the rapprochement crisis child in their transference. They cannot tolerate their strong dependency on the therapist, who may at times be viewed as excessively frustrating. For many therapists, understanding the dynamics of this period helps them understand the internal dynamics of their patients who seem both to desire and hate the care of their therapist.

Edith Jacobson

A profoundly meaningful advancement in psychoanalytic theory came from Edith Jacobson (1964). In her book *The Self and the Object World*, she attempted to integrate drive theory with the relational ideas that were being expressed by Mahler, Anna Freud, Hartmann, and others. Based on her clinical work and thinking, Jacobson suggested that drives are not to be considered a biological given; rather, they are potentials that exist at birth and develop through experience. In agreement with Spitz (1945), she suggested that infants organize their earliest experiences around the experience of pleasure and the experience of pain, which provide the infant with "affective perception." These earliest experiences of pleasure and pain become embedded in a drive, but they develop within the context of infants' experience with the caretaker. Thus, being oriented toward a caretaker becomes a motivating force in and of itself that is differentiated from the drive. For Jacobson, the mother can be *frustrating*, which relates to not have a drive met. She also can be *disappointing*, in which is anger is directed toward the mother for not meeting the drive (whose actions led to a state of frustration). Thus, libidinal and aggressive drives can develop; libido is oriented toward another person and promotes contact, whereas aggression is oriented toward a psychological separation from the object.

As noted, one of Jacobson's (1964) important modifications of drive theory is the emphasis on affective perception over drive. She noted that drive theory emphasizes the tension and displeasure felt by unfulfilled drives. As tension mounts, so does displeasure, and that pleasure only comes by way of drive reduction. This is the essence of the pleasure principle. However, Jacobson challenged that view. Some pleasure is associated with mounting tension, such as sexual excitement or the anticipation of an enjoyable event. Other times, the discharge of a tension is unpleasurable (e.g., crying), or prolonged experiences of no tension are unpleasurable (e.g., the experience of boredom). Consequently, the pleasure principle and its association to mounting tension and discharge are not as simple as Freud envisioned. Rather, it is the dynamic interplay of tension and discharge and the experience of pleasure that becomes important to understand. Greenberg and Mitchell (1983, p. 319) made some cogent observations about this theoretical change: "Once again, we are pointed toward a level of theorizing in which the importance of the interpersonal context in which pleasure is experienced will be stressed." Hence, the interpersonal world took on greater interest than the inner world of drives and conflicts.

To summarize, the work of Brenner (1982) substantially reduced the effect of Hartmann's ideas of the conflict-free ego. Likewise, Mahler (1975) and Jacobson (1964) introduced ideas that began to emphasize the importance of other people and one's sense of separateness from them. Yet, according to Wallerstein (2002), ego psychology retained a strong identification with Brenner and Hartmann in the American psychoanalytic community until the mid-1970s. In this time period, two major schools of thought began to win over American psychoanalytic theorists and therapists—that of object relations and self psychology.

Object Relations

Object relations is a major school of thought within psychoanalytic theory that departed remarkably from Freud's original ideas about neurotic conflicts and overcoming Oedipal crises. Students often find the term *object relations* a bit confusing, as it refers to *interpersonal interactions*; object relations is thus a school of thought about the nature of the interpersonal relationships and how self and other representations and the prevailing affect that connects them form the basis for the individual's sense of well-being and effectiveness. The use of the word *object* originated from Freud, who suggested that drives and their aims of seeking gratification are ultimately satisfied by the inadvertent discovery of an object, such as the mother's breast. Thus, early psychological life was founded on gratification by an object. As psychoanalytic theory evolved, many individuals came to recognize the importance and power of the "object" that satisfies drives. Indeed, it was the persons who were caregivers—often the parents—that were highly important "objects" and from whom the template for other object relations was formed.

Melanie Klein

One of the earliest and most influential individuals in developing the importance of object relations was Melanie Klein (1964, 1975). Klein was a troubled woman who had experienced a very poor relationship with her mother and had severe depressive episodes. Upon reading Freud's writings about dreams, she quickly developed an interest in his theory and how it helped account for her own suffering and disillusionment. She went on to study psychoanalysis and worked with children, interpreting their play in the same way that adult interpretations were made about free associations. Her ideas differed sharply from those of Anna Freud, such that many early followers of psychoanalytic theory and treatment rejected her ideas. Yet her ideas were found to have merit and important explanatory power. Today, many Kleinian groups and societies exist, and her ideas continue to have an influence in clinical practice.

Klein believed that all individuals suffered from deep, unconscious fears of psychological disorganization, which produced incredible anxiety and depression. She felt that such fears were inborn and that infants and very young children's mental lives were full of terrifying thoughts and ideas. To understand this process, Klein described infants as being in a *paranoid position*. In this state, children feel tremendous persecution from the object world. Objects could annihilate and destroy, which evokes very strong aggressive feelings that overcome infants. By describing infant life in this manner, Klein upheld Freud's ideas of the death instinct, which very few others had attempted to integrate into their thinking. Also as part of this position, young children were understood as having a very active fantasy life about the destructive nature of the object world. These fantasies, along with the corresponding feelings of terror and aggression, are basic features of the paranoid position.

As infants begin to interact with the object world, they quickly begin to experience pleasure from the breast. However, there also are moments of frustration with the breast, in which it is not readily available or accessible. Imagine young children hungry and ready to feed; they get close to their mother's breast, feel the touch of their mother, yet feel frustrated. This breast is "bad" in that it is not producing food. When the breast is finally accessed and the child receives the milk, the experience is satisfying and the breast is good; hence, Klein described infants' experiences of the "good breast" and the "bad breast." This separation of the good breast and the bad breast is an example of the defense of splitting, and it occurs very early in life. When children split the breast in this way, they are in the *schizoid position*, which co-occurs with the paranoid position. It is not just the breast, however, that is good or bad. As children's ability to represent objects increases, they identify their mother as not only one who gratifies but also as one who frustrates. This elicits incredible anxiety for children, as now the good breast/mother is also the bad breast/mother. The fantasized bad breast is now seen as belonging to the very person to whom the children are dependent and from whom they receive great satisfaction. Upon recognizing this, children feel tremendous anxiety and guilt, because they harbor deep anxieties and destructive feelings toward the good mother. At this point, children enter the *depressive position*. They are overwhelmed by guilt and confusion. To cope with such feelings, they may employ a *manic defense*, in which they escape from the object that has been so loved and hated. Psychological independence and separation from the caregiver are strongly pursued, yet the pursuit is futile, given the relative dependency children have on their mother. Envy also is an important part of this experience. In Kleinian terms, *envy* is such an extreme dislike of the object upon which one is dependent that one must attempt to spoil it in some way. It is more problematic than splitting, because envy destroys what is good, leaving little hope for something good to ensue. In other words, envy is a pathological manifestation of desire.

How is this conflict resolved? For Klein, children must learn over time that the loving mother—and hence their loving feelings toward her—are stronger than the fantasized, destructive, terrorizing mother. This is the process of *reparation*. Love conquers hate—that is, unless the mother is not consistent in providing good mothering and demonstrating love and acceptance toward her child. Clinically, it is the case that in some patients, it is very hard to believe that a very caring figure (i.e., the therapist) can truly be caring and that the therapist's good intentions are much stronger than any negative feelings she or he may express to patients. When such ideas cannot be accepted, envy sets in. For example, a patient expressed to her therapist that she "does not trust anyone." After months of therapy, she proclaimed that the therapist was trustworthy, because she was different—it is her job. "As for others out there, I don't fully trust any of them." She often commented that "if you [others] hurt me one time, that's it. I'm done with you." Yet her desire for relationships, and subsequently her envy, continued to grow in conjunction with her trust in the therapy relationship. As therapy progressed and her acceptance of the therapist as a good object who would not destroy her continued, she found herself having conflicts about coming back to therapy. Indeed, as she began to experience some reparation, her envy also arose in the form of wishing to discontinue therapy. By stopping therapy, she could symbolically destroy what she saw as growing goodness and trust, thereby preventing any possibility of getting hurt again.

Thus, Klein provided some of the earliest writings on the importance of internalized objects and the individual's relationships with them (Klein, 1964, 1975). Though she is most known for her discussion of early infancy, she applied such ideas to her work with both adults and children. Indeed, her revolutionary thinking led the way for others to think about the importance of the internal object world and how it affected one's well-being.

Michael Balint

Michael Balint was analyzed by Sandor Ferenczi, and according to Mitchell and Black (1995, p. 135), "Balint's contribution was an extension of Ferenczi's." Ferenczi believed that early parental deprivation played an important role in the development of psychopathology. He and Balint both thought that patients seek treatment not to overcome their sexual and aggressive urges but to engage with a new love object who could provide unconditional acceptance. Balint (1968) described the *basic fault*, which is a failure by parents in being able to meet children's needs with the requisite unconditional acceptance that was required to develop their sense of self and capacity to relate to others. He observed that patients sought treatment believing that something was missing inside of them, which in this case was a sense of knowing and understanding oneself completely. To overcome such ideas, the therapist must take on the role of a new object, who accepts and values patients who work to find their way and their sense of individuality.

Balint (1968) observed that patients sought to adapt to the basic fault through one of two mechanisms—excessive dependency on others or participation in many creative activities—which stimulated a relationship with their internal worlds. Treatment provided the mechanism by which individuals came to know themselves via favorable regard and reflection from the therapist. Balint's ideas have been criticized, however, for not describing in more depth the manner in which id, ego, and superego change as a result of this basic fault (Sutherland, 1980).

Donald W. Winnicott

Related to Balint are the ideas of Donald W. Winnicott (1965), who thought that failures of the parent to attend to the needs and potentials expressed in children led to the development of the *false self.*

Like Balint, Winnicott described patients who entered treatment feeling as if they were missing something or not really knowing who they are. The *true self*, by contrast, develops when the mother recognizes the potential and ideas of children as they are spontaneously expressed. This behavior, known as *primary maternal preoccupation*, leads to children's developing a sense of omnipotence. In this state of *subjective omnipotence*, children harbor the *illusion* that their desires can be met in the environment.

According to Winnicott, subjective omnipotence is necessary for the true self to develop. Knowing one's inner world, desires, and wishes, and seeing that they can be met by the outer world, is a fundamental developmental event that leads to knowing oneself. It is not necessary, however, that mothers be able to meet every wish of children, nor is it the case that children be perfectly protected from anything that could lead to distress. Winnicott believed that the mothering had to be "good enough," in that it created a physical world and experiences in relationships that fostered children's sense of curiosity and belief in an environment and world that met their needs. Winnicott described this as a *facilitating environment*, where children have the opportunity to explore and interact in the world in such a way that they ultimately would be protected by the caregiver from any danger while at the same time the caregivers encouraged the children's sense of independence.

An important step in the development of the true self was the early experience of *transitional objects in transitional space*. Typical transitional objects include teddy bears and blankets. These are objects in the environment to which children attribute special meaning out of their sense of omnipotence. For example, "The teddy bear has the power to make me feel better;" however, unlike the experience of total omnipotence, the teddy bear is not created by the child's wish but rather exists in the real world and is there for the child's use. Later in development, children will learn that they must seek out people and things to help comfort them, accepting the limits of their own fantasies and desires to be automatically comforted or soothed. But with the teddy bear or blanket, the transitional object is already there for them to interact with. Greenberg and Mitchell (1983) nicely described one of the many functions of the transitional object: It helps "the baby negotiate the gradual shift from the experience of himself as the center of a totally subjective world to the sense of himself as a person among other persons" (p. 195). The transitional object thus serves an important function of acting in a soothing capacity and operates as a maternal substitute for children. It is an object in the real world, yet it has magical qualities that are instilled on it by children. In their transitional space, children come to recognize that their wishes and ideas interact favorably with objects in the world.

It is particularly important to note that within object relations theories such as Winnicott's, the object world plays a very important role in psychological development. Wallerstein (2002) described object relations approaches as "two-person psychology" that is focused on the "interpsychic, or interpersonal, experience within the transference-countertransference matrix, of two interacting personalities or subjectives—of patient and analyst—together constructing the meaning of their shared experience of the interactive process…" (p. 151). Unlike the Freudian and ego psychological focus on inner conflict of id and superego, and the defenses used to ward off the anxiety, Winnicott and object relations theorists spend much time talking about developmental experience and what children needed to develop meaningful connectedness to others. It was through relatedness that children's inner life was formed and developed. Consequently, in terms of therapeutic technique, Winnicott suggested that what was crucial was the presence of "good enough" therapists who accepted individuals and fostered their own internal exploration. Interpretations of transference and conflict took on a secondary role, only in that they helped patients understand how their object relations were affecting current problems.

William R. D. Fairbairn

William R. D. Fairbairn (1952) articulated perhaps the most extreme departure from Freudian theory. Fairbairn believed that the structure of the ego had its own energy, unlike Freud who thought that energy was found only in the impulses of the id. Fairbairn reasoned that because the ego was a psychic structure, it must contain energy. Freud, by contrast, thought that impulses of energy sought an outlet in the object world and that it was the task of the ego to assist in this outlet. More fundamentally, Fairbairn suggested that people seek and desire relationships—they are object seeking, not pleasure seeking. Although psychosexual stages and erogenous zones were still acknowledged by Fairbairn, they were part of the psychological processes by which the object-seeking libido operated. As is discussed later, Fairbairn's ideas were supported by advances in ethnology and attachment theory.

Because people are object seeking, Fairbairn believed they are fundamentally motivated toward relatedness. However, when experiences become frustrating or too painful, the individual withdraws from external real objects/people and reverts to an inner world of objects. Fairbairn believed that this process began very early in childhood, such that the frustrating person becomes an internalized object. Once it is internalized, and as frustration (Fairbairn's equivalent of Freudian aggression) builds, the object is split into an *exciting object*, a *rejecting object,* and *an ideal object.* The exciting object incites longing for interaction with the real person of the caregiver; the rejecting object is associated with frustrating experiences with the caregiver; and the ideal object is the memory of the satisfying and fulfilling caregiver. Thus, children continue to experience their mother, but as an internal object. Energy is devoted to these inner representations, and the self-representation is also split, so that different experiences and understandings of one's sense of self are developed for the exciting, rejecting, and idealized maternal object. Once this system was established, Fairbairn stated that the *central ego* (comparable to Freud's ego) would be split so that part of it gets directed toward the exciting object. This part of the ego was known as the *libidinal ego.* Another part of the split ego is directed toward the rejecting object and was known as the *antilibidinal ego.* The ideal object remained associated with the central ego, which also was invested in the outer world of relationships. To state this approach simply, Fairbairn described how various thoughts, feelings, and experiences (conscious and unconscious) were directed toward different elements of a relationship with the mother that were experienced in the ego. Each of these ego units took on a life of its own. Hence, conflict (and subsequent psychopathology) was the product of interactions of object representations in the ego, much different from id–superego–defense analysis seen in Freudian and ego psychology.

Marcus (1999), Greenberg and Mitchell (1983), and others have suggested that Winnicott's and Fairbairn's theories are not comprehensive theories; they explain elements in the child's early dependency but fail to account for other roles (both positive and negative) that parents take on. They also did not provide comprehensive descriptions of therapeutic technique and, without careful attention, could lead to problematic alterations in psychoanalytic technique. Yet it is certainly the case that these ideas have not fallen out of favor. Pine (1998, p. 41) astutely observed that psychoanalysis and psychoanalytic theory are better because of the influence of object relations theorists:

> Therefore, we are dependent on objects—primary caregivers—for long years in order to insure survival. This fact guarantees the impact of those caretakers on the psychic life of the individual .... Object relations concepts underlie Freud's views of transference, identification, superego formation, and the Oedipus complex; they are inescapable and have been part of psychoanalysis from the start, although, like the ego, received full systematic recognition only later on. Through our study of identification, they help us understand character, defensive style, and the choice of sublimations. They have also given us a view of the "representational world" (Sandler and Rosenblatt, 1962), the internal map that develops progressively and governs our expectancies with regard to human relationships ... that is, reading them in terms of the schema of expectancies based on past experience. This assimilation of new experience into the internal map of expectancies underlies the repetitiveness of object relations.

As is discussed throughout this text, it is not surprising, therefore, that underlying the success of most psychotherapies (not just analytic or dynamic ones) is the development of a positive therapeutic relationship, one that consists of the therapist as a good object (Norcross, 2002).

Harry Guntrip

Fairbairn analyzed Harry Guntrip (1961, 1969) after becoming very interested in his developing ideas. Like Fairbairn, Guntrip believed in the centrality of interpersonal relatedness. He thought the libido was object seeking and that drives attached to a larger psychic process that oriented itself toward interrelatedness. Like Fairbairn and Winnicott, Guntrip's ideas have been criticized for being too divorced from drive theory. More in contrast to Fairbairn, however, was Guntrip's assertion that the ego is fundamentally oriented toward regression, more so than relatedness. In part a function of his work with very mentally ill patients, Guntrip saw that even the libidinal ego could be split off into a *regressed ego*, in which patients completely detached themselves from the object world altogether. This included objects in the outside world and those in the inner world. Patients with such problems experienced a pervasive sense of hopelessness and helplessness. Because patients still retained a libidinal ego that was fundamentally oriented toward object relatedness, Guntrip would find himself varying from the traditional psychoanalytic technique to ensure that patients continued to remain interested in their work with him, ergo their own development and happiness. Again, like Winnicott and Fairbairn, Guntrip's ideas reflected a strong interpersonal element and a de-emphasis on libido. While practicing psychoanalysis, object relations theorists' treatment focused more on the nature of patients' relationships, what patients wanted from the analyst in the treatment, and their inner representations of others and how that affected other relationships, particularly in the transference. Many of Freud's major premises continued to be understood and adhered to in conceptualization and treatment, yet what treatment was like with these theorists was notably different from what one might see with an ego analyst.

Harry Stack Sullivan

In some ways, it is a misnomer to place Harry Stack Sullivan's (1953) ideas into an object-relations category. Some consider his ideas to be a major category by themselves, yet Sullivan spoke very much about the interpersonal nature of personality development and treatment as it certainly is the case that his theoretical developments are about object relatedness. Sullivan is credited with founding the interpersonal psychoanalysis movement in the 1920s, which still has an important place today in analytic training, most prominently at New York's William Alanson White Psychoanalytic Institute. Sullivan believed that understanding individuals must occur in the context of understanding the interpersonal environment in which they have developed and operate. Consequently, psychoanalysis and any psychiatric treatment must consider the interpersonal context and patterns that have shaped each person.

Sullivan (1953) believed that individuals are oriented toward maintaining a homeostatic inner state through their *needs for satisfaction*. These needs occur interpersonally, since they are met exclusively in early infancy by the parent. He described *integrating tendencies*, which are natural activities of children that draw others to them in mutually satisfying ways. For instance, when children cry it elicits a caring, loving, or feeding response from their caregiver. Anxiety, from Sullivan's perspective, had a *dis-integrating* function, in that it creates a diffuse sense of uneasiness and tension that can be hard to gratify. Mitchell and Black (1995) stated that, to Sullivan, anxiety was the "fly in the ointment" (p. 67) that serves to undermine virtually all human activities and that a critical role of the caregivers is to help their children manage the anxiety so that they come to view themselves as being effective in having their needs met through mutually gratifying relationships with others. Such skills foster the development of the self-system, which allows individuals to be effective in this way. Similar to defenses, Sullivan described *security operations* that individuals learn early on in life as ways to reduce anxiety and maintain the self-system. It is through a careful and detailed analysis of the interpersonal interactions learned in childhood in which treatment is conducted. Countertransference serves as a means by which these security operations and self-system come to be understood by the analyst or therapist so that their origins may be uncovered and worked through. More contemporary interpersonal psychoanalysis was developed by Clara Thompson (1964), who was influenced by Ferenczi and Erich Fromm. Thompson's ideas have put the focus of interpersonal analysis on present-day relationships (and less on past relationships) and on the engaged, interactive aspects of the analyst.

Self Psychology

Not surprisingly, with an increased interest in object relations and the role of others in shaping the individual's psyche, there grew an interest in the sense of self—how it came to be formed and the factors that positively and adversely shaped its development. Throughout Freud's writings, there were references to one's sense of self. Sometimes, this was reflected in his writings about the ego, while at other times the self was described loosely as a separate entity.[5] Ego psychologists, such as Hartmann and Jacobson, also made reference to the self. However, it was Heinz Kohut who revolutionized the way the self developed and was understood.

Kohut (1971, 1977) noticed in his work with narcissistic patients that they seemed to develop certain kinds of transference reactions to him. One type of transference, a *mirroring transference*, reflected concerns on part of the patient of being understood and appreciated by the therapist. Here, patients looked for the therapist to understand and recognize what they said, did, or felt. Kohut thought this transference represented the absence of mirroring type reactions from their mother or caregiver, which fostered children's sense of self-understanding and self-acceptance. He speculated that children have a *grandiose-exhibitionistic self*, which seeks to capture the gleam in their mother's eye for her approval of their actions, ideas, and desires. Patients with mirroring transferences may work very hard to please the therapist, which is part of their grandiose-exhibitionistic self that seeks approval and recognition. Kohut also observed *idealizing transferences* in his patients. Here, patients found themselves seeing therapists as being highly powerful and influential, such that they wanted to become as much like their therapist as they could. This kind of transference reflected either the lack of modeling by the parent for their children or the parent's indifference to this need in their children, such that the children felt traumatized and neglected.

Kohut found classical explanations of narcissism to be insufficient to explain his patients' difficulties in their developing sense of self. In the traditional Freudian view, young children are in a state of primary narcissism, which must be outgrown so that object love develops. In other words, primary narcissism is outgrown when the needs of others take on as much or more importance than one's own needs. Without this transition, the ego becomes the object of love; hence, the individual becomes narcissistic. Kohut believed that all children have *narcissistic needs*; they are normal and necessary for appropriate development of the self. These needs consist of mirroring and idealizing. Mirroring allows children to develop an attunement to their sense of their inner life, thoughts, feelings, and desires. It leads to the development of ambitions and goals. Idealizing provides children with values and ideals that are important to live by. These processes initially provide important guideposts and standards for children, which attain greater definition as children mature and develop their own values. In contrast to outgrowing primary narcissism, Kohut believed that individuals always had narcissistic needs vis-à-vis their relationships with others. In other words, self-love and object love are reciprocally influential. Because others take on a tremendous importance in the development of the self, Kohut referred to the representation of others as *self-objects*. These are people that we experience as part of our self and who shape who we are and who we become. Hence, Kohut's theory is often referred to as the *double-axis theory* of development, which describes a *bipolar self*, composed of mirroring and idealizing narcissistic needs.

Kohut's ideas have had a significant impact in clinical work (Kohut & Wolf, 1978). Pathology of the self results from anxiety that results from a fear of *fragmentation*. In its most extreme form, Kohut thought that psychosis could result. Borderline states are less severe yet still represent a feeble, poorly developed sense of self. Patients with narcissistic personalities or narcissistic disorders may present in two ways: (1) with a sense of grandiosity and superiority that reflects their unmet mirroring needs; or (2) with a view of others as grandiose and powerful, reflecting their own unmet idealizing needs. The latter individuals often attribute tremendous power to others in shaping their sense of identity and how much influence another's thoughts, feelings, or ideas may have on them. This idea is reflected in the concept of *covert narcissism* (Wink, 1991) or *hypervigilant narcissism* (Gabbard, 1989), a type of narcissism not detected in the *Diagnostic and Statistical Manual of Mental Disorders* (DSM) system. Covert or hypervigilant narcissists are highly sensitive to the reactions of others, may be very shy or even self-effacing, and dislike being the center of attention. They can be hurt easily and react to even slight criticism very negatively.

Kohut's ideas and approach to treatment have been criticized. Kohut (1971, 1977) suggested that there should be an emphasis on empathic understanding with maximal effort directed toward *not directly* meeting the patient's narcissistic needs; rather, nonjudgmental interpretation in the context of an empathic relationship was viewed as key. By way of contrast, Bacal (1985) and Lindon (1994) emphasized an optimal level of responsiveness on part of the therapist as opposed to "optimal frustration." Rangell (1982) suggested that Kohut's ideas were already included in ego psychological viewpoints, whereas Bacal and Newman (1990) suggested that Kohut emphasized the self too much in the context of a self and object relationship. Nevertheless, Kohut's ideas about the development of the self have played an important role in understanding what the self is and how it develops.

Summary

In this chapter, the major developments in psychoanalytic theory have been described. While it is mostly theoretical, this chapter has described the major ideas that influence the practice of psychoanalytic and psychodynamic psychotherapy today. A significant trend in the development of theory has been how we understand the self and the individual's relationship with others. As I discuss in the next several chapters, the therapy relationship is highly prognostic of the outcome of treatment, and it is no surprise that psychoanalytic and psychodynamic theory have come to incorporate the salience of the relationship in its thinking. The next chapter describes some additional theories that have been important in shaping the psychoanalytic and psychodynamic thinking and practice. Knowing these basic principles is important later on when we examine how theory interfaces with research and practice.

Notes

1. This phrase is taken from the title of an excellent book by Fred Pine (1990), titled *Drive, Ego, Object, Self: A Synthesis for Clinical Work.*
2. Note that this example is based on heterosexual parents, which is the framework for which Freud described his theories. Less has been written about same-sex parents and the development of sexual and gender identity.
3. Many analysts and nonanalysts consider Charles Socarides's writings to be hostile toward gay and lesbian individuals. Some have even suggested that his work is an outlier in the burgeoning psychoanalytic and psychodynamic literature on sexual orientation and gender identity development.
4. Infant research has found that this perspective is not entirely accurate. Infants have considerable awareness of things going on around them, which can be documented even in utero. For example, it has been well established that infants recognize and prefer their mother's voice to other voices well before they are born (DeCasper, Lecanuet, Busnel, & Granier-Deferre, 1994; DeCasper & Spence, 1988).
5. Confusion arose from the use of the phrase, "das Ich," which sometimes seemed to suggest the ego whereas at other times seemed to imply the sense of "I" or "me."

4

The Evolution of Theory II

Integration and Expansion

When Pine (1990) described the history of psychoanalytic theory as drive–ego–object–self, he nicely captured the major theoretical shifts within psychoanalytic and psychodynamic theory. Yet many others have made important contributions to the development of theory that have had notable implications for conceptualization and treatment. Many of these advances have been reformulations or expansions of important ideas that were contained within the original theories or an integration of a different domain of study into psychodynamic ideas (e.g., cognitive psychology). In some cases, there have been important attempts at integrating the major ideas into one expansive theory. This chapter provides a selective review of more recent attempts to enrich psychoanalytic and psychodynamic theory.

Integrating Theoretical Models: The Contribution of Otto Kernberg

It would be misleading to suggest that Otto Kernberg is the only theorist who has attempted to integrate ideas of various theorists into one unified theory. However, I mention some of the works of Kernberg here because he has arguably made the most highly recognized contributions in integrating important theoretical developments in drive theory, ego psychology, and object-relations theory (Kernberg, 1970, 1975, 1983, 1984). He also has had a substantial influence in explaining and elaborating upon personality development and the treatment of character pathology.

Kernberg's ideas are an integration of the theories of Edith Jacobson, Melanie Klein, Margaret Mahler, William Fairbairn, and Sigmund Freud. Like Jacobson (1964), Kernberg believes that the earliest experience of the infant is organized around that of pleasure and pain. These experiences occur mainly in the relationship with the primary caregiver, and out of these experiences drive and affect are embedded. While *instincts* are biologically organized and present at birth, *drives* are highly individualized, malleable, and formed out of the affective experience with the caregiver. They are unconscious motivational systems that are oriented toward another person. "The basic units of self- and object representations and the affects linking them bring together these characteristics of drives" (Kernberg, 2001, p. 610). In other words, drives can be considered to be embedded within an object-relations unit.

Development occurs in three distinct stages. In the first stage, the most critical task becomes the differentiation of self and other, which occurs through the evaluation of experiences with others as either pleasurable or painful. Positive affects is associated with libidinal drive, and negative affect is associated with the aggressive drive, much in the way Jacobson (1964) described. Because self and other representations are not fully integrated—the good mother and the bad mother are not recognized as the same person—there is a psychological splitting of these representations, much as Klein (1964) described. When the first stage does not occur successfully, splitting processes become impaired. Consequently, psychotic pathology can emerge, as the fusion of self and other leads to significant deficits in reality testing. In the second phase, splitting that occurs must be overcome. The good and bad representations of self and other must be brought together into a distinct sense of self, who has both good and bad qualities, and a sense of the other—usually the caregiver—as having good and bad qualities. When this process does not occur, borderline conditions can occur—conditions similar to those described by Klein (1964) and Mahler, Pine, and Bergman (1975). This also means that powerful internal objects can influence a person's relationship to others in significant ways, much as Fairbairn (1952) described. In the third phase, self and other representations are clearly intact. How impulses are experienced and controlled can lead to neurotic conditions, much as Freud described in many of his writings.

The idea that conflicts in a particular stage of development could influence and dictate the nature of the adult's personality was introduced by Freud (1908, 1931) and further elaborated upon by his student Karl Abraham (1921/1953, 1924/1953). Oral and anal characters were early concepts in psychoanalytic theory, and further descriptions of other character types were offered by Reich (1933), Fenichel (1945), and Schneider (1958). In 1970, Kernberg proposed a classification system of character pathology that reflected a hierarchical organization of pathology in the ego and superego, pathology in object relations, and pathology in the development of libidinal and aggressive drives. His organization reflected the ongoing expansion of analytic theory at the time, and even today, one can see the influence of this system in the *Diagnostic and Statistical Manual of Mental Disorders* (DSM) and contemporary analytic thinking of about personality pathology (McWilliams, 1994; *PDM* Task Force, 2006; Shedler & Westen, 2004a, 2004b; Westen & Shedler, 1999a, 1999b).

Kernberg (1970) identified three types of character organization. In the higher level of organization individuals have relatively well-developed psychic structures (id, ego, and superego), but their superego tends to be overly punitive and too severe. Typically, such individuals use repression and related defenses, which are primarily avoidant of unwanted impulses. Socially, individuals are relatively well adapted, but their conflicts may limit their general satisfaction. Individuals at the higher level have meaningful object relations, but the expression of drives and impulses is partly inhibited. Personality pathology at this level is seen in hysterical, obsessive-compulsive, and depressive-masochistic personalities.

At the intermediate level of organization, patients have an even more punitive superego, but it is less well integrated into the personality. As such, persons show inconsistent patterns of behavior, in which there may be some failures of effective impulse regulation and appropriate adaptation while at other times there may be very high ideals and standards for behavior and ways of being. While repression is still an important defense, there are some trends toward splitting, projection, and denial. Oral-stage conflicts are commonly observed, such as conflicts over dependency, relatedness, and trust. The ability for stable relationships is there, but there is much ambivalence or conflict associated with such relationships. Included here are passive aggressive, sadomasochistic, "better functioning infantile personalities" (Kernberg 1970, p. 807), and certain narcissistic personalities. Kernberg (1970) added that well-established sexual deviations are indicative of this type of organization, provided that object relations remain stable.

At the lower level of character pathology, there is minimal integration of the superego into everyday life; as such, persons are freer to act on their aggressive and sadistic desires. There is little capacity to experience guilt, and persons have much difficulty looking critically at themselves. Defenses tend to be reactive as opposed to avoidant; projection and projective identification are commonly observed, as is splitting, denial, and the unconscious use of a fantasy of omnipotence to ward off evidence to the contrary. Good and bad representations of self and other are very much separated, and others are treated for their need-gratifying abilities. Not surprisingly, empathy is sorely impaired. Individuals at this level have infantile, narcissistic, antisocial, and "impulse-ridden character disorders" (Kernberg, 1970, p. 809). Prepsychotic personalities are seen here, such as hypomanic, schizoid, and paranoid personalities. Individuals who self-mutilate or who have multiple sexual deviations or a sexual deviation and drug addiction often are organized at this level.

Anaclitic and Introjective Configurations of Development and Psychopathology

Besides being a prolific researcher on psychoanalytic and psychodynamic theory and their application to psychotherapy, Sidney Blatt has expanded the understanding of developmental processes as they affect later functioning and psychopathology. Blatt's early work focused on schizophrenia and depression. Blatt and colleagues (Blatt, 1974; Blatt, D'Afflitti, & Quinlan, 1976; Blatt, Wein, Chevron, & Quinlan, 1979) identified and described two types of depression that were based on early experiences with caregivers. In *anaclitic depression*, individuals experienced significant deprivation or loss of caregivers in childhood. These experiences led to feelings of neediness and unrequited dependency, where individuals became particularly sensitive to the presence or absence of caregivers and significant others. When these important people were unavailable, children were vulnerable to and could easily experience depressive episodes. This type of depression was centered on the need for relatedness and connection, which was experienced as painfully absent. In its more pathological forms, even slight levels of deprivation or unavailability of others could trigger severe depression.

In *introjective depression*, individuals were vulnerable to depression when their sense of identity and esteem was threatened. This form of depression resulted when individuals failed to meet an important goal or experienced some threat to their sense of effectiveness, agency, or abilities. Such individuals often have high levels of perfectionism and are very achievement oriented, as these qualities and achievements help individuals retain a favorable sense of self, which, when compromised or attacked, leads to depression. Introjective depression is believed to originate in childhood experiences with caregivers who are perceived as critical or lacking in praise and encouragement. Because criticism and a lack of nurturing was absent, individuals sought to perform or act in ways that captured the attention of the caregiver, who would then provide the praise and encouragement that was so much desired.

Blatt also provided a template by which cognitive abilities and object relations develop in early childhood and how these are related to later psychopathology. Based on the ideas of Piaget (1954) and Werner (1948), Blatt (1974) suggested that object relations undergo a series of changes in how they become represented. His model describes five stages (with four intermediate or transitional stages) beginning with *sensorimotor-preoperational* representations, in which significant others are represented as existing solely for the needs of the other. Sensorimotor-preoperational representations reveal little appreciation for the separate existence of others apart from the gratification that they provide or the frustration that they cause. The next level of development involves *concrete-perceptual* representations. At this stage, individuals are represented in concrete ways with little appreciation for their inner qualities and experiences. At the *external iconic* level, others are represented in terms of what they do and the functions that they serve rather than who they are as people. *Internal iconic* representations are ones that begin to include internal psychological dimensions such as thoughts, feelings, beliefs, and values. And finally, *conceptual*-level representations integrate previous levels of the others' external and internal dimensions and qualities. Descriptions of others at the *conceptual* level may include inner conflicts that one has toward the person but are done so in a complex and integrated manner so that the richness of an individual's personality is captured.

To assess object relations, Blatt and colleagues developed the Concept of Object Scale (Blatt, Brenneis, Schimek, & Glick, 1976), which is used to assess the way representations of human and human-like figures are described on the Rorschach Inkblot Test. In a series of multiple studies with children, adolescents, and adults, Blatt and colleagues found evidence to support the idea that the severity of psychopathology was related to the quality of the object representation (reviewed in Huprich & Greenberg, 2003).

Blatt and colleagues also developed a set of procedures for evaluating the content of open-ended descriptions of self and significant others as a way to investigate object representations. These procedures have been slightly modified through the years but have come to be known as the Object Relations Inventory (Blatt, Chevron, Quinlan, Schaffer, & Wein, 1988, 1992; Blatt et al., 1979; Diamond, Kaslow, Coonerty, & Blatt, 1990). Like the Concept of Object Scale, these procedures are rooted in cognitive developmental theory, which posits that object representation changes over development. Studies with this measure have demonstrated an association between level of psychopathology and level of object relations, with more mature object relations being characterized by less psychopathology (see Huprich & Greenberg, 2003, for a recent review of this literature).

In addition to his work on cognitive development and object relations theories, Blatt and colleagues have offered an expansive description of two developmental trajectories that may become associated with various forms of psychopathology (Blatt and Shichman, 1983). These lines, or configurations, are based on the ideas of Anna Freud (1963, 1965), Fairbairn (1952), Jacobson (1964), and Shapiro (1965, 1981), who focused on the cognitive, affective, and interpersonal styles related to certain personality configurations. Blatt and Shichman, (1983) identified anaclitic and introjective configurations of development and related psychopathologies. In the *anaclitic configuration*, the predominant concerns are about interpersonal relationships and the desire to be close and intimate with another person. Defenses of this configuration are primarily avoidant, such as denial and repression. Cognitively, individuals focus on images and affects, and have thought processes that center on the simultaneous, interactive nature of relating to each other. Because there have been depriving, rejecting, or unpredictable relationships, individuals in this configuration are conflicted around libidinal issues of care, affection, love, and sexuality. The individual's sense of self is not given attention, as seeking and obtaining satisfying relationships consumes one's mental energy. More severe pathology in this configuration is associated with disruptions in the mother–infant dyad, while less severe pathology is associated with relatedness in the triadic, Oedipal period (mother–father–child).

In the *introjective configuration*, individuals focus on self-definition, self-worth, and identity. The typical defenses used are counteractive, such as projection, splitting, externalization, doing and undoing, reaction formation, isolation, intellectualization, rationalization, and overcompensation. Cognitively, individuals tend to be more literal than symbolic and focus more on thoughts and deeds rather than on people and interpersonal concerns. Such individuals tend to be analytical, critical, and linear in their thinking. They do not like contradictions or uncertainty and, subsequently, are quite focused on control. Attempts to secure and establish one's identity are key and supersede relationship desires. More severe psychopathology is associated with more extreme forms of criticism and hostility, while less severe is associated with criticism and inconsistency experienced during the Oedipal period.

In both configurations, the most extreme psychopathologies are schizophrenia and borderline conditions. In the anaclitic form, nonparanoid (i.e., Type II, negative symptoms) schizophrenia and hysterical, attentional seeking borderline pathologies are observed, while the introjective form includes paranoid schizophrenia and overideational borderline pathology. Pathologies in a less severe range, though still causing clinically significant distress, range along a continuum of neurotic symptoms and personality types. In the anaclitic continuum of neuroses, hysterical forms of disorders are seen, from more severe histrionic (infantile) personalities to hysterical symptoms or tendencies, which are predominated by concerns of how to relate to different kinds of people (e.g., mother figures, father figures, those for whom sexual desire is experienced). In the introjective continuum of neuroses, paranoia, obsessive-compulsive, introjective/depressive personalities, and phallic/overt narcissism are observed. Throughout this continuum, the sense of preserving one's integrity is the focus, in which others may be represented as hostile and malevolent (paranoia) or, in less extreme forms, as being competitors who might expose one's inferiority or limitations. In the case of phallic narcissism, this may be seen as inferiority regarding one's bodily assets.

Sadomasochism and Two Systems of Self-Regulation

Patients who present with sadomasochistic conflicts pose a real challenge for clinicians. Here, patients have come to associate pleasure with pain, something that seems counterintuitive to the assumption of the pleasure principle. Some very interesting work on sadomasochism has been done by Jack and Kerry Kelly Novick. In developing their ideas, they noted Freud's (1940) diffculty in understanding masochistic pathology: "We are specially inadequate in dealing with masochistic patients (p. 180)" (cited in Novick & Novick, 2004, p. 235). Furthermore, they suggested that each major shift in psychoanalytic theory, including the development of the idea of a superego as one of three psychic structures, was associated with Freud's experience of sadomasochistic phenomena (Novick & Novick, 1996). Having expanded these ideas over the years, Novick and Novick's ideas about sadomasochistic pathology are understood by many as being quintessential to successful treatment.

Though they initially began their writing and theoretical developments on the treatment of sadomasochistic pathology, the Novicks suggest that at the heart of virtually all psychopathology is embedded in some kind of sadomasochistic conflict, specifically based in how to resolve conflict and self-regulate (Novick & Novick, 1987, 1996, 2001, 2004). These systems of self-regulation and conflict management may be described as closed and open systems. In the *closed system*, individuals turn away from reality to preserve a sense of safety. Such a strategy originates in childhood, in which the child is faced with some internal or external overwhelming experience. Very often, this is the result of extreme demands from the parents or insensitivity to the needs of the children, which force the children into a painful experience that is not wanted. If the outer world of reality (i.e., appropriately attuned parents) does not help resolve this distress, children turn inward to some idea, fantasy, or belief that helps maintain a sense of safety in the face of such overwhelming helplessness. These fantasies include the ideas that they deserve this kind of mistreatment and that extraordinary standards of behavior and conduct are necessary to please others. Hence, a very strong superego develops. However, the fantasy of tolerating the mistreatment goes further, in that children who experience rage toward the abusive parent or caregiver also believes that were their anger to be expressed, it would conquer and overtake the caregiver. In developing this kind of fantasy, children feel a sense of *omnipotence* in being able to conquer such upsetting material. It, therefore, becomes very resistant to change because it is highly rewarding to feel such omnipotence against such upsetting feelings of helplessness. According to the Novicks, if personality does not develop adequately, this strategy may become a more permanent structure that provides feelings of control, safety, excitement, power, and a favorable self-esteem. By contrast, an *open system* of self-regulation is "competent and effective, based on mutually respectful, pleasurable relationships formed through realistic perceptions of self and others, open to experience from inside and outside and thus generative of creativity in life and work" (Novick & Novick, 2001, pp. 100–101). Open systems are created through parenting that involves appropriate levels of attunement to children's emotional state and desires, the capacity to tolerate children's anger and aggression (while also providing love and adaptive alternatives to such aggression), and fostering children's autonomy and independence with oversight and availability for emotional and physical comfort when needed. Novick and Novick (2003) noted that how the open system develops has been elaborated in the psychoanalytic literature by many others, such as John Bowlby, Erik Erikson, Anna Freud, Sigmund Freud, Heinz Hartmann, and Donald Winnicott.

The Novicks recognize the importance of mastering masochistic experiences throughout the lifetime, particularly salient in early life. Here, all children must come to learn that a certain amount of pain or discomfort is necessary for living adaptively in the world. But the need to adapt may transform into an unhealthy preoccupation or reliance on pain for one to feel capable of mastery and efficacy. This is the essence of masochism, which Novick and Novick (1987, p. 381) defined as "the active pursuit of psychic or physical pain, suffering, or humiliation in the service of adaptation, defense, and instinctual gratification at oral, anal, and phallic levels." It is when pain, suffering, or humiliation helps to meet needs associated with dependency, nurturing, control, submission, jealousy, competition, or desire (sexual or aggressive) that masochism results.

As their ideas have developed, Novick and Novick (1996, 2004) suggested that masoschism and sadism are always connected. Masochistic suffering gives way to acting out the sadistically the fantasy of destruction that comes from the omnipotent belief that one's anger could destroy those who induce suffering. It is not hard to imagine, then, that sadomasochistic conflicts could have significant effects on the therapeutic alliance. Sadomasochistic conflicts could easily set up transference dynamics in which therapists are approached as the ones who could inflict pain or punishment; patients, therefore, are oriented toward the fantasy of omnipotence in being able to tolerate the demands of their therapist (which could be distortions of basic requests of the therapist, such as saying more about a topic or to look with curiosity at why they find themselves in such frustrating relationships). The therapist also may be one who must be conquered in some way by patients' sadism (Novick & Novick, 1998). Since patients with these kinds of conflicts operate within a closed system, the idea of working together "is incompatible with sadomasochism" (ibid., p. 832). Thus, treatment needs to focus on working with the patient within the open system, in which the open system of patients' ego is aligned to the treatment process. Staying within the open system, therapists can highlight for patients ways the closed system presents conflicts and challenges to a satisfying life (Novick & Novick, 2003). Closed-system mechanisms, however, are highly effective for patients with sadomasochistic conflicts. Hence, they are difficult to change. Recognizing and accepting the value of the patients' closed system approach is highly important, as is being curious with the patient about the ways these solutions have affected them, so that patients do not perceive the therapist's interest in the maladaptivity of the system as an attack.

Attachment Theory

In developmental psychology, the study of the attachment process of the young to their parents has been a topic of study for decades. Beginning with Harry Harlow's (1958) work with baby monkeys and Rene Spitz's (1945, 1946a, 1946b) important papers on the life-or-death nature of touch and affection for the infant's survival, the evolutionary importance and necessity of good attachment—and consequences of a not-so-good attachment—is now common knowledge and accepted as a core developmental process (Bowlby, 1977, 1988). More specifically, Bowlby wrote that attachment "has its own internal motivation distinct from feeding and sex, and of no less importance for survival" (Bowlby, 1988, p. 27). Thus, in the tradition of Fairbairn and Winnicott, relatedness to another person is seen as a fundamental motivating force in human behavior. Bartholomew, Kwong, and Hart (2001) indicated that the goal of attachment—besides the fundamental necessity of basic care—is to provide children with a *sense of safety* such that they can explore, learn, and understand the environment yet have support and help when the environment becomes too difficult to understand on their own.

Implicit to attachment theory are two major premises:

1. Responsible and accessible caregivers need to create a secure base for children, thus providing children with the sense that the caregivers are accessible and dependable.
2. The way the emotional bond develops becomes internalized, and internal working models—or representations—are formed.

Infants are not passive in this regard. They actively construct a basic understanding of the attachment relationship (Bowlby, 1977). To assess these representations, Mary Ainsworth and colleagues (Ainsworth, Blehar, Waters, & Wall, 1978) created the *strange-situation technique*. This involved a period in which the mother and infant are in a playroom alone. Then, a stranger comes into the room, and after a few minutes the stranger begins to interact with the child. The mother then goes away for brief intervals. In the first interval, the infant is left just with the stranger, and in the second interval, the child is left alone. What is assessed in this technique is the infant's response to the mother when she returns. It is in this interval that a child's conception or representation of the mother as a source of comfort can be detected.

Based on the infants' behavior in this situation, Ainsworth et al. (1978) described three kinds of attachment. *Secure* infants are happy to see their mother return to the room and go to them for brief comfort. They quickly return to play. *Anxious-resistant* (or ambivalent) infants show a mix of comfort seeking and anger toward the mother when she returns to the room. They are less confident in their exploration of the playroom and are not readily comforted. *Avoidant* infants do not make contact with the mother when she returns. They do not seek comfort from the mother, and mothers of such children are often seen to be rejecting or affectively bland with their child. Other patterns of attachment were added to the theory later, including an *avoidant/ambivalent* pattern (Crittenden, 1988) and a *disorganized-disoriented* pattern (Main & Solomon, 1986), in which infants showed contradictory or disoriented strategies for going to the mother for seeking comfort. This type of attachment is found in 80% of maltreated infants (Carlson, Cicchetti, Barnett, & Braunwald, 1989, as cited in Schore, 2002).

Bowlby (1980) believed that infant attachment patterns affect the types of affective bonds they make with others later in life. Not surprisingly, some have assessed adult attachment patterns based on their reports of past family relationships or current romantic relationships. Mary Main and colleagues (George, Kaplan, & Main, 1985; Main, Kaplan, & Cassiday, 1985) described secure, dismissing, and preoccupied attachment patterns in adults, which were derived from their descriptions of their childhood family relationships during the Adult Attachment Interview. Cindy Hazan and Philip Shaver (1987) were interested in adult romantic relationships and developed a brief, self-report measure of attachment style. They described secure, ambivalent (or preoccupied), and avoidant adults, who were found, respectively, to have comfort with trust, anxiety or overdependency, or distrust and distance in their closest adult relationships. Subsequent research with this measure has found that it predicts adult relationship patterns rather well and is related to expected patterns of experience in relationships (Shaver & Clark, 1994).

Having evaluated the attachment styles reported by Main and colleagues (1985) and by Hazan and Shaver (1987), Brennan, Clark, and Shaver (1998) suggested that two dimensions underlie attachment patterns observed in both infants and adults: *anxiety* and *avoidance*. Anxiety relates to the individual's fear of rejection, separation, and abandonment and is a dimension related to representations of the self in relationships. Avoidance relates to how well others can and will provide comfort and reassurance. This dimension is related to representations of others. As a means of combining these dimensions with the types, Kim Bartholomew and colleagues (e.g., Bartholomew & Horowitz, 1991) described a two-dimension, four-category model of attachment. Low anxiety and low avoidance characterize secure attachments; high anxiety and high approach characterize preoccupied attachments; low anxiety and high avoidance characterize dismissing attachments; and high anxiety and avoidance characterize fearful attachments. What is appealing about this model is that self and other representations are described, as is the nature of an affect; hence, there is a strong parallel to object-relations theory and a categorization of individuals by their interpersonal relatedness. While there is not yet a consensus about which model of attachment is most representative of reality (Bartholomew et al., 2001), there is considerable empirical support for this model, making it widely appealing to clinicians and researchers in their conceptualization of patients. Particularly impressive about the attachment literature in general is the evidence for the long-term stability of attachment patterns and the behavioral expressions of attachment into adulthood (e.g., Main et al., 1985; Waters, Merrick, Treboux, Crowell, & Albersheim, 2000).

Fonagy (1999a) observed important similarities in attachment theory and psychoanalytic/psychodynamic theory. These include an interest in the internal psychic life of the child (particularly during events of the earliest years), maternal sensitivity and mirroring, the importance of relationships in human motivation, the representation of relationships, and the importance of the maternal relationship and its mentalization. Fonagy suggested that attachment theory would benefit by attending more to the distortions children have of their early experience, by de-emphasizing the categories of attachment and looking more at the situations and context in which certain attachment paradigms are in operation, and by putting greater emphasis on children's perception of the psychological and physical integrity of their caregivers.

The biological mechanisms of attachment and their implications for treatment have been described in much detail by Allan Schore (1994, 2000). In reviewing the work of Bowlby (1973), Schore (2000) noted that Bowlby saw attachment as being fundamentally rooted in a neurobiological process, much like Freud believed that neurobiological processes underlay unconscious processes. Bowlby (1973) speculated that the reticular formation, in conjunction with the midbrain nuclei and limbic system, plays an important role in self-regulation, which ultimately is the goal of the attachment system. He thought this attachment system was represented in the prefrontal lobes. In expanding these ideas, Schore (2000) suggested that it is the orbitofrontal cortex that is actively involved in the process of establishing attachment pattern representations. As children experience face-to-face interactions with their caregiver, Schore explained that the emotional matching of children by their mother affects the neural pathways laid down in the orbitofrontal cortex. Not only does this region have connections to the prefrontal regions, but it also is connected to autonomic pathways. Thus, one can see how patterns of attachment can become easily associated with sympathetic, parasympathetic, and autonomic patterns of behavior. Schore (1994, 2000) emphasized that the internal working models of the child–caregiver relationship get represented in this region, as it is during the first 10–12 months of life when the orbitofrontal cortex pathways begin to mature the most (up to 2 years, which happens to coincide with the onset of the attachment patterns first described by Ainsworth et al., 1978). Schore (2000) noted that the orbitofrontal cortex is actively involved in emotional-related learning and that empirical studies have shown that there is a plasticity, or fluidity, to these processes, such that new kinds of emotional learning may occur. He suggested that understanding more about these processes may unlock the door to the biological mechanism of how psychoanalytic or psychodynamic therapy works.

Schore (2002) also spoke about trauma and its impact on the developing person. In referring to the role of the orbitofrontal cortex again, Schore noted that severe abuse and neglect leads to deficits associated with right brain activity, such as a lack of empathy, an inability to read others' facial cues, a poor ability to read social cues, and difficulty understanding one's own internal bodily state. These deficits result from an inability of mothers or caregivers to appropriately identify the affective state of infants and to provide a soothing or comforting response. In other words, caregivers teach children about the nature of their inner response and impart an ability to remain secure despite the distress. This phenomenon may be understood as right-brain-to-right-brain communication between children and caregivers.

However, when caregivers are unable to attend to their children's cues, perhaps because of their own deficits in recognition and self-understanding, the child is left with a state of underlying and unremitting distress. When comfort does not come despite this despair, children can be seen to engage in dissociation from the world around them. This automatic, psychological removal of one's experience from the outer world to the inner world serves a protective function, but it comes with a price. Children have not internalized the sense of felt safety and security from experiencing distress; their right brain suffers the consequence of learning how to return to safety. Schore (2002) suggested that this overwhelming fear followed by extreme withdrawal is what Kohut (1971) understood as fear of disintegration. To some extent, all individuals experience some degree to which they are not appropriately mirrored or comforted; however, the absence of "good enough" caregiving produces significant structural changes in the brain, which can be seen in adults who were severely abused in childhood or who have a diagnosis of posttraumatic stress disorder (PTSD). This phenomenon has been observed empirically. In an emotional processing task, individuals with PTSD have decreased activity in the right hemisphere (Galletly, Clark, McFarlane, & Weber, 2001; Raine et al., 2001) compared with controls. Therapeutically, Schore (2002) suggested it may be that patients can only express their internal distress through their transference and through projective identification. In this sense, therapists must "listen" with the right brain to understand what patients are trying to communicate. Subsequently, therapists can then provide an interpretation and help the patients reformulate their experience with a greater sense of mastery and felt security.

Mentalization and Reflective Functioning

Closely related to attachment theory is the concept of mentalization and its key activity, reflective functioning. These ideas were proposed by Peter Fonagy and Mary Target (Fonagy & Target, 1996, 1997, 2006; Fonagy, Gergely, Jurist, & Target, 2002). *Mentalization,* or *reflective capacity,* is the ability to conceive of and understand the mental states of self and others as explanations of behavior and experience, a process known as *interpersonal interpretive functioning.* Mentalization is necessary for the development of a fully developed sense of self and is acquired in the context of early attachments, specifically primary-object relationships. Inherent to developing mentalization is the development of self and other representations, or object relations: "The baby's experience of himself as having a mind or self is not a genetic given; it evolves from infancy through childhood, and its development critically depends upon interaction with more mature minds, assuming these are benign, reflective, and sufficiently attuned" (Fonagy & Target, 2006, p. 545). Thus, the role of the caretaker in developing the child's capacity for mentalization is crucial. Specifically, caretakers must be able to mirror accurately for children their mental state while at the same time doing so in a way that shows it is the children's state being expressed and not their own mental state. If mirroring is not accurate, Fonagy and Target (2006) suggested that the inner state as it is represented will not match the inner subjective state, which could lead to the development of a false self, as Winnicott (1965) described. If the mirroring does not differentiate children's emotions from caregivers' emotions, individuals may come to experience emotions only through other people, such as is found in borderline personality disorder and other severe personality pathology.

Fonagy and Target (2006) described four points of interest in the course of development that delineate important process toward the development of mentalization:

1. Between 6 and 12 months, children begin to construct causal relationships in which persons' actions come from their own volition, or *agency*, and have an effect on the environment. It is not that children have an understanding of the mental state of others; rather, they detect simple cause-and-effect relationships in the physical world.
2. In the second year, children develop a psychological understanding of agency. Children then understand that they and others have intentions toward action that are caused by some preexisting motive or desire. These actions of self and other then bring about changes in the minds and bodies of self and others. However, children at this point do not yet have the capacity to separate the sense of mind from the sense of body. This is readily seen when a child becomes enraged toward another child who innocently takes away a toy, such that the child strikes out at the innocent offender.
3. Around 3–4 years, children begin to understand that agency comes from their own inner state of mind. What is seen about their own or another person's actions does not automatically reflect what is happening in their minds. In this time period, playing with peers becomes more important than playing with adults, as it is believed that for play children now do not require adults, who helped them understand their own experiences or the experiences of others when they did not have the skills, and subsequent ability to self-regulate, during earlier times.
4. Around age 6, children now have the capacity to recall times when their actions were caused by their agency or volition, which leads to a temporally stable sense of themselves as active and intentional persons.

All of these events introduce another important concept: *intersubjectivity*. This is the ability of individuals to recognize that they have a perception of reality and that when engaging in experiences with others, they, too, have a perception of reality. Early recognition of this intersubjectivity is very narcissistic—what children know and experience is believed to be known and experienced in exactly the same way by other people. As development proceeds, including the growing capacity for mentalization, children now recognize that what they know and experience is not the same as what other people know—hence, a greater capacity for children to relate to others and to tolerate slightly different desires or goals is experienced, as is an appreciation of the uniqueness of what other people may be able to share.

What are the implications of these theoretical developments for the conceptualization and understanding of psychopathology? When the attachment process goes awry, mentalization does not occur in an optimal manner. Most problematic is the disorganized pattern of attachment. Here, individuals live in a mode that predates the representation of others as being able to accurately define and mirror their inner state. This sets up an orientation toward self-protection, in which others are seen as potentially hostile to individuals' own sense of self, albeit frail and incomplete. Trauma histories in the attachment upset the mentalization process. Playfulness, which fosters the interpersonal interpretive function, is decreased; affect regulation and attentional processes are impaired; and an unconscious defensive avoidance of mentalization processes occurs. This avoidance protects the individual from the fearful states of mind experienced in the hands of an abusive caregiver; subsequently, differentiation of self and other's inner world and experience is compromised. Research has supported these ideas. For example, Fonagy et al. (1996) found that patients with borderline personality disorder have difficulty with mentalization after experiencing maltreatment. Fonagy, Stein, Allen, and Fultz (2003) also found that difficulty detecting facial emotional expressions was positively associated with more severe maltreatment.

Intersubjectivity: Two-Persons and Constructed Reality in Psychotherapy

Modifications of theory have also had an effect on issues surrounding treatment. As noted already, Fonagy and colleagues (1996, 1997, 2002, 2006) discussed the importance of intersubjectivity in the development of healthy relatedness and a definition of one's sense of self and one's agency. Related to these ideas, and as an outgrowth of interest in object relations and self psychology theories, Stolorow, Atwood, and Brandchaft (1994) described an *intersubjective view* of the treatment situation. Intersubjective approaches to treatment recognize that there are two persons in the treatment room and that the actions and behaviors of the treatment provider have an effect on the patient. In other words, not only is the unconscious mind of the patient operating, but so is the unconscious mind of the therapist. If one is to take seriously the significant role of the unconscious in determining conscious thoughts, feelings, attitudes, judgments, and behaviors, then one must consider that the same processes work in the mind of the therapist and that these processes can and do have an effect on what the therapist says and does with the patient. This means that, in Fonagy's sense of intersubjectivity, what the therapist attends to from the verbal and nonverbal aspects of the patient reflects the therapist's ability to see, hear, recognize, and respond to the needs and desires of the patient (Fonagy et al., 2002). It also means that what becomes understood in the conscious minds of the patient and therapist is a construction of their making. Consequently, no longer can transference be viewed just as the product of the patient's mind; rather, transference reflects "the patient's here-and-now experience" of the treatment provider (Mitchell & Black, 1995, p. 166). This issue will be revisited in chapter 7 when discussing mechanisms of therapeutic effectiveness.

Cognitive Experiential Self-Theory

Seymour Epstein (1973, 1991, 1994) sought to integrate psychoanalytic theory with more recent findings from cognitive psychology. He suggested that the Freudian unconscious does not make sense from an evolutionary perspective; that is, why would an unconscious that is so maladaptive and powerful have such a strong influence on behavior? How could it have evolved (and remained) throughout human history? For Epstein (1994, p. 709), the suggestion of secondary process thinking was an "ad hoc solution" to this problem. Instead, he suggested that the cognitive unconscious, as identified in cognitive psychology research, is a more adaptive system. This system contains multiple, automatic processes that occur effortlessly, is more palatable from an evolutionary perspective, and, by Epstein's account, is better suited for psychodynamic theory.

According to Epstein (1994, p. 715), *cognitive-experiential self theory* (CEST) holds that "people automatically construct an implicit model of the world, or a "theory of reality," that has two major divisions—a world theory and a self-theory—and connecting propositions .... A theory of reality is not developed for its own sake, but in order to make life as livable, meaning as emotionally satisfying, as possible." CEST proposes that there are two major psychological systems in place: the rational and the experiential. The ideas of the self and the world contain *beliefs*, which are contained in the rational system, and *implicit beliefs* (or schema), which are contained in the experiential system.

The rational system operates with logic and analytic thinking. It works to make logical connections among symbols, words, and numbers, and it processes information more slowly than the experiential system. However, it can change course more rapidly than the experiential system, as seen in the rapid pace by which thoughts can change. Behavior is mediated in this system through conscious understanding of events.

The experiential system is oriented toward judging experience by pleasure and pain. It forms associative connections among experiences, which affect behavior in either nonconscious or preconscious ways (i.e., "I had a sense that things were not right here"). It processes experience more quickly than the rational system but is slower to change, as repetitive or intense experiences are needed to change the associations that have been laid down. Epstein noted that this theory encompasses four different motivating principles that have been espoused in prior analytic and dynamic theorists: (1) the need to maximize pleasure and to minimize pain; (2) the need to maintain a relatively stable internal state and sense of self; (3) the need for relatedness; and (4) the need to overcome feelings of inferiority and to enhance self-esteem. Resulting behavior can be understood as a compromise among the four needs, and the needs work to moderate each other.

Epstein (1994) highlighted three implications from CEST for how therapeutic change can occur:

1. The rational system can be used to influence the experiential system, such as is found in cognitive therapy.
2. Learning about emotionally significant experiences can occur in working through troublesome life experiences or by understanding the relationships individuals have with others or with the therapist.
3. Using fantasy could help to understand components of the experiential system that are not readily discernible.

In short, Epstein's (1994) approach appears to be an integrative hybrid of theory both inside and outside of psychoanalytic and psychodynamic theory.

Summary

In this chapter, I have reviewed more recent advances in the development of psychoanalytic and psychodynamic theory. There are many individuals who have advanced theory that were not discussed, and it was not my intention to provide a comprehensive overview. Rather, I sought to demonstrate that psychoanalytic and psychodynamic theory have evolved quite a bit since the life and times of Sigmund Freud. Most obvious in this evolution has been the increasing importance of the psychological life of the individual as it exists in relationship to others. Even in the practice of psychoanalysis, the importance and meaning of the relationship takes on tremendous importance, more so than in the days of analysis when the "blank screen" singularity of clinical practice dominated.

As I noted in chapter 2, psychoanalytic and psychodynamic ideas have been under attack for some time (see Bornstein, 2001, 2002b, 2005). Some of this criticism reflects the fact that psychoanalysts were rather insular and avoidant of those with different theoretical points of view. It may be that another reason for this disdain, particularly in the professional community, is that evidence was accruing in psychotherapy research, indicating that, regardless of theoretical orientation, the *therapeutic relationship* was the best predictor of the progress and outcome of psychotherapy (Lambert & Barley, 2002). Although psychoanalysts and proponents of psychoanalytic and psychodynamic theory are far from disinterested in the therapy relationship—in fact, they arguably are more interested in the relationship than most schools of therapy—it may have been the case that the failure to acknowledge the success of other modes of treatment was the result of their theory not evolving more quickly to the place that it now is. That is, the nature of the intimate relationship between one person and another has a profound influence on a person's development and that the earliest types of intimate relationships set templates for all future relationships. Perhaps it could be said that "good enough" relationships produce "good enough" outcomes.

Nonetheless, there are multiple strengths that psychoanalytic and psychodynamic theory offers to the practice of psychotherapy that are not found in other schools of thought. Among these are the richness and comprehensiveness of the theory, a century's worth of clinical practice and empirical support, and the countless lives of those who have benefited from the practice of psychoanalytic or psychodynamic therapy. The next chapters discuss basic principles of treatment, what mechanisms account for therapeutic effectiveness, and what the research suggests about the effectiveness of psychoanalytic and psychodynamic therapy. Contrary to the skepticism of many academically oriented psychologists and psychiatrists, Freud's ideas are not dead; they are quite alive, and they are supported by good empirical research.

Section II

Treatment Principles and Empirical Support

5

Basic Principles of Treatment

The focus of this chapter is on the basic principles of treatment within the psychoanalytic and psychodynamic tradition. Mastering the skills to implement these principles is learned through practice, good supervision, more practice, and additional supervision. In essence, it is a lifelong process that ought never to stop. Some might add (including myself) that personal, dynamically oriented therapy is also a valuable—if not the most valuable—tool for one's development as both a professional and as a person who happens to conduct individual, dynamically oriented psychotherapy. Indeed, most therapists say that most of the learning of *how* to do psychotherapy comes from real contact with the patient and what it is like *to be with* a patient. This is no different within the psychodynamic tradition, though virtually all psychodynamically oriented clinicians will indicate that their technique is distinctively influenced by psychodynamic and psychoanalytic principles. It is, therefore, a knowledge and understanding of the principles that creates a framework on which to begin practice from a dynamically oriented perspective.

Ways of Practicing within a Psychodynamic Approach

Types of Psychoanalytic and Psychodynamic Therapies

As I have noted throughout this book, many Freudian ideas are the foundation to the psychodynamic tradition, although practice within a psychodynamic framework is different from the practice of *psychoanalysis*. Traditional psychoanalysis can vary from four to five times a week and lasts for several years. The time needed depends on the nature of the pathology and a number of other factors. Patients lie on a couch and engage in the process of free association; analysts sit behind the patients and provide interpretations as they see fit. Traditional psychoanalysis aims to provide meaningful change in psychological structures (e.g., a more adapted ego, a less punitive superego). It also seeks to foster and understand transference and some degree of psychological regression so that the childhood origins of the conflicts and the consequent effects on psychological structures may be identified and worked through to a greater level of adaptation. In more modern times, psychoanalysis often is conducted with less frequent weekly appointments and, as already noted, may continue for briefer periods of time than was once the case. For instance, a patient may be in treatment three days per week or may complete his analysis in less than three years. Duration depends on a number of factors, including the nature of the problem and patients' resources in terms of both time and finances.

In contrast, psychoanalytic and psychodynamic psychotherapy are conducted on a less frequent basis with patients sitting directly across from their therapist. Patients may meet with their therapist once per week or two to three times per week. Often, there is no set limit on the amount of time spent in treatment, as it is understood that treatment progresses until patients' level of functioning, amount of conflict experienced, and overall level of life satisfaction have reached a point where therapists and patients agree that treatment may be discontinued. Free association and interpretations are used, though therapists may take on a bit more of an active role than in typical psychoanalysis.

Goldstein (1998) differentiated forms of therapy that have been derived from psychoanalysis. On a continuum, the range is as follows:

- Psychoanalysis
- Analytically oriented psychotherapy
- Modified analytically oriented psychotherapy
- Dynamically oriented psychotherapy
- Supportive therapy

Goldstein notes how analytic and dynamic treatment are based on psychoanalytic ideas and that the technique and goals of treatment vary somewhat. The more analytically oriented approaches continue to focus on identifying and working through transference, whereas dynamically oriented therapy focuses more on present-day relationships and on improving those relationships and ways of managing distress and conflict. There also are several brief psychodynamic therapies that seek to work in a time-sensitive fashion (Messer & Warren, 1995). To a large extent, however, psychotherapy (not analysis) as it is practiced by many analytically and dynamically oriented therapists is probably difficult to discriminate along this continuum, given the dynamics and fluidity of patients' lives and difficulties.

Psychoanalytic and psychodynamic approaches take the perspective of *understanding the inner world and mental life* of the patient. There are few other theoretical orientations and models of psychotherapy that direct so much of their efforts to understanding the private thoughts, feelings, ideas, wishes, fantasies, goals, attitudes, desires, conflicts, and needs like the psychoanalytic and psychodynamic approach. In academic and American psychology, behavioral therapy has long been avoidant of examining the inner life of the patient. Being strongly rooted in an empirical philosophical orientation, behavior therapy stresses that it is only what is observed that can become the focus of attention. It assumes that causative factors can be identified, modified, and changed in the outer world so that a patient may experience less distress and greater satisfaction. The founding fathers of behaviorism had an almost incredulous stance toward clinical work—they sought to treat individual, *personally and internally experienced* suffering and distress through avenues that did not focus on the personal and internal experience. Over time, this position became untenable both theoretically and practically. Behavioral therapy gave way to cognitive-behavioral therapy (CBT), though it was only recently that the Association for the Advancement of Behavior Therapy (AABT) formally changed its name to the Association for Behavioral and Cognitive Therapies (ABCT). Cognitive therapy and CBT address the inner world of thoughts and more pervasive schemas that direct and shape one's orientation to the world. CBT recognizes that these thoughts are often formed and established through early experience and are based on irrational assumptions. By changing the irrational bases of these assumptions and beliefs, patients should get better. While this is certainly a favorable step toward the integration of cognitive and psychodynamic ideas, CBT often fails to appreciate the power of unconscious, affective motivation and maintenance of problematic ways of being (Huprich, 2004a). CBT assumes that change will occur readily with the identification of more adaptive and rational ways of viewing the world. While this certainly is the case for many people and many kinds of problems, it assumes that the irrational bases will dissipate readily over time. It also assumes the following:

1. Resistance to change is minimal.
2. Defensive processes will fail to impede the progress.
3. The adaptive bases of the old ways of viewing the world can be readily discarded.
4. Generalization across situations (a principle of learning theory) will occur.

Yet, as Westen and colleagues (Westen & Morrison, 2001; Westen, Novotny, & Thompson-Brenner, 2004) have suggested, it may be that the failure to attend to these issues is why many types of empirically supported, behavioral, and CBT interventions fail to produce long-standing changes in many of the people who receive the treatment.

The Expressive and Supportive Continuum of Interventions

Forms of psychoanalytic and psychodynamic intervention have been discussed in the literature from a historical perspective. The form that therapy takes assumes that therapists have an adequate understanding of their patients' level of personality organization and functioning, in which they can thereby decide how to practice. The major orientation toward practice outside of psychoanalysis was first offered by Knight (1945), who distinguished expressive and supportive psychotherapies. *Expressive therapies* are designed to increase persons' insight into their suffering, to identify significant intrapsychic conflicts, and to lead to structural changes in the psyche (e.g., reduce the influence of the superego and increase the ego's capacity to find adaptive ways to have particular needs and desire met). Attention is provided to the development, expression, and understanding of transference, as is understanding and interpreting resistance and defense (Dewald, 1996). *Supportive therapies* are designed to bolster the patients' defenses and coping abilities, so that they may return to previous levels of functioning. Therapists provide some gratification of transference desires (i.e., to be cared for by a kind and wise parent) and often take a more active role in correcting patients' distortions in the transference, their defenses, and resistances. They also may become a model in which patients identify and learn more adaptive ego and superego functions (ibid.). Specific examples of supportive interventions have been described by Dewald (1996) and Huprich (2004b).

Gabbard (2000, 2004) suggested that patients with neurotic levels of personality organization are appropriate candidates for expressive therapies, whereas those with borderline organization are better suited for supportive therapies. Indications for expressive therapies include the following:

- A strong motivation to understand
- The ability to tolerate frustration and to regress somewhat while conflicts are identified and worked through
- A capacity for insight
- Intact reality testing
- Good interpersonal (object) relatedness
- Good impulse control
- The ability to think in terms of metaphor and analogy

By contrast, indications for supportive therapy include the following:

- Significant ego deficits
- Low anxiety and frustration tolerance
- A severe life crisis
- A lack of psychological mindedness
- Poor reality testing and poor interpersonal (object) relatedness
- Any organic or other factor that would impair the patient's ability to form a therapeutic alliance

The application of a particular type of therapy to patients' level of functioning cannot be emphasized enough. In fact, one of the myths of psychodynamic and psychoanalytic therapy is that "one treatment works for all." It has been long recognized that different types of analytic and dynamic therapies exist and are appropriate for certain kinds of patients (Gabbard, 2000, 2004; Kernberg, 1970; Knight, 1945; Trimboli & Farr, 2000; Wallerstein, 1989). Unstable patients, or those with a strongly compromised ability to manage stress and conflict, will simply not do well when asked to explore in depth the origins of their suffering. I often describe this to my students by saying that when a person's inner world is crumbling, it is important not to take apart and examine the fragile psychological walls that hold them together. Patients in significant distress do not necessarily need insight-oriented answers at that time, though many very much want this at some point in their treatment. To do effective insight-oriented work, patients need to have sufficient walls of defense to tolerate an examination of those long-standing, conflicted areas of their life that are often associated with painful childhood experiences. It should be noted, however, that expressive and supportive work is not to be viewed dichotomously. Gabbard (2000) noted how most psychotherapy involves some mixture of expressive and supportive activities. Some patients undergoing expressive work may encounter a significant life crisis that requires appropriate supportive interventions. Likewise, patients may begin treatment requiring supportive kinds of activities, given the nature of the life crisis or their personality structure. However, as time goes on and the patients stabilize, therapists and their patients may be able to move to a stance in which they seek to understand the origins of the conflicts and issues that were associated with the life crisis, hence leading to a more expressive orientation. Thus, supportive therapies should not be viewed as offering no opportunities or interest in fostering persons' awareness of the powerful unconscious motivators of their behavior.[1]

Expressive and supportive orientations can be easily applied to the cases presented in chapter 1. These two cases were rather different: Mr. Shelby was a very quiet, reserved young man who had little capacity for psychological insight, depended on his parents for his physical and psychological protection, and had little interest in interpersonal relationships. Ms. Murdock, on the other hand, was a pleasant, engaging woman who easily developed and maintained relationships. She was interested in why her most recent relationship failed and entered treatment with significant depressive symptoms. For Mr. Shelby, the therapist adopted an orientation of simply trying to build a relationship and some level of attachment to him. As the patient had very poor ego functions and object relatedness, and his only distressing experience was that of some panic attacks, he was not appropriate for insight-oriented, or expressive, work. As it turned out, the patient was referred for behavioral treatment of his anxiety symptoms. This is not to say that a dynamic conceptualization and approach was not useful; it was in the context of conceptualizing this young man from a dynamic perspective that the treatment provider was able to assess how motivated and appropriate this patient was for therapy and what his major obstacles and defenses were to treatment, to understand the internal life of this patient, and to make a recommendation about a treatment approach that could be useful. In this case, the recommendation was for behaviorally oriented treatment that focused on helping him manage his panic symptoms. When the idea was presented to the patient, it was not a surprise that the patient experienced reluctance to the idea. His resistance solidified, however, when his parents (to whom he felt much ambivalence) endorsed the idea. This case, too, demonstrates that even in patients who are relatively low-functioning it is so important for the therapist to attend to the therapeutic relationship to maximize the probability of a successful treatment.

By contrast, Ms. Murdock had good ego functions and object relations. She wanted to find the answers to why a relationship had failed. Her expressive treatment ultimately identified a history of relationships with men, beginning with her father, who were very attentive to her, who idealized her to some extent, and for whom she did not identify any significant interpersonal qualities that could have been a warning sign of things to come. She identified how this pattern stemmed from her childhood experiences with her father, during a time in her life when she did not have the life experience or maturity to recognize potentially problematic qualities in him. Subsequently, she had entered adult relationships with a level of naiveté that prohibited her from recognizing these men's shortcomings.

As alluded to earlier, the activities of the therapist are indicators of whether the therapist is adopting mainly a supportive or expressive orientation. Gabbard (2000) described and (Gabbard, 2004) expanded the idea of an expressive-supportive continuum of interventions, which were derived from the Menninger Clinic Treatment Interventions Project (Horowitz et al., 1996). Gabbard's (2000, 2004) collective description of the continuum includes the following (from most supportive to most expressive):

- Affirmation: Showing patients that the therapist understands what they mean with simple statements such as, "uh huh" or "right."
- Advice and praise: Two kinds of interventions that are very direct and self-evident.
- Psychoeducational interventions: Provide information to patients that they may not be aware of. They are designed to strengthen patients' ability to effectively engage their ego skills and to provide knowledge that is believed to quickly be helpful.

- Empathic validation: Occurs when therapists demonstrate that they are clearly attuned to and understand patients' internal state.
- Encouragement to elaborate: Designed to increase patients' verbalizations and associations about a particular topic or issue. Sometimes, therapists may not understand what their patients mean, so this request is made. Other times, patients may say something suggesting that there is rich material to be better understood (e.g., "I've always thought I was unattractive").
- Clarification: An activity in which therapists try to make clearer or more understandable points their patients are raising. Sometimes, a short phrase is all that is necessary, such as, "So, you really are feeling pretty despondent."
- Confrontation: Designed to address an issue that patients may not wish to talk about. It should not be understood as a negative or critical comment; rather, it is meant to bring patients' attention to something that they are not focusing on.
- Observation: Can be a very powerful technique of bringing to patients' awareness important material without offering an explanation for it. For instance, therapists may say, "I notice that you are pretty avoidant each time I ask you about your relationship history."
- Interpretation: An offered explanation, or a hypothesis, for why patients are experiencing what they do. Weiner (1998) suggested that interpretations only be offered when therapists believe they have enough material to support the interpretation and that patients will be receptive to hearing it. Therapists also must be ready to address resistance or defensiveness about the interpretation.

Brief Dynamic Therapies

In addition to expressive and supportive orientations to therapy, a significant number of brief dynamic therapies have entered into practice within the past 30 years (Messer & Warren, 1995). These therapies employ supportive and expressive techniques, although in some ways it is difficult to place brief therapies into this dimension. Therapists are often much more directive, and less time is devoted to allowing the therapeutic relationship and transference to evolve. It is often the case that brief dynamic therapies are targeted to a very specific problem in which patients are carefully selected (much like supportive approaches). At the same time, patients need to be able to tolerate focused and direct attention to interpretation of their defenses and their maladapative relationship patterns (much like expressive approaches). They must be able to withstand some uncomfortable ideas suggested by their therapist without significant regression, as well as the capacity to integrate the ideas provided by the therapist into their life more quickly and efficiently than is the case in long-term therapy.

Messer and Warren (1995) noted that patients with severe disturbances are not appropriate for brief work. They suggested that one way to operationalize this criterion is to examine the behaviors in which patients engage that preclude their participation in brief therapy, including serious suicide attempts or the potential for suicidality, a history of alcohol or drug problems, severe depression, poor impulse control, severe obsessional or phobic symptoms, poor reality testing, and some psychosomatic conditions. Malan (1976, as cited in Messer & Warren, 1995) suggested that patients with the inability to make interpersonal contact, poor motivation, rigid defense processes, complex/deep-seated problems, severe dependency, or intensified depressive or psychotic symptoms all should be excluded from brief treatment. Sifneos (1992) suggested that short-term therapy is best suited for patients with anxiety without other symptoms, interpersonal difficulties, phobias along with obsessive thoughts, and mild depression. Strupp and Binder (1984) suggested that patients having emotional discomfort, the capacity to establish basic trust, a willingness to consider conflicts in interpersonal terms, a willingness to examine feelings, the capacity for mature relationships (others are seen as separate individuals with their own thoughts, feelings, and desires that are separate from the patients'), and the motivation for brief treatment are good candidates for brief interventions. All of these examples demonstrate that brief therapy as it is conceptualized is specifically targeted for certain kinds of patients.

Major Principles of Psychoanalytic and Psychodynamic Psychotherapy

The Therapeutic Alliance

The nature of the relationship between patients and therapists is the most important component of operating within a psychoanalytic or psychodynamic framework. Many terms are used to describe this relationship, though the concept of the *alliance* is most used in this capacity. The alliance is the understanding between patients and therapists that therapists are invested in assisting their patients to reach their therapeutic goals in effective, caring, and compassionate ways and that patients are actively invested in achieving new levels of understanding and awareness that promote long-lasting changes in thoughts, feelings, behaviors, and relationships. The alliance term was introduced first by Zetzel (1956) and Greenson (1967) to capture the idea that patients and therapists work together for a common goal. Even Sigmund Freud (1915a) had some interest in the nature of the relationship, which he called an unobjectionable positive transference. A strong alliance has clearly been established when therapists make statements that are uncomfortable for their patients. While patients may find temporary dislike of their therapist at these times, patients who have a positive therapeutic alliance will come to evaluate, accept, and enact the interventions of their therapist. This acceptance and action, however, occurs because the relationship has been established and a sense of trust and safety between patients and therapists has been developed. Herein lies the essence of a good alliance: the development of a sense of trust in the treating professional, the process, and the physical environment, along with a sense of safety provided by therapists when examining upsetting and conflicting material. As such, attending to the therapeutic alliance at the outset and throughout the duration of treatment is essential for good psychodynamic therapy to occur.

Gabbard (2000) described three important concepts related to the therapeutic alliance. First is the concept of *neutrality*. Anna Freud (1936/1966) suggested that this means therapists maintain an equal distance from patients' id, ego, and superego, seeking not to be too identified with any one part of patients' psyche. Neutrality, according to Gabbard (2000, p. 95), is "the assumption of a nonjudgmental stance regarding the patient's behaviors, thoughts, wishes, and feelings." Greenberg (1986) considered neutrality to be therapists' development of a relationship with patients that reflects both elements of the new object relationship (with therapists) and the old object relationship (revealed in the transference with therapists). Stated somewhat differently, neutrality may be considered to be therapists' attitude of nonjudgment toward patients while at the same time maintaining the appropriate psychological distance from their subjective experience to think in more objective and theoretically informed ways about patients to plan and act in therapeutically beneficial ways.

Although the idea of being neutral originated from Freud's papers on analytic technique, Gabbard (2000) noted that there is considerable evidence showing how Freud did not abide by this concept. Other contemporary therapists have written about how they have not fully abided by the principle of neutrality. For example, Greenberg (2001a) provided six examples of instances in which therapists describe how their neutrality was broken. These include things such as admitting they lied to a patient, confessing erotic feelings to a patient, bringing a patient a blanket because she was cold, and screaming at a patient. Of course, many of these examples are highly idiosyncratic to the specific interaction of very experienced therapists and their patient. Consequently, they are to be considered out of the norm of standard practice. What remains of crucial importance in these circumstances is to recognize why these therapists did what they did and how patients experienced and benefited from such activities. For all therapists, when considering whether to break analytic neutrality the rule of thumb remains that if in doubt, remain neutral.

Second, Gabbard (2000) described the concept of anonymity, which is the "mythical construct" that personal effects, self-disclosure, and the "blank screen" approach are not to be utilized in dynamic psychotherapy. Early models of psychoanalysis stressed the idea that the analyst be "opaque," revealing nothing of himself to the patient (Marcus, 1999; Wallerstein, 2002). However, it is now considered impossible for analysts (or therapists) to be a blank screen, as the unconscious mind of therapist and the unconscious mind of patient work in a dynamic, reciprocal fashion that affects what each says and does in the presence of the other (Greenberg, 2001b; Stolorow, Atwood, & Brandchaft, 1994). Gabbard (2000), McWilliams (1999, 2004), Greenberg (2001a), and many others have dissuaded therapists from acting from the assumption of being a blank screen. More specifically, McWilliams (1999, p. 15) suggested that it is impossible for the personal, idiosyncratic interpretative processes of therapists not to impact therapy: "The term implies that patient and therapist have created together, from their combined subjectivities and quality of the relationship that evokes between them, a narrative that makes sense of the client's background and predicament—a narrative truth rather than a historical one (Levenson, 1972; Spence, 1982; Atwood & Stolorow, 1984; Schafer, 1992; Gill, 1994)." Nevertheless, anonymity is an important therapeutic ideal, in which therapists are cautioned to select their words and actions very carefully. Although one cannot be truly anonymous, one can be circumspect in what one says, does, or reveals.

Finally, Gabbard (2000, p. 96) described the construct of abstinence, which is the "deliberate withholding of gratification wishes so that those wishes could be analyzed rather than satisfied." In other words, patients are not always provided with what they immediately want. This is important for many reasons. Mainly, therapy is designed to bring insight into what patients desire and how they have gone about getting these desires met. Providing frequent gratification undermines this process. Additionally, when therapists do not abstain, they foster dependency in their patients, which likely will cloud the analytic process and the way patients feel toward their therapist. Unlike many psychotherapies, psychoanalytic, and at times psychodynamic, approaches to treatment are most interested in the wishes and fantasies of patients and the means by which these fantasies and wishes are gratified. Systematic exploration and analysis of these wishes is a defining feature of treatment. Gabbard noted that partial gratification of these wishes occurs automatically, simply by the nature of the therapy process itself. Here, therapists listen empathically to their patients and respond accordingly, such as laughing at something funny patients say or acknowledging a comment from patients not related to the therapy (e.g., "It sure is cold outside today"). Wish gratification also occurs with greater frequency when a supportive approach to treatment is undertaken. By its very nature, supportive therapy attempts to restore patients to their previous level of functioning and to bolster their coping and defense mechanisms. For many beginning therapists, adopting an orientation toward abstinence is difficult to master, given their own wishes and desires to help, save, or rescue the patient. This was reflected very well by one of my supervisees, who said of his patient, "I don't want her to walk out of here not feeling good."

Goals of Psychoanalytic and Psychodynamic Therapy

Freud asserted, and it still is the case today, that the purpose of psychoanalytic treatment is to make the unconscious conscious. Greenberg (2001a) noted how Freud (1916–1917) was somewhat modest in what he thought analysis could do; that is, making more of mental life accessible to consciousness and being open to more effective management was the best analysis could hope for. Gabbard (2004) offered several goals that can be accomplished in psychodynamic therapy:

- The resolution of conflict
- The search for truth
- An improved capacity to seek out self-objects
- Improved relationships as a result of a gain in understanding about one's internal object relationships
- The generation of meaning within the therapeutic dialogue
- Improved reflective functioning

Indeed, it is these goals that often are associated with most forms of psychoanalytic and psychodynamic psychotherapies.

This is not to suggest that more specific goals may not be part of the treatment. For example, fewer arguments with one's spouse, the ability to go out on dates and seek a long-term life partner, or discontinuing smoking are valid goals and are typical of the things patients mention as reasons for entering psychotherapy. In fact, these kinds of goals are very often reached as part of the treatment. Behavioral and cognitive-behavioral therapists often are critical of psychoanalytic and psychodynamic treatment for the lack of attention to such specific, behavioral goals and behavioral interventions in treatment. Yet attention to one's inner life, conflicts, and pursuit of interpersonal relationships can very much lead to significant improvement. Empirical support for the utility of psychodynamic therapy in the treatment of these problems is discussed in the next chapter.

Insight is often discussed in the context of goals, as it is believed that insight is a significant part of psychoanalytic and psychodynamic treatment that is associated with a favorable outcome. Interestingly, Freud only used the word *insight* one time, and not in the way it is typically understood (Messer & McWilliams, 2007). Rather, many ego psychologists attribute to Strachey (1934) the implicit introduction of the necessity of insight in treatment. Insight has been defined and understood in many ways. Insight may come to the patient by way of the interpretations and suggestions of the therapist. Alternatively, relationally oriented therapists tend to view insight as a product of mutual discovery that arises from the meaningful relationship that develops between patients and therapists. In this case, both patients and therapists are considered to have important ideas to share that leads patients to new ways of thinking about and experiencing things.

Messer and McWilliams (2007) provided important criteria by which to determine whether insight is occurring. Implicit in these criteria are important outcomes of psychoanalytic and psychodynamic treatment:

- Recognition of patterns of connections
- The ability to observe one's own internal processes, personality, or psychopathology
- The revision of pathological beliefs
- Recognition of the motives of oneself and others

These criteria speak well about the direction and focus of psychoanalytic and psychodynamic treatment.

Free Association

Free association is a technique that was created for psychoanalysis in which patients are to speak freely—without censorship—about whatever comes to mind. This is done while patients are lying on the couch with the analyst behind them to hear, reflect on, and guide the associative process. Initially, free association was used to detect and overcome the resistance patients experienced by conscious censorship of their ideas and desires (Freud, 1913). Free association also allows therapists to examine why certain material is resisted from being verbalized (Busch, 1994) and is considered to be part of what fosters patients' ability to get better; that is, they learn how to self-observe. In many ways, free association guides the psychoanalytic and psychodynamic psychotherapy process today. Once the process of therapy has begun, patients say whatever is on their minds—the therapist very rarely begins the session with the intent of exploring certain material or themes. Rather, this is left up to patients. Often, patients' ability to free associate is an important assessment tool to understand their psychological mindedness, their awareness of upsetting and troubling material, and the manner by which they cope with or defend against such material. Using behavioral language to describe the process, interpretation is a process whereby patients are simply allowed to engage in a particular form of verbal behavior that is then observed by the trained mind of their therapists, who reflect on what they have observed in their patients so additional opportunities for observation can occur.

Often, free association is understood as being carried on by patients, with therapists remaining passive. While it is the task of patients to speak about what is on their mind, it is the task of therapists to *actively and carefully listen* to what is offered, what is not offered, and how it is offered. At the same time, therapists should be formulating ideas for what it is that is bothering patients and what the best avenue is for examining this material. For example, a patient who has come to therapy because of dissatisfaction in her marriage may begin the session by speaking about the events of the past few days. She may recall with quite a bit of detail what happened, how people responded, and what her course of action was in specific situations. Listening actively to the patient, the therapist may observe that she has left out a description of her inner or private world when speaking. The patient also may be observed to avoid specific material (e.g., discussions about her reactions to her husband's egregious behaviors) or to show little connection from her past sessions to the events of the past few days and what she is learning or thinking about the most recent events. Thus, what may initially appear to be irrelevant or useless information becomes quite meaningful in telling the therapist about the patient's insightfulness, defensiveness, conflict, ego strengths, qualities of her object relatedness, and sense of self or agency in an upsetting situation.

Free association is a therapy technique that is believed to provide therapists with important information about their patients' inner world. Certainly it is the case that as an end product of the free association process, therapists can select from one or more important issues or topics that were brought up so that they can employ one of the several interventions that are part of the expressive-supportive continuum. But this is not to suggest that free association is the only method to be used. Some patients require structure to begin the session or assistance in deciding where to focus their attention. Patients who are more impulsive or highly guarded may require some direction from therapists to make the session time together meaningful. Such activities demonstrate a sense of competence and care on the part of therapists, as well as fostering the alliance. In more brief forms of psychodynamic therapy, therapists may be more explicit about where to begin or what to focus on in the course of the session. Davanloo (1980), for instance, suggested that trial interpretations be made in the first session to determine patients' openness to the more direct and confrontational nature of his model of brief therapy. In the model proposed by Luborsky and Crits-Cristoph (1990), therapists seek to identify early in treatment what are called core conflictual relationship themes (CCRTs). These themes are reflected in the transference and consist of a wish or need, a response from the other person, and the response of the self to that need. CCRTs become the focus of the treatment, and attention is directed to identifying and understanding them in the context of patients' interpersonal relationships. In both cases, free association is not a predominant method that is utilized.

Transference

Huprich and Keaschuk (2006, p. 476) defined transference as "an inaccurate perception, representation, and interaction the patient experiences with the therapist, often reflecting the patient's experience with someone similar in his or her past." In the context of psychoanalytically oriented psychotherapy, transference is considered a fundamental process that will foster patients' exploration and discovery of the origins of their conflicts. In the context of psychodynamic psychotherapy, transference is also expected to occur and be examined and be worked through; however, it does not take on the magnitude of importance for the technique as it does in psychoanalytically oriented treatment. Gabbard (2000) wrote that transference may be generated when therapists act out of anonymity and, at times, abstinence. Thus, transference is very closely tied to the nature of the alliance.

In traditional American ego psychology, all experiences, comments, attitudes, desires, wishes, thoughts, and feelings of patients toward their analysts reflect transference. However, more contemporary views of transference recognize that it is *one part of* the relationship between patients and therapists. A patient who reacts with some anger or frustration toward a therapist who makes a disparaging or insensitive comment to the patient is not necessarily reacting out of transference. Or, consider a more dramatic example, in which the therapist forgets the patient's appointment and the patient becomes angry. In both cases, the patient's reaction is to the behavior of the therapist and is justified. This represents a patient's reaction to the *real relationship* between the patient and the therapist. However, it is *how* the frustration is expressed that can help uncover any transference component that may be present. Extreme reactions of anger or acting out may represent a transferential element to the situation, and in such cases it is important for the therapist to carefully tease apart the reasonable reaction to the behavior of the therapist versus the patient's reaction to a past parental figure.

The transference relationship may be positive or negative toward the therapist. Transference also may be an admixture of positive and negative feelings. It may be sexual or aggressive or filled with ambivalence. It also may be relatively problematic in how it interferes with the therapy goals, or it may be circumscribed in its effect. Thus, transference is fundamentally associated with the concept of resistance. Ellman (2001) observed how many analysts believe that transference is always present and should be interpreted early on in the therapy relationship. Others, such as Weiner (1998), take a more cautious approach to the interpretation of transference. Weiner provided three guidelines for when to interpret transference: (1) when it is producing resistance; (2) when it is of moderate intensity and interferes with treatment; and (3) when significant information is believed to come from the exploration. Depending on the type and length of therapy, the extent to which the transference is examined and worked through will vary.

Countertransference

Countertransference certainly is bound to occur in the context of psychotherapy. As living, thinking, and feeling individuals, therapists come to experience their patients in many ways and develop particular affects, desires, and attitudes toward them. Countertransference has traditionally been considered a distortion made by the therapist about a patient. Freud identified this process after struggling with his own reactions to patients who were resistant and defensive toward certain material and content. Later, he came to see it as an important obstacle to successful treatment. When it occurs, countertransference has traditionally been viewed as inappropriate or irrational, needing careful scrutiny by therapists so as to prevent it from interfering with their ability to be objective.

Alternative views of countertransference also have been posited. Theodore Jacobs (1987, 1991, 1993) arguably has made the most influential contributions to modern understandings of countertransference. Going beyond the idea that countertransference is a hindrance to psychotherapy, he has suggested that therapists ought to evaluate their internal experience to see what it can tell them about their patients and the nature of the transference that is being played out. Similar ideas were reflected earlier by Racker (1968, p. 17), who boldly stated, "If the analyst is well identified with the patient and he has fewer repressions than the patient, then the thoughts and feelings which emerge in him (i.e., the analyst) will be, precisely, those which did emerge in the patient, i.e., the repressed and the unconscious." Racker's ideas stem from the concepts of *concordant* and *complementary identifications*. In the former, therapists identify with the thoughts, feelings, and desires (i.e., id and ego) of their patients. In the latter, therapists identify with internalized relationship roles assigned to them by patients' thoughts, feelings, and desires. In this way, therapists experience the wants and desires of patients and their representations of others who may or may not provide gratification. Eagle (2000) wrote that Racker's statement about countertransference reflects an overemphasis on complementary identifications, thereby reinforcing the idea that therapists can truly function as a blank slate without projecting any of their wishes or ideas onto patients. As discussed earlier, it is the belief of most therapists that it is impossible for therapists to function in such a neutral and abstinent role. Consequently, Eagle recommended that countertransference be viewed in a more balanced manner; that is, therapists' feelings and thoughts toward patients may reflect either therapists' or patients' inner life. Most psychodynamic therapists today tend to view countertransference in this balanced manner.

It is often difficult for beginning therapists to speak about or to acknowledge their countertransference. Often, such ideas are viewed as being shameful or fearful (i.e., "What does it mean if I really don't like this person?"). Coming to accept and learn from one's own countertransference is an important skill to master and is virtually identical to the process that occurs in psychoanalytic and psychodynamic therapy. That is, understanding one's inner life and private world is viewed as paramount in being able to live and function with less conflict and greater adaptation. I find it interesting that some beginning therapists are highly reluctant to discuss these experiences, despite the fact they very much want to learn and operate from a dynamic or analytic process. This may reflect a different kind of transference–countertransference dynamic: between therapists and their supervisors. To come to recognize and accept thoughts, feelings, desires, and attitudes toward others—including supervisors or patients—is part of being human and related, and it is part of personal maturity and professional development to recognize and understand them.

Interpretation

Interpretation "is a speculation or hypothesis provided by the therapist about the nature of the patient's problem of which the patient is not currently aware. It is an explanation [made] with the intent of providing insight and meaning to the patient" (Huprich & Keashcuk, 2006, p. 475). Interpretations are considered one of the hallmarks of psychoanalytic and psychodynamic psychotherapies and are founded entirely on the ideas and values of therapists. That is, they are the hypothesis of therapists that are offered to patients for their consideration as possible explanations for why a particular problem exists. Thus, therapists' understanding of personality and psychopathology theories is necessary for them to offer an idea that is plausible for both them and their patients to consider. Brenner (1973), for instance, noted how good interpretations include a comment about the nature of the wish patients hope to have fulfilled, the anticipated danger associated with fulfilling the wish, the affects that are aroused when the wish occurs, the defense that is used to help keep the conflict out of awareness, and the resulting compromise formation that is observed. While this sounds like a lot to address in an interpretation, it can be put forth in a rather straightforward way: "The thought of expressing your desire to have a closer relationship with her is so frightening that you have feel you must block it out of awareness for fear that you might embarrass yourself if you were to express it. This seems to have created much dissatisfaction in your current relationship and the distance you now experience with her."

Spence (1992) was critical of the nature by which interpretation works. He suggested that there are few examples in the literature of how an interpretation was made, accepted, and provided meaning and subsequent change in patients. He added that little attention has been given to the developmental level of patients and their readiness to hear an interpretation. For instance, a patient may be overwhelmed with frustration at an employer for what is perceived to be unfair treatment. The patient may find herself feeling "in a daze" and "drawing a blank" as to how she might deal with the frustrating aspects of her relationship with the employer. The therapist may make the interpretation, based on the patient's history and on sound theoretical grounds, that her experience of the employer is much like the time in her early childhood when she became so angry with her mother, yet so fearful of her, that she had no way of expressing what was happening internally. While the interpretation may indeed identify the reasons why the patient's here-and-now experience occurs as it does, the patient may be experiencing the therapist as a parental figure so that she cannot take the ideas of her therapist and consider them in a reasoned way as she might consider other ideas from her therapist. Thus, the interpretation may not be processed or understood as something that may be helpful in understanding her experience.

Some good ideas have been offered on how to make interpretations meaningful to the patient. Weiner (1998) stated that an interpretation must be made when patients are ready to accept a new understanding of their problems. This is known to happen when the therapeutic relationship has been well established and patients are low in their resistance to treatment. Weiner (1998) also noted that interpretation of the therapy process should occur before the content, since a focus on the here-and-now exchange between patient and therapist that is observed by the therapist will lay the foundation for the patient to hear a content-oriented explanation. For instance, in the case just described, the therapist may have started by observing to the patient what she saw, such as, "You seem to be having a hard time putting words into your experience." At this point, the patient would have the opportunity to describe what she was experiencing, thereby making her experience more understood rationally and in the here-and-now relationship with the therapist than in the experience of the confused, frustrated child. The therapist could observe this to the patient with the comment, "It seems like you have a better understanding of what it was like for you when you were with your boss." As the patient hears and accepts this statement, the therapist could then suggest to the patient, "Perhaps what you were experiencing with your boss was similar to the feelings you have had in the past with your mother—feeling so frustrated and angry that you did not know how or what to say to her." Moving from the patient's here-and-now experience to a deeper, more interpretive understanding makes the process easier for both the patient and therapist and, consequently, more effective.

By its very nature, interpretation offers a new, though potentially challenging, way by which patients understand their current way of thinking, feeling, and behaving. An interpretation either implicitly or explicitly suggests that the patients' current way of understanding their situation is not as complete as it could be. It may even be that the patients' understanding is inaccurate. Thus, interpretations can be met with resistance and may require time to work through and understand. For instance, the interpretation, "You find yourself feeling attracted to this woman because she offers something you aren't experiencing in your wife right now," suggests a reason for the patient's unhappiness that he may not have known before. It is for this reason that the stereotypical response of "Aha, now I see it all!" is infrequently observed with an interpretation. Rather, interpretations are worked through, often many times.

Alternatively, interpretations can sometimes provide a sense of relief to the patient. It can be quite encouraging to hear an interpretation that offers meaning and hope to a situation that seemed hopeless, confusing, or bewildering. The same interpretation previously exemplified could be met with relief by a man who is feeling highly guilty for having sexual feelings toward another woman or who is confused about why he could possibly have such feelings when he has always found his current wife to be very attractive.

Resistance

One of the ironies of psychotherapy is that patients resist making changes despite their conscious efforts to be alleviated from their problems and difficulties. This is certainly observed in psychodynamic and psychoanalytic treatment. In fact, good psychoanalytic and psychodynamic psychotherapy should elicit, identify, and address resistances when they occur. Resistance often occurs via a defense or in the transference, and it is present because it serves a protective function, much like a cast on a broken arm or leg. Those with a cast will say after an extended period of time that they are ready to have it removed. But anyone who has been in a cast will tell you it is very difficult to remove it without the right kind of tools. Thus, by way of analogy, it often takes time and the right psychological tools to bring the nature of the problem into full conscious awareness and for the resistance to addressing the problem (i.e., the psychological "cast") to be overcome so that it can be removed. Thus, a tension exists between wanting to resolve the problem (i.e., "get better") and the protective nature of one's psyche of the conflict underlying the problem.

There are numerous reasons why patients are resistant. Weiner (1998) proposed several mechanisms: (1) resistance related to a secondary gain of being a patient or of holding onto specific problems or symptoms; (2) resistance to changing the relationship patterns with others; (3) resistance to specific content; (4) resistance to being in the patient role; and (5) self-criticism persons experience because of their psychological growth. Some resistances, too, are very gratifying. For instance, a man who refuses to listen to his wife's complaints during couples therapy about their relationship will continue to reap the benefits of her nurturing and caregiving if she is unable to separate herself from him for financial or emotional reasons. McWilliams (2004) added that sometimes resistance occurs because patients are not attuned to what the role of being a patient requires of them. Cultures that encourage deference to authority or suppression of one's emotional life or individual inner world produce patients who are resistant to treatment. She suggested that patients sometimes need to be informed and educated about the role of the patient and what to expect in psychotherapy. Menninger (1958) astutely noted that resistance may also be observed in acting out and erotization of the therapy process. For instance, patients who provoke the therapist or who make sexual advances toward the therapist may successfully avoid addressing the underlying conflicts that are so difficult to experience. Finally, resistance can also be rooted in one's personality. Reich (1949) and Shapiro (1965) observed that characterological resistances are tied into the stereotypical use of defense mechanisms and tend to be difficult to overcome. Thus, an individual with an obsessive-compulsive personality is very likely to use intellectualization and rationalization as a means to avoid important emotionally conflicted material, whereas an individual who is more paranoid is likely to use projection and projective identification as a means by which to avoid conflicted material.

It should be apparent by now that a discussion of resistance does not just include patients who say to their therapist, "No, I'm not talking about that." Nor is it just about patients who skip appointments or come in late. Rather, even in the most motivated and engaged patients, there is a reluctance to engage in certain material that is associated with tension and discomfort. Resistance is often buried in the unconscious mind, such that persons have no awareness whatsoever of information or content that is very painful, that is highly relevant to the presenting issue, and that has much potential to improve their well-being if it were addressed.

Psychodynamic and psychoanalytic therapy is often criticized for producing insight without corresponding behavioral change. This is clearly a misrepresentation of this genre of treatment in that it does not consider the role of resistance in producing behavioral change. Resistance operates at many levels and affects how change occurs. Some types of problems can be resolved by insight alone, like the kind that comes from having a greater understanding of one's conflicts and the subsequent lessening of self-directed criticism for having such thoughts or ideas. Some problems are overcome by both insight and subsequent changes in one's attitudes and orientation to particular problems, such that the overt behavioral changes may seem minimal but the subjective suffering is significantly lessened. For instance, a man who feels very angry toward a spouse for her excessive spending may recognize that many angry feelings stem from his own conflicts over using money for self-gratification. By adopting a more understanding attitude toward his own conflicts over experiencing pleasure, he may find that he feels less critical of her behavior and more understanding of why he has those feelings and may be able to communicate his concerns about her spending only after first being clear in his own mind what part of his anger toward her is related to his own conflicts. Finally, some problems are overcome via both insight and notable behavior change, which is usually observed in most patients. Insight provides a sense of mastery and competence in understanding the problem. Yet resistance to notable behavioral changes is often associated with the substantial power of the underlying affect and sense of danger that is felt by making change. An insightful patient who is socially anxious may find himself feeling quite unsettled when it comes time to initiating a date with someone. Among the many factors that are associated with this action could be the considerable anxiety that is experienced by making himself look physically and interpersonally attractive to his date. Not only is there significant self-denigration he may experience regarding his sense of inadequacy, but there also is likely significant arousal that is felt and very highly desired in looking attractive to another person. In other words, the resistance to behavior change comes from, among other things, his own high level of arousal and desire that is felt when thinking of and making himself look attractive. To overcome his anxiety, the patient must dress and groom himself in a way that makes him look attractive, something that had been associated with fear and anxiety in the past.

Summary

In this chapter, I discussed orientations toward clinical practice (expressive and supportive), as well as major principles involved in psychodynamic and psychoanalytic therapy. Knowledge of these concepts is absolutely essential for good therapy to proceed. Yet knowledge alone does not make a good therapist. It is the nature of the interpersonal relationship and therapists' ability to be attuned to relationship dynamics that become important components of therapeutic change. While therapists' relational skills clearly overlap with many of the principles discussed herein, it is the case that good relationship skills contribute to a good outcome (Norcross, 2002b). The next chapter discusses the research evidence that supports the principles and concepts described herein, along with evidence about the components of therapy most strongly associated with a favorable outcome.

Note

1. An even stronger position that advocates the mixing of therapeutic techniques has been offered by Westen (2000); this issue is discussed further in chapter 7.

6

Empirical Studies of Psychoanalytic and Psychodynamic Psychotherapy

Patients, clinicians, and researchers all have interests in psychotherapy. While the motivation behind their interests varies, all agree that two fundamental questions about psychotherapy are of great importance: (1) Does psychotherapy work? And if so, (2) how does therapy work? These issues have been the focus of much attention over the years (e.g., Bergin & Lambert, 1978; Lambert & Bergin, 1994; Lambert & Ogles, 2003; Luborsky, Singer, & Luborsky, 1975; Luborsky et al., 2003; Shapiro & Shapiro, 1982; Smith, Glass, & Miller, 1980; Wampold et al., 1997, Wampold, 2001). In particular, these questions came to the forefront of the psychotherapy literature in 1993, when Division 12 of the American Psychological Association worked to publish a list of criteria for what constitutes *empirically supported treatment* (EST; Chambless et al., 1996; Task Force on Promotion and Dissemination of Psychological Procedures, 1995; Task Force on Psychological Intervention Guidelines, 1995). A subsequent list of those treatments was published that were empirically supported. Very few psychodynamic treatments were included, nor were interpersonal or humanistic therapies included. Not surprisingly, these guidelines and this list became anything but unifying for psychotherapists and psychotherapy researchers.

Westen, Novotny, and Thompson-Brenner (2004) made some important critiques of the literature on ESTs. They noted that ESTs are often designed for a single, Axis I disorder, and patients are screened to maximize their homogeneity and to minimize their diagnostic comorbidity. Treatments are manualized and brief, and outcomes are assessed often by reductions in the primary symptom reduction for that disorder. Westen et al. suggested that EST researchers also assume the following:

- Psychopathology is highly malleable.
- Most patients can be treated for a single problem or disorder.
- Psychiatric disorders can be treated without much attention to underlying personality factors.
- Experimental methodology used to develop the EST has ecological validity in clinical practice.

Westen et al. (2004) contended, however, that these assumptions are not valid. There is considerable diagnostic comorbidity, making most patients ineligible to participate in EST research trials. There also is considerable stability of psychopathology of psychiatric symptoms, even after "successful" completion of the EST. And clinicians of all theoretical orientations see patients well beyond the time frame allotted in treatment manuals (see Morrison, Bradley, & Westen, 2003; Thompson-Brenner, Glass, & Westen, 2003; Westen & Morrisson, 2001 for an excellent review of these issues).

Norcross (2002a) offered an additional perspective on why the EST literature has been so controversial. First, he suggested that EST research seldom addresses the fact "that the therapist is a person, however much he may strive to make himself an instrument of the patient's treatment" (Orlinsky & Howard, 1977, p. 567 as cited by norcross 2002a). This idea has been demonstrated well in the empirical literature. For instance, Wampold (2001) concluded in a meta-analysis of psychotherapy studies that the qualities of the therapist play a much stronger role in the outcome than does the treatment itself. Second, Norcross stated that therapy research has grossly neglected the important question of studying the therapy relationship. Instead, the focus has been more on the application and mastery of a technique (not a relationship). Third, who the patient is affects treatment outcome. As attention has been directed toward the study and implementation of psychotherapy techniques to different categories of disorders, scant attention has been paid to the patient characteristics that affect treatment outcome, such as comorbid conditions, capacity for insight, and history of interpersonal relatedness.

Psychoanalytic and psychodynamic therapies certainly are related to these issues. Analytic and dynamic models of therapy are very focused on the behavior and qualities of the therapist, with special attention to issues of the therapeutic alliance, neutrality, transference, and countertransference. As I noted in other chapters, much of one's training in how to conduct psychoanalytic or psychodynamic psychotherapy is focused on how therapists presents themselves and how patients respond to this. Such a focus automatically puts the therapeutic alliance at the center of attention, something that has taken on more interest over the years (Fairbairn, 1952; Greenberg, 1986, 2001a; Pine, 1998; Stolorow, Atwood, & Brandchaft, 1994; Wallerstein, 2002). Psychoanalytic and psychodynamic therapists also have recognized that the personality and qualities of the patient affect how therapy should be conducted (e.g., Gabbard, 2000, 2004); that is, one approach to working with patients does not fit all patients. From a more critical perspective, however, it has taken analytic and dynamic clinicians a long time to recognize that the real person (not the neutral, "blank screen") of the therapist has an effect on treatment (Gabbard, 2000; Greenberg, 2001a; McWilliams, 1999; Pine, 1998; Wallerstein, 2002). The fact that other types of therapy are effective without enacting a "blank screen" approach was largely ignored by psychoanalytic therapists. Moreover, many analytic practitioners have been reluctant to allow their therapy relationships to be subject to empirical investigation (Bornstein, 2005), making it very difficult to provide more objective data that support the validity of analytic and dynamic therapy. In contrast, the many cognitive and behavioral therapies included on the EST list have very willingly been tested for their empirical efficacy.

The focus of this chapter is to provide a review of selected studies that demonstrate the effectiveness of psychoanalytic and psychodynamic psychotherapies and related clinical phenomena. I begin by reviewing arguments for the use of psychoanalytic and psychodynamic therapies in modern clinical psychology and psychiatry. Then I move into a review of studies that address many issues relevant to psychoanalytic and psychodynamic treatment, which include the length of treatment and its relationship to therapeutic outcome, the therapeutic alliance, transference, countertransference, and patient characteristics that affect outcome. This review is not meant to be comprehensive; rather, it is meant to provide an overview of some of the rich empirical support that exists for psychoanalytic and psychodynamic psychotherapy.

Does Psychoanalytic and Psychodynamic Treatment Work?

A considerable body of research has been performed on the efficacy of psychoanalysis, psychoanalytic, and psychodynamic psychotherapies. One of the most recent comprehensive reviews of the treatment research was provided by Wallerstein (2006). In this review, he described four generations of research, each of which was marked by increasing methodological sensitivity and empirical rigor. The earliest generation consists of studies between 1917 and 1968, in which patient improvement was assessed subjectively by clinicians' judgments (and not more standardized measures of functioning). These studies also were retrospective and did not utilize agreed on criteria for diagnostic assessment or clinical improvement. The second generation of research consisted of studies at the Boston and New York Psychoanalytic Institutes and the Columbia Psychoanalytic Center, along with separate lines of research by Pfeffer (1959, 1961, 1963), Norman and colleagues (Norman, 1975; Norman, Blacker, Oremland, & Barrett, 1976), and Schlessinger and Robins (1974, 1975, 1983). Overall, these studies found moderate support for the effectiveness of psychoanalysis, which was defined in some studies as the successful resolution of transference neuroses or overcoming the debilitating effects of neurotic conflict.

The third generation of studies was performed in the 1980s and early 1990s and includes studies of psychoanalytic psychotherapy. Wallerstein (2006) noted that these studies have analyzed data by groups (e.g., comparing a treatment group with a nontreatment group) or by single-subject case analyses. He noted that terms and ratings scales in this generation were more carefully designed and that longitudinal designs were implemented. Such studies also examined improvement beyond the time in treatment. Included in these studies were those from the Boston Psychoanalytic Institute (Kantrowitz, Paolitto, Sashin, Solomon, & Katz, 1986; Kantrowitz, Katz, Paolitto, Sashin, & Solomon, 1987a, 1987b; Kantrowitz et al., 1989) and from the Menninger Clinic (Wallerstein, 1986, 1988). These studies yielded some fascinating results. For instance, the former studies reported on the outcome of 22 patients who underwent psychoanalysis. In this sample, a large majority reported considerable improvement, though no variables could be identified that successfully predicted improvement. Kantrowitz (1986) speculated that patient–therapist match may have been an important predictive variable that was not assessed, and, indeed, research in other domains of psychotherapy at the time certainly supported the importance of such a variable (e.g., Miller, Taylor, & West, 1980; Orlinsky & Howard, 1980; Shapiro, Firth-Cozens, & Stiles, 1989). Follow-up studies of these patients 5 and 10 years later found that many patients had maintained the gains from treatment or were able to successfully overcome a problem with additional treatment (Kantrowitz, Katz, & Paolitto, 1990a, 1990b, 1990c); however, the stability of the gains could not be predicted by any variable identified in the earlier study. Kantrowitz et al. (1990c) later evaluated the degree of match between the analyst and patient and found that 12 of the 17 patients' outcomes were favorably affected by the nature of the therapeutic relationship. In this case, match referred to the interaction between analysts' and patients' personal qualities.

Perhaps one of the most well-known research studies of psychoanalysis and psychoanalytic psychotherapy is the Psychotherapy Research Project (PRP) of the Menninger Foundation. Wallerstein (2006) stated that the aims of the PRP were to learn what changes take place in treatment and how these changes come about. A total of 42 patients were followed over the course of their treatments (ranging between 6 months and 12 years). All of them were evaluated again 2 to 3 years after treatment, and one third were studied 12 to 24 years posttreatment. Patients were seen in psychoanalysis, expressive analytic psychotherapy, or supportive analytic psychotherapy. Wallerstein (1986) reached six major conclusions at the end of the study:

1. There appeared to be about as much structural change in supportive therapy as in the expressive therapies. The stability, durability, and capacity to tolerate life stress were just as strong in the supportive cases as in the expressive cases.
2. The amount of change that occurs is proportional to the degree to which there is conflict.
3. Changes in personality and overall functioning occur just as much in supportive modes as they do in expressive modes, including psychoanalysis.
4. Supportive therapies often achieved results that would only have been expected in expressive types of therapies, such that the changes were hard to distinguish from structural changes obtained in psychoanalysis.
5. Psychoanalysis as a whole did not achieve the magnitude of results expected when compared with expressive and supportive analytic therapies.

6. More substantial and enduring change was found in expressive therapy and psychoanalysis patients than the supportive therapy patients; however, supportive interventions were often utilized in analysis and had a notable effect on patient outcome.

Summing up his review of treatment research, Wallerstein (2006) described the fourth generation of psychotherapy research. This consists of studies that have examined psychotherapy process and psychotherapy outcome conjointly. Wallerstein (2001) proposed a Collaborative Analytic Multisite Program (CAMP) to the American Psychoanalytic Association that would evaluate both process and outcome. Although CAMP did not take hold at the time of its proposal, Wallerstein (2006) noted that many psychotherapy researchers are incorporating the ideas of CAMP into their research (something discussed in chapter 7).

Traditionally psychodynamic forms of therapy have been long term and high frequency. It is commonly believed that long-term treatments produce better outcomes than short-term treatments, and findings from dose–response relationship studies suggest that longer-term treatment may benefit a higher proportion of patients (Shapiro et al., 2003). Even the famous *Consumer Reports* (1995) study reported by Martin Seligman demonstrated that improvement is proportional to the length of time in treatment. Research also has suggested that there is a tendency for long-term therapies to show long-lasting benefits, especially with regards to posttreatment maintenance of gains (Luborsky, 2001; Sandell et al., 2000; Shapiro et al., 2003). In addition, significant differences in patients' perception of the effectiveness of psychotherapy have been found between patients receiving 6 months or 24 months of psychotherapy, with patients in therapy longer viewing their therapy as more effective (Freedman, Hoffenberg, Vorus, & Frosch, 1999).

However, in the current state of managed care there has been a sentiment to decrease the cost and length of treatment. As such, there has been an increase in research investigating the efficacy of short-term psychodynamic therapy. This research has challenged the long-standing assumption about the necessity of long-lasting psychotherapy. In short, meta-analyses have shown that short-term psychodynamic treatments are as efficacious as other forms of brief treatment, are slightly better than minimal treatments, and are significantly better than control treatments (Anderson & Lambert, 1995; Crits-Christoph, 1992). Support for brief dynamic therapy is not without controversy, however. Sandell, Blomberg, & Lazar (2002) suggested that there is no set effective dose of psychotherapy and that session frequency and duration interact in determining eventual treatment outcome. Research has supported this idea. In a comparison of short- and long-term therapies, Luborsky (2001) found that both forms of treatment show positive benefits for some patients. Patient characteristics and diagnostic classification also appear to differentially impact response to treatment in both short- and long-term therapies. For example, patients with personality disorders have been found to have a slower, positive response to short-term dynamic therapies (Barber, Morse, Krakauer, Chittams, & Crits-Cristoph, 1997; Hardy et al., 1995). It also has been demonstrated that characterological changes will occur more slowly than changes in acute and chronic distress (Kopta, Howard, Lowry, & Beutler, 1994). These findings suggest that one should consider carefully the desired outcome when deciding on what type of therapy to implement.

There have been at least three recent published reviews of efficacy and outcome studies on psychoanalytic and psychodynamic therapy. The first of these (Fonagy, 2006) is a comprehensive review of short-term psychodynamic psychotherapy efficacy studies (less than 24 sessions) that was published in the *Psychodynamic Diagnostic Manual (PDM; PDM* Task Force, 2006). In conducting this review, Fonagy (2006, p. 766) sought to determine: "1) are there any disorders for which short-term psychodynamic psychotherapy (STPP) can be considered as evidence-based; 2) are there any disorders for which STPP is uniquely effective as either the only evidence-based treatment or as a treatment that is more effective than alternatives." Fonagy organized his review of STPP by disorder or diagnostic category and included the following: major depression, anxiety disorders, eating disorders, substance misuse, and personality disorders. His conclusions are presented in Table 6.1. Although these findings are mixed, Fonagy (2006) noted that the absence of evidence for treatment efficacy should not be confused with evidence of the treatment's ineffectiveness. Particularly relevant to this issue is the fact that most empirically supported treatments attempt to address a single disorder with virtually no comorbid conditions. They also use a treatment manual that attempts to work in a time-effective fashion such that the intervention may be systematically applied to all individuals. Fonagy noted that the kind of patients for which brief therapy is targeted are not typical in clinical practice and that comorbidity is the rule, not the exception.

TABLE 6.1 Fonagy's (2006) Summary of Efficacy Studies on Short-Term Psychodynamic Psychotherapies

Efficacy Study	Summary
Major depression	"The current evidence base of psychodynamic therapy for depression is weak, relative to the number of psychoanalytic therapists and the rate at which evidence is accumulating for other approaches. The psychodynamic approach may be marginalized, not by its relative lack of effectiveness, but by the sparseness of compelling demonstrations of its comparability to 'empirically supported' alternatives. There is some evidence relating to brief psychodynamic therapy (up to 24 sessions), but no evidence for long-term therapy or psychoanalysis, despite the fact that data from trials of depression indicate the need for more intensive treatment."
Anxiety disorders	"One controlled trial suggested that STPP might have something to offer…A controlled trial comparing an unspecified form of STPP to cognitive therapy showed the latter to be substantially more effective in the short and medium term… There is a promising psychodynamic therapeutic approach to panic that might match CBT in efficacy that requires extension and replication in multi-center controlled trials …. It is striking that so little research has been done to establish the pertinence of psychodynamic approaches to anxiety, which is so central to both psychoanalytic theory and practice."
Eating disorders	"There have been four trials of psychodynamic psychotherapy for anorexia nervosa, all of which found it to be as effective as other treatments, including intensive behavioral and strategic family therapy …. STPP fares less well in the treatment of bulimia."
Substance misuse	"For alcohol problems of low severity, brief interventions seem to be the interventions of choice. Psychodynamic psychotherapy, along with other formal psychological therapies, appears not to be particularly helpful when offered as a stand-alone treatment …. Supportive expressive psychotherapy appears of almost no value in the context of cocaine misuse …. A different picture emerges in the context of opiate abuse where psychodynamic treatment was shown to be efficacious in two trials, unfortunately (from the standpoint of EST criteria) carried out by the same team …. There is prima facie case for the unique effectiveness of supportive expressive therapy, as neither IPT nor certain cognitive therapies appear to have quite the same impact."
Personality disorders	"The limited number of studies, compounded by the heterogeneity of clinical populations and methods applied, suggests that meta-analysis at this stage may be premature …. The broad conclusion from these aggregated figures would be that CBT and psychodynamic therapy are equally effective."

Source: From *PDM* Task Force, *Psychodynamic diagnostic manual.* Silver Spring, MD: Alliance of Psychoanalytic Organizations, 2006. (With permission.)

Thus, when reviewing the literature on empirically supported STPP, Fonagy, along with others (e.g., Westen & Morrison, 2001; Westen et al., 2004), suggested that caution be employed in making premature conclusions about the efficacy of STPP. Nonetheless, he suggested that ongoing research on psychoanalytic and psychodynamic treatments is necessary so that, among other things, it may compete in contemporary health-care settings and be valued for its utility from a more scientifically grounded perspective.

A slightly more optimistic conclusion about the efficacy of STPP was provided by Leichsenring (2006), who also published his review in the *Psychodynamic Diagnostic Manual* (*PDM* Task Force, 2006). His review included many German studies not included in other papers, such as Fonagy (2006). Having reviewed studies of personality disorders (especially Borderline) and Axis I disorders, Leichsenring (2006, p. 830) concluded that "the available meta-analyses provided some evidence that psychodynamic psychotherapy is an efficacious treatment of psychiatric disorders which is superior to TAU (treatment as usual) or wait list conditions and as effective as other forms of psychotherapy such as CBT." He noted that the studies he reviewed came from randominzed controlled trials (in which patients were carefully screened and randomly assigned to one of the treatment conditions possible) and added that further STPP research is needed, particularly with anxiety disorders.

Another review was also published by Leichsenring and colleagues (Leichsenring, Hiller, Weissberg, & Leibing, 2006) in which cognitive-behavioral and psychodynamic therapies were compared. His review consisted only of studies of randomized control trials and included psychodynamic studies ranging in duration between 7 sessions and 18 months. The studies reviewed included empirical support for psychodynamic treatment of depressive disorders, social phobia, generalized anxiety disorder, panic disorder, posttraumatic stress disorder, borderline personality disorder, *DSM*, 4th ed. (*DSM-IV*; American Psychiatric Association, 1994), Cluster C personality disorders, anorexia nervosa, bulimia nervosa, somatoform disorders, and alcohol and opiate dependence. Leichsenring and colleagues concluded that there is substantial evidence for the efficacy of both cognitive behavioral and psychodynamic therapies, although more studies exist for cognitive behavioral interventions. "However, for specific disorders the rates of treatment responders are not yet sufficient" (ibid., p. 234) in the cognitive behavioral conditions. Leichsenring et al. concluded that more studies of psychodynamic interventions for specific disorders are needed to support the current evidence that supports psychodynamic treatment.

Since these reviews were published, additional research has supported the effectiveness of psychoanalytic and psychodynamic therapy as well as psychoanalysis. In the paragraphs that follow, I provide five examples that have studied the efficacy of all three types of interventions.

A very intriguing case study was recently published by Porcerelli, Dauphin, Ablon, Leitman, and Bambery (2007). The patient was a man in his 50s who agreed to participate in psychoanalysis four times per week. He was initially diagnosed with avoidant personality disorder and complained of long-standing anxiety and fears about driving. His treatment lasted more than five years, and he was assessed at intake and once per year around the anniversary of his treatment. He also was evaluated one and two years after his treatment ended. Porcerelli et al. assessed the patient's symptoms via a self-report measure, and his personality organization was measured with an observer-rated measure of normal and pathological personality traits. The patient was also evaluated for the quality of his object relations and for the quality of the therapist–patient interaction. Overall, the patient's symptoms steadily declined, his overall level of functioning improved (he no longer met criteria for avoidant personality disorder after one year in treatment), and the quality of his object relations improved. The analytic process was characterized by the patient's active involvement in treatment, by attention to the patient's fantasies and dreams, and by the analyst drawing attention to conflicted and unacceptable feelings and content. More important, the patient continued to improve after the analysis was completed.

Levy and colleagues (2006) were interested in the effect of transference-focused psychotherapy (TFP), dialectical behavior therapy (DBT), and modified supportive psychodynamic psychotherapy (MSP) on patients' attachment patterns and reflective functioning. They recruited 90 patients with borderline personality disorder and randomly assigned them to one of the three treatment conditions (i.e., types of psychotherapy). Patients were followed for 3 years and were assessed with reliable and valid interviews for Axis I and Axis II diagnoses, attachment patterns, and reflective functioning. At the 1-year point, patients were again assessed for their attachment pattern and capacity for reflective functioning. A significant number of patients in the TFP group changed from an insecure to a secure attachment pattern, but this pattern was not observed at a level of statistical significance in the DBT or MSP groups. Reflective functioning and narrative coherence of one's attachment patterns also were significantly different between time 1 and time 2 for the TFP group, but not the DBT or MSP groups. In this case, reflective functioning and narrative coherence improved over time. Levy et al. concluded that TFP improves patients reflective functioning and attachment patterns over time. They suggested that future research should look to identify the mechanisms by which these patterns change and how stable such changes remain once therapy has completed.

Another study of 88 outpatients diagnosed with borderline personality disorder was conducted by Giesen-Bloo and colleagues (2006). This study was a multicenter, randomized, two-group comparison conducted in the Netherlands. Patients were assigned to either schema-focused therapy (SFT) treatment or transference-focused therapy and were evaluated at multiple points throughout treatment on multiple variables, including frequency and severity of borderline symptoms, quality of life, general psychiatric symptoms, self-esteem, self-perception, schemas, and defensive style. Giesen-Bloo et al. found that both treatment conditions led to a reduction in borderline and other psychiatric symptoms and improvement in quality of life. However, across all outcome measures, patients in the SFT group did better; the authors noted, however, that there was a higher attrition rate in the TFP group. Moreover, their data indicate that the TFP group patients had a statistical trend ($p = .09$) toward a higher rate of recent suicide planning and a significantly higher rate of recent nonsuicidal injuries. There also was not consistent agreement about the enactment of TFP procedures by therapists in the TFP group. Consequently, it may be that there were some ways the TFP group was more impaired or important ways treatment integrity was not maintained in the TFP group, which affected the overall outcome. Nonetheless, these findings stand in contrast to the previous study, in which the TFP group had better outcomes than comparable therapy groups.

Milrod and colleagues (2007) evaluated the efficacy of panic-focused psychoanalytic psychotherapy in a sample of patients who met *DSM-IV* (American Psychiatric Association, 1994) criteria for panic disorder with or without agoraphobia. Of the sample, 26 received psychoanalytic therapy while 23 received applied relaxation training, which is a behaviorally based treatment involving in vivo exercises and homework. Panic-focused psychotherapy is a 24-session, twice-weekly manualized psychoanalytic psychotherapy that has no homework or exposure to panic-inducing situations. There has been prior empirical support for the efficacy of both treatments (e.g., Milrod et al., 2001; Chambless & Peterman, in press), although this was the first study to compare the psychoanalytic treatment with another form of treatment targeted to this disorder. It also was the first published efficacy study of manualized psychoanalytic psychotherapy for panic disorder that was conducted in a randomized controlled clinical trial. Milrod et al. (2007) found that 73% of the psychoanalytic group met predefined criteria for improvement compared with the 39% in the applied relaxation training group. Furthermore, only 7% of the psychoanalytic group discontinued treatment prematurely compared with 34% of the behavioral group. Milrod et al. concluded that, contrary to past ideas, it is not just manualized behavioral therapy that is efficacious in the treatment of panic disorder.

Another study recently reported the efficacy of psychoanalytic and psychodynamic psychotherapy in a sample of 473 outpatients in Germany. Puschner, Kraft, Kachele, and Kordy (2007) collected data over the course of two years from patients who were in treatment for a wide variety of disorders (e.g., mood, anxiety, somatoform, and personality disorders). They were assessed on measures of psychiatric symptoms, overall level of functioning and impairment, interpersonal problems, physical complaints, and life satisfaction. Therapists and patients also completed a measure of the alliance. Puschner et al. computed linear models of improvement and found that patients in both psychoanalytic and psychodynamic psychotherapy made notable strides over the course of 27 months, regardless of whether they were in treatment the entire time or only a portion of the time. Furthermore, all patients had a rapid decline of their symptomatic distress, with lesser, though continued, improvements in symptoms over the course of treatment.

Much research demonstrates the empirical efficacy of certain types of psychotherapy. Likewise, many professional organizations (e.g., American Psychological Association) and clinical educators advocate the use of empirically supported treatments (which to date have been mostly behavioral and cognitive). What is done in clinical practice, however, is rather different from what researchers and academics advocate. Two studies highlight this issue well. First, in a survey conducted in summer 2001, psychologists in Division 29 (Psychotherapy) of the American Psychological Association were surveyed about their practice of psychotherapy (Norcross, Hedges, & Castle, 2002). The most widely endorsed theoretical orientation was "eclectic/integrative," which consisted of 35.8% of the 531 surveyed. Presumably, many of those who self-identified as eclectic/integrative incorporate psychoanalytic and psychodynamic ideas into their treatment. The next highest percentage was "psychodynamic" (20.9%), which rose to 28.9% when "psychoanalytic" was included. Thus, it may be that as many as two thirds of all clinicians in this study incorporate some aspect of psychoanalytic or psychodynamic theory and technique into their clinical practice. Second, in the treatment of anxiety disorders, for which there are many behavioral and cognitive behavioral therapies that have received empirical support, most patients receive psychodynamic or psychoanalytically oriented treatment (Goisman, Warshaw, & Keller, 1999; Goisman et al., 1993). This finding is quite interesting, given that much of the research on empirically supported treatment for anxiety disorders comes out of the same treatment centers reported by Goisman and colleagues in which psychodynamic or psychoanalytic treatment regularly occurs. On one hand, it could be argued that these findings reflect the fact that most of the clinicians have not been exposed to empirically supported treatments, either in their professional training or postgraduate education. On the other hand, it could be the case that experienced clinicians recognize that psychoanalytic and psychodynamic modalities offer something very important that is not found in other therapies. In all likelihood, both of these suppositions help explain the observed, real-world practice of psychoanalytic and psychodynamic psychotherapy. Likewise, it is the case that these two studies demonstrate the ecological validity of psychoanalytic and psychodynamic ideas in real-world, clinical practice.

Therapeutic Alliance

As noted throughout this text, the therapeutic alliance has been identified as a common treatment factor that mediates psychotherapy outcomes across theoretical orientations (Gaston, 1990; Horvath, Gaston, & Luborsky, 1993; Horvath & Greenberg, 1994; Horvath

& Luborsky, 1993; Horvath & Symonds, 1991; Luborsky, 1990, 1996; Norcross, 2002a). In a recent review of 90 studies of the therapeutic alliance, Horvath and Bedi (2002) computed the effect size[1] of the alliance on therapeutic outcome across multiple types of psychotherapy. They found that the average effect size of the therapeutic alliance is between .21 and .25. They note that while this is not a particularly large effect, Wampold (2001) concluded that the alliance, along with therapist variables, accounts for the most variance in psychotherapy outcome. When looking more specifically at the alliance–outcome relationship, alliance appears to be more predictive of a positive outcome when outcome is measured as change in the patient's target complaint rather than as symptoms (Horvath et al., 1993) and when a positive alliance is formed early in treatment (Luborsky, 1996). Alliances that are initially more negative do not seem to share this same relationship, as it appears that initial negativity in the alliance is a relatively irregular predictor of outcome (ibid.).

Empirical evidence also lends support to the idea that the therapeutic alliance will undergo change throughout treatment duration, a result of a cycle of relationship rupture and repair, as it has been suggested that positive early alliances occur because strain has not yet been placed on the therapeutic relationship (Safran, Muran, & Samstag, 1994). Consequently, it may be the case that these changes in alliance possibly affect the predictive validity of a positive therapeutic alliance. To address this concern, it has been suggested that a more accurate prediction of outcome could occur if alliance measures were averaged across sessions. In fact, Krupnick et al. (1996) found *stronger* associations between outcome and alliance when measures of alliance were averaged across several sessions than when measured during early sessions. However, one potential confound in measuring alliance during later sessions is that an improved therapeutic relationship may actually be an early indicator of positive treatment effects, which would decrease the predictive value of these measurements.

Because the therapeutic alliance is interaction between the patient and the therapist, research has investigated the attributes of both patients and therapists that contribute to positive therapeutic alliances. A review of 25 studies identified therapist personal attributes that contribute positively to the alliance, including flexibility, trustworthiness, experience, confidence, clear communication, enthusiasm, warmth, and interest (Ackerman & Hilsenroth, 2003). This analysis also identified therapeutic techniques that positively contributed to the alliance, including clear communication, accurate interpretation, exploration, affirmation, understanding, facilitation of affect expression, and attention to patients' experience.

Transference

The concept of transference has been examined in both laboratory and clinical settings and has been found to impact both clinical relationships and social functioning. Analogue laboratory studies of transference within social relationships have found that fictional characters that activate subjects' representations of a significant other will likely be misremembered as possessing characteristics of the significant other (Andersen & Cole, 1990). This finding suggests that the perception of new people is influenced by representations of meaningful others from one's past. In addition to influencing perceptions of new people, representations of significant others have also been found to influence affective responses to new people when representations of significant others are activated (Andersen & Baum, 1994).

Within the context of psychotherapy, Luborsky and colleagues (1985) used the Core Conflictual Relationship Theme (CCRT) method to examine narratives relating to the therapist and significant others of eight patients at different points in psychodynamic treatment. The CCRT identifies a transference pattern based on patients' wishes, needs, and intentions toward another person, the responses of the other person to these wishes, and the responses of the patients. The most frequent pattern found is labeled as being the CCRT. The results of these case studies supported nine of Freud's hypotheses about transference. In particular, individual patients were found to have one specific core transference pattern (but may possess other patterns as well), which is repeated in a relationship with the therapist and is also carried out in outside relationships.

Further empirical investigation of the specificity and pervasiveness of the transference pattern as measured with the CCRT in larger samples has yielded more generalizable results. Investigation of the pervasiveness of relationship themes found that 66.3% of patient narratives (n = 33 patients) contained the patient's main wishes as determined using the CCRT (Crits-Christoph & Luborsky, 1990). When looking at transference in the therapeutic relationship in particular,

Fried, Crits-Christoph, and Luborsky (1992) compared the patients' CCRTs derived from relationships with significant others to narratives about the therapist. They found that patients' own CCRT was similar to their narratives about the therapist. In addition, the transference toward the therapist appeared to be patient specific, as patients' narratives about the therapist were found to be more closely related to their CCRT than to the CCRTs of other patients.

Connolly et al. (1996) investigated transference relationships using a different measure of transference: the Quantitative Assessment of Interpersonal Themes (QUAINT). They examined the narratives of 35 male opiate addicts seeking dynamic or cognitive therapy and found that patients generally displayed repetitive patterns of interaction with significant others in their lives; however, patients appeared to have several different interpersonal patterns with specific subsets of people in their lives. Connolly et al. also found that the most pervasive pattern may not be the one transferred onto the therapist. However, the majority (60%) of patients who give a narrative about the therapist early in treatment report similar interactions with others in their lives.

A more recent study on therapeutic effectiveness of transference interpretation processes was conducted by Høglend and colleagues (2006) in a sample of 100 Norwegian patients who were randomly assigned to one of two treatment groups: psychodynamic therapy with "moderate levels of transference interpretations" (p. 1739) or psychodynamic therapy without any transference interpretation. Patients were assigned a diagnosis based on expert consensus discussion and were evaluated by their clinicians on their level of psychodynamic functioning, which included ratings on the patients' quality of family relationships, quality of friendships, quality of romantic/sexual relationships, tolerance for affects, insight, and problem-solving capacity. Clinicians also rated the patients' quality of object relations and assigned a Global Assessment of Functioning (GAF) score from the *DSM,* 3rd ed., revised (*DSM-III-R*; American Psychiatric Association, 1987). Patients completed a symptom checklist and measure of interpersonal problems. Overall, the two groups did not differ significantly on any outcome measure at pretreatment, midtreatment, or posttreatment, which was contrary to what Høglend et al. hypothesized. However, the quality of object relations scale was found to moderate the relationship between type of therapy and psychodynamic functioning and GAF score. In this case, patients with poorer quality of object relations were observed to benefit more from transference-based psychotherapy than were patients with higher quality of object relations. This finding was in contrast to what was expected, as past studies have noted how transference-based therapies tend to have a stronger effect for patients who enter therapy at an overall level of higher functioning. Høglend et al. did note, however, that some studies have found a negative effect of *high-frequency* transference interpretations in patients with higher level of object relatedness (Høglend, 1993a; Piper, Azim, Joyce, & McCallum, 1991b). Thus, it is possible that for some patients who enter therapy functioning at a higher level, transference interpretations can have a negative effect. Clearly, this issue requires further investigation.

Countertransference

Research in the area of countertransference was rarely done prior to the 1980s. Until recently, this area has primarily been investigated using analogue research, which has raised questions about the generalizability of these findings to clinical settings. Despite this, analogue research has contributed to the operationalization of countertransference and has improved in measurement methodology (Rosenberger & Hayes, 2002). Analogue research has lent support to several hypotheses including the following:

- Self-integration and anxiety management on the part of the clinician can beneficially impact the management of countertransference behavior (Gelso, Fassinger, Gomez, & Latts, 1995).
- Clinician gender is a moderator of countertransference—in particular, male therapists have a tendency to withdraw when they are anxious (Gelso et al., 1995).
- Clinician awareness of countertransference feelings in concert with adherence to a theoretical orientation decreases countertransference behavior (Latts & Gelso, 1995).

In an effort to provide a framework of countertransference that could be used to direct empirical research, Hayes (1995) proposed a structural model of countertransference consisting of five factors: origins, triggers, manifestations, effects, and management. In his model, countertransference was defined as therapist reactions identified (by the therapist) as being related to unresolved personal intrapsychic conflict. In a qualitative field study, Hayes et al. (1998) examined postsession interview data from eight clinicians who practiced brief psychodynamic treatment. They found that countertransference was present in 80% of the sessions and found support for the first three elements of the model (origins, triggers, and manifestations) as well as relationships among these three elements. Common origins of countertransference included family issues (family of origin, parenting, and partnering), therapist needs and values, issues related to the role of the therapist (competence and termination), and cultural issues (gender and race). Common triggers of countertransference behavior were identified as including the content of patient material, therapists comparing their patients to others, a change in therapy structure, the progress of therapy, therapists' perception of their patients, and emotional arousal on the part of therapists and their patients. The relationship between origins and triggers was found to be a strong predictor of whether countertransference will be experienced by a particular therapist with a particular patient. In general, an incident in session will trigger countertransference only if that incident is related to relevant origins for the specific therapist. More specifically, countertransference has been found to be more prevalent when the patient reminds the therapist of significant people in the therapist's life (including the therapist's identification with the client), when the patient's therapy content is similar to the therapist's unresolved issues, and when the therapist positively or negatively evaluates the client's progress in therapy (Hayes et al., 1998; Williams, Judge, Hill, & Hoffman, 1997).

Using the interview data from therapists, Hayes et al. (1998) also were able to categorize therapist manifestations of countertransference behavior into four categories:

1. Approach: Thoughts, feelings, and behaviors on the part of the therapist that decrease distance between therapist and patient.
2. Avoidance: Thoughts, feelings, and behaviors on the part of the therapist that increase distance between therapist and patient.
3. Negative feelings: Uncomfortable therapist emotions.
4. Treatment planning: Therapist decisions relating to the therapy process.

All of the therapists reported countertransference manifestations that included the categories of approach, avoidance, and negative feelings. The type of countertransference manifestation that occurred was found to be related to specific origins and triggers. For example, when therapists' family of origin issues were aroused by patients, the therapists tended to identify with the patients; when the trigger of countertransference was patients discussing their family of origin issues, therapists tended to respond with compassionate understanding.

Few empirical studies have examined the relationship between countertransference and therapy outcome, and results from these investigations have been mixed. Yet it appears that countertransference can interfere with therapists' ability to be maximally effective (Williams et al., 1997) and that countertransference behavior is inversely related to treatment outcome in cases with poor outcome (Hayes, 1995). For this reason, the management of countertransference is an important issue. In fact, studies have found that therapists who possess better self-integration appear to have fewer countertransference reactions (Gelso et al., 1995; Hayes, Riker, & Ingram, 1997). Therapist personal qualities including empathy, self-insight, and the ability to manage anxiety have also been related to better management of countertransference (Hayes et al., 1997; Van Wagoner, Gelso, Hayes, & Diemer, 1991).

Patient Characteristics

Psychodynamic therapy requires engagement on the part of both therapists and patients. A significant amount of empirical research has been directed toward identifying patient characteristics that can positively impact treatment outcome in psychodynamic therapy. Patient characteristics have also been applied to outcome in different forms of psychodynamic therapy. Several of these characteristics—including motivation, health sickness, ego integration, object relations, and interpersonal relations—have been found to consistently impact therapy outcome.

Motivation has consistently been emphasized in the empirical research. Measures of motivation have examined patients' ability for the following (Keithly, Samples, & Strupp, 1980; Sifneos, 1978):

- Recognition of the psychological nature of symptoms
- Tendency toward introspection
- Willingness to participate in treatment process
- Ability to become emotionally involved in treatment
- Willingness to understand themselves

- Willingness to change
- Willingness to make reasonable sacrifices
- Realistic expectations of therapy outcome
- Degree of autonomy in seeking therapy

In general, early ratings of patient motivation have a significant, positive relation to participation and outcome in psychodynamic therapy (Frayn, 1992; Keithly et al., 1980; Sifneos, 1978).

Initial psychological "health" and "sickness" of a patient can be generally described as emotional stability and mental health. Luborsky et al.'s (1993) review of health-sickness research found that higher initial levels of psychological health were related to more positive treatment outcomes. The authors noted, however, that this finding does not directly imply that psychodynamic therapy should be avoided for patients with less favorable ratings of health-sickness.

Psychodynamic therapy involves a significant relational element. For this reason the impact of patients' initial quality of interpersonal relations and object relations have been investigated. A history of good interpersonal relations has not been associated with symptomatic change, but has been related to improvement in dynamic processes (e.g., improved interpersonal relations and self-understanding) during the course of psychotherapy (Høglend, 1993b). Quality of object relations has been significantly related to the patient's ability to form a therapeutic alliance and to positive treatment outcomes (Piper, Azim, Joyce, & McCallum, 1991a; Piper & Duncan, 1999; Piper, Joyce, McCallum, & Azim, 1998). Prediction of treatment outcome from the quality of object relations was found to be particularly relevant when evaluating patients who were in interpretative psychodynamic therapy but was not significant for patients in supportive psychotherapy (Piper, McCallum, Joyce, Azim, & Ogrodniczuk, 1999). This implies that the match between patient characteristics and treatment process may be of particular importance.

Further support for the proposition that treatment outcomes may be related to matching treatment with patient variables (i.e., treatment congruence with patient variables) comes from Blatt's (1992) reanalysis of the data from the Menninger PRP. Kernberg (1973) reported that patients in the PRP with higher levels of inital ego strength appeared to improve regardless of the treatment modality. Results from the PRP, however, demonstrated negligible differences between the outcomes of patients in psychoanalysis and in psychotherapy (Wallerstein, 1986). In Blatt's reanalysis, he distinguished between anaclitic patients, whose pathology is related to interpersonal disruptions, and introjective patients, whose pathology is related to self-definition and autonomy. His analysis found that anaclitic patients have better outcome in psychotherapy, possibly because of the relational nature of this form of treatment. In contrast, introjective patients had more positive outcome in psychoanalysis, which may be related to the focus on insight and understanding in this modality. Although this congruence appears related to treatment outcomes, Blatt suggested that both types of patients require integration of the needs for integration and relatedness, and, as such, both processes need to be addressed during the course of treatment.[2]

The abilities of patients to engage in the process of dynamic therapy have been investigated using the Capacity for Dynamic Process Scale (CDPS; Thackrey, Butler, & Strupp, 1993), which is a clinician-rated scale that combines measurement of patient characteristics across several domains. The CDPS assesses several basic patient skills:

1. The capacity to be introspective
2. The capacity to integrate affect
3. Verbal fluency
4. Insightfulness
5. The ability to perceive affective aspects of problems
6. The capacity to differentiate affect
7. The capacity to differentiate interpersonal events
8. Therapeutic collaboration

Baumann et al. (2001) found the CDPS to effectively discriminate patients' persistence in treatment. In particular, patients with higher CDPS scores were more likely to remain in psychodynamic treatment and to continue their involvement in the psychotherapy process.

Summary

There is significant empirical support for the efficacy for psychoanalytic and psychodynamic therapy. There also is empirical support for the efficacy of psychoanalysis, although few studies have employed the methodological rigor that is often required of psychotherapy research. It is interesting that psychoanalysis, psychoanalytic therapy, and psychodynamic therapy are often dismissed in academic psychology (Bornstein, 1988, 2005; Westen, 1998), particularly when the academic community beatifies training in empirically supported treatment.[3] Criticisms of empirically supported treatments have been clearly articulated (e.g., Westen et al., 2004), yet there is not much openness in many graduate and postdoctoral training programs to training students in psychoanalytic and psychodynamic theory and therapy. The next two chapters discuss research on the mechanisms of therapeutic action and cognitive neuroscience and how these "nonpsychodynamic" domains of research actually provide significant support for psychoanalytic and psychodynamic ideas. It is time for the fantasies and resistance to these ideas to be brought more to conscious understanding and professional public awareness so that any philosophy of training that believes in the value of science informing practice becomes once again open to discovering truth, wherever it leads. In short, it is time that the empirical status of psychoanalytic and psychodynamic therapy becomes reflected accurately and frequently in the training and development of mental health professionals.

Notes

1. Effect size is a statistical representation of the power of one's finding, with larger numbers representing larger effect sizes. Cohen (1988) noted that effect sizes of .20, .50, and .80 are of small, medium, and large magnitude, respectively.
2. More recently, Blatt, Auerbach, Zuroff, and Shahar (2006) advocated the use of insight-oriented, psychoanalytic therapy for introjective patients but not for anaclitic patients.
3. These ideas would be well heeded by those who advocate the use of ESTs as they currently exist (e.g., Anthony, Ledley, & Heimberg, 2005; Barlow, Levitt, & Bufka, 1999; Herbert, 2003; Nelson-Gray, 2003).

7

Theories and Empirical Studies of Therapeutic Action

In the previous chapter, I provided a selected review on the research evidence that supported the efficacy of psychoanalytic and psychodynamic psychotherapy. I noted that there are two questions of interest for psychotherapy patients, clinicians, and researchers: (1) Does psychotherapy work? And if so, (2) how does it work? The focus of this chapter is on the latter question of how psychoanalytic and psychodynamic psychotherapy works. The theoretical literature has much to say about this, and increasing research on the psychotherapy process is finding that, across theoretical orientations, psychoanalytic and psychodynamic ideas and interventions are quite helpful.

How and Why Treatment Works from a Psychoanalytic/Psychodynamic Perspective

For many years, an immutable principle of psychoanalytic technique was the primacy of *interpretation* as part of the curative process (Strachey, 1934). In this process, analysts serve as an "auxiliary superego," which provides permission for patients to speak about unconscious content and material that might not otherwise be discussed. In the course of speaking, the patient begins to be aware of feelings or desires that can be observed by the analyst, with particular attention to transference reactions. The patient becomes consciously aware of his transference feelings and that they seem peculiar, given the manner by which the analyst has treated the patient. At this point, the analyst makes an interpretation about why these feelings are there and from where they may have originated. This provides the patient with the opportunity to better understand

and master them. For instance, a patient who comes to treatment for increasing feelings of anger toward his wife may find that, although he can speak openly about his wife's inadequacies, he cannot speak a negative word about his mother. When the therapist observes this to the patient, he becomes highly resentful toward her for suggesting such a terrible thing and eventually gets angry at such a "terrible idea." The therapist then interprets that that patient's anger toward her may reflect some pent-up feelings he has had for years toward his mother, who discouraged the expression of any negative feelings toward her or any loved ones. In traditional approaches, this interpretation could then be used to foster insight into the reasons why the patient experiences such conflict in expressing his angry feelings toward his wife.

Yet many have come to be critical of the traditional understanding of interpretation. Binder, Strupp, and Rock (1992, p. 610) wrote, "There are no clearly articulated, published guidelines for when and how to provide an interpretation." Spence (1992, p. 564) noted how Fenichel (1941) and Schafer (1976), who described with greater richness what was meant by interpretation, failed to provide "convincing clinical confirmation of its validity." In fact, Spence boldly suggested that few models exist in the published literature that demonstrate the therapeutic value and potency of interpretation. Even more disturbing, Spence cited examples of how analysts each tend to provide unique interpretations of the same material taken from one patient. This leads to many questions about whether interpretations can be "accurate" and how such interpreted material actually leads to a therapeutic effect in patients. For instance, it would not be at all surprising to find that ego-analytic therapists make interpretations centering on patients' conflicts and defenses, whereas object-relations therapists make interpretations centering on patients' representations of themselves or others.

Spence (1992) offered some ideas as to why the mechanism of interpretation has been hard to identify and understand. First, he noted that interpretations need to be understood in the context of patients' psychological developmental level. Patients are all too often assumed to have an adult-functioning ego that can hear and understand issues that are being reenacted in treatment from a much younger period of development, often times preverbal. This means that an interpretation that may indeed explain the reason for patients' problems cannot be heard by patients who are not psychologically ready to hear it. For instance, the man previously described, who was angry at his wife, may not recognize how his conflicted feelings toward his wife may be strongly related to his feelings toward his mother as reflected in the transference. Second, Spence highlighted the fact that patients must have a good working alliance with the therapist and be oriented to hearing the interpretation that is provided. Even when interpretations may not be accurate or may miss important content, Spence noted that "the voice of the analyst takes on added significance that goes far beyond the utterances themselves, and endows whatever is expressed with a persuasive power that is something more than its semantic content alone" (p. 569). I saw this happen not too long ago with a relative who sought out analytic treatment. Although he found his therapist to be quite helpful, he found that her comments were hard to take because he had not yet developed the positive alliance and trust that made such interventions really powerful. Regretfully, he ended treatment with her (though he was able to find a psychodynamic therapist with whom he felt more comfortable).

Cooper (1989) also evaluated theories of therapeutic effectiveness, with particular attention devoted to the nature of interpretation. In describing how traditional analytic treatment works, he provided part of a hypothetical "catechism" of how analysis—and analytic therapy for that matter—works. The process sets out to make "the unconscious conscious. How is that done? By interpreting defense and resistance in the context of the transference. What is it that changes? The rational demands of the ego expands [sic] its domain at the expense of the irrational id. There is thus a structural and dynamic change; the ego is strengthened, and it has a greater repertoire of more flexible defenses available to it for its necessary protective purposes" (p. 9).

Such ideas about interpretation had been prominent in American psychoanalysis for many years, but Cooper (1989) drew attention to the increasing influence of object relations theories in explaining therapeutic action. He noted that as early as 1960, Loewald (1960) observed that the process of change is not based on the interpretive skills of analysts or therapists but on the fact that patients' relationship with the analyst becomes a new type of object relationship. Here, patients establish a relationship with the therapist that is not as traumatic as the childhood environment in which it occurred. This new relationship allows a "corrective emotional experience" (p. 13, in reference to Alexander, 1956) to occur. Specifically, as a new relationship is created with the therapist, older representations may "shatter," which "allows the flowering of previously thwarted positive emotional and relational capacities" (ibid.). Thus, Cooper (1989) observed a meaningful theoretical change from the sanctity of interpretation to that of elements rooted in the therapeutic dyad. Similar to Michels (1986), Cooper suggested that therapeutic action is composed of insight (which is inherently linked with interpretation), the intensity of the emotional experience (which occurs with new learning in the context of powerful affect), and the new relationship with the therapist.

This trend toward the influence of the therapy relationship has been observed elsewhere, and it is certainly the case that interpretation, though a fundamental component of psychoanalytic and psychodynamic treatment, is not as powerful as a mechanism as it had been originally understood to be (e.g., Frederickson, 1999; Gabbard, 2000, 2004; McWilliams, 2004; Weiner, 1998). Many theorists and clinicians now accept that the acquisition of new knowledge (insight via interpretation), along with the experience of the therapy relationship, are what accounts for the success of many treatments. Pulver (1992, p. 204) described these two domains as being fundamentally related: "An understanding relationship cannot be maintained without insight into the dynamics of the relationship itself." Stern and colleagues (1998) specifically described this relational element as "implicit relational knowing." They considered this as a type of procedural memory based on knowledge of how relationships work. Implicit relational knowing integrates affect, cognition, and behavioral interactions in the interpersonal domain and is acquired early in life. Transference, therefore, is a phenomenon rooted in this memory system, and interpretation "rearranges the patient's conscious declarative knowledge" (p. 906) of relationships. Stern and colleagues went on to articulate in great detail elements of the relationship and how particular moments in the course of interaction provide important pathways toward meaningful change in patients' way of experiencing relationships. Stated somewhat differently, effective psychotherapy may be understood, in part, as helping persons develop their memory systems of meaningful interpersonal relationships that allow them to become happier and more adapted.

In more contemporary times, therapeutic action is seen as being multiply determined. Gabbard and Westen (2003) described three broad categories of interventions that are associated with therapeutic action: (1) those that foster insight; (2) those that make use of aspects of the therapeutic relationship; and (3) those that use secondary strategies, such as direct confrontation of dysfunctional beliefs, working with patients' problem-solving skills, and exposure. As previously noted, insight occurs in the context of two therapeutic techniques: free association and interpretation. By its very nature, free association allows patients to give voice to ideas and thoughts when they would normally would not. In this sense, patients can "discover" mental content that would otherwise not be given much, if any, conscious awareness. Consequently, therapists, guided by theory, can offer interpretive hypotheses or ideas about what the newly discovered material may mean.

There are many ways the therapy relationship serves as a vehicle of therapeutic action according to Gabbard and Westen (2003). First, it allows for the experience of a relationship that can correct or repair damage done from past, intimate relationships with meaningful others (e.g., parents). A kind and caring parental figure, for instance, can help undo the damage or a destructive and overly critical father or mother. Second, patients learn how to internalize and comfort themselves by hearing and experiencing such things from the therapist. Third, patients can internalize a more favorable, accepting, and curious attitude toward their affective experience that is demonstrated by their therapist. For instance, the man described earlier who found it horrifying to speak negative thoughts about his mother may be able to examine such ideas and thoughts with curiosity and with less danger than he previously though such ideas carried. Fourth, and related to that previously mentioned, patients can internalize the ability to self-reflect, or to enhance their reflective functioning capacities. Finally, therapeutic action occurs by way of the identification and interpretation of the transference–countertransference dynamics. In all of these processes, implicit, procedural memory networks that have been maladaptive become the focus of attention such that patients can learn a more adaptive, healthy way of experiencing their life.

A final, but very interesting, aspect of Gabbard and Westen's (2003) discussion of therapeutic action is in their overview of secondary strategies. These are activities not commonly associated with psychoanalytic and psychodynamic treatment yet that nevertheless are believed to be therapeutic. Two ways this occurs are through implicit and explicit confrontation of particular content. For instance, when therapists say, "That's an interesting thought," there is an implicit message that patients should direct their attention to that thought. In a more direct way, therapists may ask patients to engage in more direction exploration of their inner world. A patient who believes that most people do not have anxiety when it comes to asking out a person on a date may hear her therapist say, "I'm not sure I see it that way—everybody has anxiety in these situations." Here, the patient is told head-on that she is not unique in this regard. Such a comment can provide an avenue by which the patient and therapist can look at why the patient's anxiety seems so different from others. Another secondary strategy is to examine directly a patient's manner by which he problem solves. Such a strategy involves a current situation in which the patient seeks to address a problem area. Here, the therapist and patient can look at the way a patient's defenses are operating, can address self and object representations that may be distorted in the situation, and then can work together on how to better address the problem. Such a strategy could be used with the patient described earlier, when he finds himself angry with his wife when discussing a financial matter. He and the therapist could look at ways he distorted some of his perceptions toward his wife in that situation and could consider ways to interact with her that are less conflicted and more based on rational ways of thinking about the situation.

Another secondary strategy is to use the technique of exposure. This technique was developed from behavioral interventions for many anxiety disorders, yet its idea is very much part of psychoanalytic history: It is only when patients come in direct psychological contact with the feared object or situation that they can experience in more adaptive ways the feared stimulus and can use more rational and adaptive means by which to experience it. What makes exposure different from a psychoanalytic and psychodynamic orientation is that self and object representations may be examined, as can common patterns of defense and the developmental origins of such fears. Unlike behavior therapy, which focuses mostly on how to perform the technique of exposure to get the patient to respond a particular way, psychoanalytic and psychodynamic approaches take much interest in the inner experience and development of the anxiety, which ultimately increases the chances of better mastery and recovery from the disabling anxiety symptoms.

Another secondary strategy described by Gabbard and Westen (2003) includes the use of therapist self-disclosure. Patients' ability to identify with their therapist is fostered by self-disclosure and subsequently the ability to internalize their experience as part of the human experience, not to mention their ability to master their world by drawing on the representation of the therapist who had successfully managed such conflicted feelings. As an example of this process, I will share an experience from my own analytic treatment. During one session, I was speaking about my frustration and feelings of inferiority and inadequacy after a manuscript I had submitted for publication was not accepted. My therapist indicated that he, too, was resubmitting a manuscript that he thought was one of the best articles he had written. His self-disclosure then brought to my conscious awareness comments made in the past by two of my colleagues, both of whom had been very successful in their scholarship. One had told me the very same thing about having trouble publishing one of his very best pieces of scholarship. The other told me how frustrated he had become with certain kinds of journals, which seemed disinterested in his program of research. Consequently, he found other outlets for his work, which have allowed his work to become very widely cited and respected. The net effect of my analyst's self-disclosure was an increase in my ability to internalize my past successes and to realize that I was just as capable as others whom earlier I had thought were more competent than I was.

A final set of secondary strategies described by Gabbard and Westen (2003) is therapists' use of affirmation and validation, along with other facilitative strategies. Although this is not typically thought of as a technique in insight-oriented psychotherapy, affirmation and validation are quite useful in helping patients better develop their sense of self-awareness and self-acceptance. Facilitative strategies can include psychoeducation or the use of humor to help patients to better understand their inner world. For instance, patients new to therapy may need some direction about how psychotherapy works and what to expect from their therapist.

Therapeutic Action in and outside of Psychoanalytic and Psychodynamic Theory

As can be seen from the previous material, psychoanalytic and psychodynamic treatment can incorporate multiple types of interventions to reach their therapeutic aims and goals. It is not surprising, therefore, to see that some are beginning to integrate psychoanalytic and psychodynamic theory and therapeutic approaches with ideas and techniques from other theories in an effort to achieve maximal therapeutic effectiveness. This has occurred primarily in the union of cognitive behavioral theory with psychoanalytic and psychodynamic theory. In fact, the idea that psychoanalysis could be merged with behavioral theory is not new to psychology. Dollard and Miller (1950) were some of the first to note that, by repressing or blocking one's awareness of anxiety, individuals were likely to use the same processes again. This is a basic principle of learning—that individuals are likely to repeat a "behavior" if it is associated with favorable outcomes (i.e., reinforcement). In this case, the behavior in question is the mental act. Clark Hull (1951), too, tried to create a mathematical formula of how drives interacted with features of a situation to produce certain behaviors. In fact, there multiple articles and books now address how analytic theory and therapy can be integrated with cognitive-behavioral theory and therapy (e.g., Bornstein, 2005; Bucci, 1997; Epstein, 1994; Horowitz, 1987; Kohlenberg & Tsai, 1991; Messer, 1986; Shevrin, Bond, Brakel, Hertel, & Williams, 1996; Singer & Singer, 1992; Wachtel, 1977, 1987; Westen, 2000).

A well-articulated discussion about integrating psychodynamic and cognitive-behavioral therapies was provided by Westen (2000). Although a detailed review of this paper is outside of the scope of this chapter, I highlight a few of the critical points he made about this issue. First, he suggested that although psychodynamic theory is comprehensive and integrative in its description of how mental processes lead to behavior, it all too often does not operationalize its terms in an easy-to-understand, mechanism-specific way. By way of contrast, he noted that cognitive-behavioral approaches focus on specific processes and provide directed instructions on how to intervene. This approach, however, does not provide the richness and complexity of the interactive processes that account more completely for the processes observed in clinical practice. Second, he noted that psychodynamic theory assumes that behavior will change by focusing on the internal processes behind them; in contrast, cognitive-behavioral theory focuses on skills and behaviors needed to obtain real change with less attention to the complexity of the internal cognitive processes. Both approaches, he suggested, are important, and depending on the needs of the patient, greater attention may be needed to internal versus external processes (or vice versa). Third, psychodynamic approaches attend much more to unconscious processes and mechanisms, whereas cognitive-behavioral approaches take greater interest in what is conscious and immediate in awareness. Both unconscious and conscious mechanisms account for psychological conflict, distress, and disrupted behavior. Thus, targeting both processes is important and likely necessary for patients to achieve the results they desire. Because of these basic differences, Westen suggested that psychodynamic and cognitive-behavioral therapy can and should be integrated to maximize therapeutic effectiveness.

It should not be assumed that Westen's (2000) ideas are widely agreed on. For instance, the imposition of more cognitive-behavioral techniques has much potential to affect the transference. Patients' experience of therapists' directiveness may activate transference phenomena that complicate treatment; they may invoke different kinds of representations of therapists that heretofore had not been seen, experienced, or understood. For instance, a therapist who has a very Socratic, didactic orientation toward cognitive-behavioral psychoeducation could invoke in patients a representation of the therapist as a teacher and educator. This could elicit all kinds of feelings and attitudes, both positive and negative. These experiences are part of the transference, although they may be part of understanding the real person of the therapist if, for instance, the therapist has poor tolerance of a patient's failure to quickly acquire the material that is being taught or the therapist has poorly developed skills in educating or explaining important concepts to a patient. Another potential problem is that a failure to understand the complexity and contributing variables toward a patient's conflicts and problems may lead to the implementation of a cognitive-behavioral technique that could not work or may produce contradictory results. By contrast, if the treatment is "too successful," patients may erroneously believe that they have mastered their difficulties and decide they have benefited all they can from treatment, when the therapist may have good reason to believe otherwise.

This being said, it is nonetheless true that different types of psychotherapy (e.g., cognitive-behavioral, brief) have been reported to have therapeutic efficacy. Moreover, it is true that many psychoanalytic and psychodynamic therapists and researchers believe that other theories of treatment can be integrated with psychodynamic therapy so that maximal therapeutic effectiveness can be obtained. Thus, two additional questions arise that are important to understand about therapeutic action: (1) Are there *common mechanisms* of therapeutic action in many forms of treatment that account for therapeutic success? And if so, (2) are these mechanisms *specific to* psychoanalytic and psychodynamic interventions? To address these questions, I now turn attention to the psychotherapy research literature and what it has to tell us about these issues.

Empirical Studies of Therapeutic Action

There have been multiple studies on psychotherapy outcomes, with attention devoted to what accounts for the favorable outcome across theoretical models and various techniques. In a review of several meta-analyses of this issue, Lambert and Barley (2002) devised an empirical summary of what the literature says about psychotherapy outcome: 40% of the improvement is accounted for by *extratherapeutic change*; 30% is accounted for by *common factors*; 15% is accounted for by *techniques*; and 15% is accounted for by *expectancy factors*. Extratherapeutic change is a general term that describes patients' efforts to seek help and reassurance from others, either while in treatment or waiting for treatment. This includes the support of family, friends, clergy, and support groups. This also accounts for the finding that people who wait for treatment report getting better on their own without treatment (which is highly variable by person, based on many individual factors).

A substantial component of treatment success is related to common factors, which specifically relates to certain aspects of therapists and their therapeutic relationship. These include therapists' interpersonal style, attributes, and qualities (e.g., empathy, warmth, showing positive regard, kindness, compassion), and the therapist–client relationship. This finding is robust across decades of psychotherapy research (more than 60 years) and multiple meta-analyses of this literature and is independent of theoretical model. It is clear that some therapists are better than others and that their skills are strongly linked to outcome. Although the implementation of specific therapy techniques is believed to account for some degree of improvement (15% in their analysis), Lambert and Barley (2002, p. 19) concluded, "Conventional reviewing procedures of the comparative studies of different psychotherapies have not consistently demonstrated the preeminence of any particular school of therapy in treating clients across the broad categories of anxiety, depression, and interpersonal problems." They added that what appears to be consistent in the literature is that individuals who seek some form of psychotherapy tend to be about 80% better than their counterparts who do not seek treatment. Their conclusion, which is consistent with recent others (e.g., Beutler & Harwood, 2002; Castonguay & Beutler, 2006; Wampold, 2001), is that therapists need to be highly attuned to their own behavior and attitude toward their patients and focused on the quality of the therapeutic alliance. As for students who are beginning to learn how to do psychotherapy, Lambert and Barley wrote, "Training in relationship skills is crucial for the beginning therapist" (p. 27). More so, they encouraged experienced professionals to keep very focused on their ability to foster and to maintain a favorable therapeutic relationship.

As a means by which to assess common factors that are responsible for therapeutic effectiveness, Goldfried, Newman, and Hayes (1989) developed the Coding System of Therapeutic Focus (CSTF). This is a rating system designed for coders to evaluate the types of interventions performed in psychotherapy sessions. Five "axes" are assessed:

1. Components of the client's functioning (e.g., emotions and thoughts)
2. Connections that are made between intrapersonal or interpersonal themes
3. General types of interventions used (e.g., support)
4. The persons who are the focus of the intervention
5. The time frame of the focus

Goldfried, Castonguay, Hayes, Drozde, and Shapiro (1997) used the CSTF system to compare manually driven cognitive-behavioral and interpersonal-psychodynamic treatments for depression. They found that the interpersonal-psychodynamic treatment consisted more of therapists' exploration of clients' problematic interpersonal relationships, their misperceptions of others, and how these patterns were part of their life. Attention also was directed toward the historical origins of these problems and how the problems may manifest themselves in the interaction with the therapist. By way of contrast, cognitive-behavioral therapists focused more on the future and what clients might do to function more effectively.

Because this study was done via treatment manuals, Goldfried, Raue, and Castonguay (1998) were interested in the naturalistic practice of cognitive-behavioral and psychodynamic-interpersonal psychotherapies. Past research had suggested that master psychodynamic-interpersonal therapists believed that the most important parts of a session consisted of greater levels of emotion; in contrast, cognitive-behavioral therapists believed the most important portion of a session was associated with a decrease in patients' emotional experiencing. Given these past issues, Goldfried et al. recruited 22 master cognitive-behavioral and 14 master psychodynamic-interpersonal therapists to participate in a study in which their work with a patient would be evaluated with the CSTF. They were asked to identify therapeutically significant portions of their session to evaluate what the therapists actually were doing at that time. Therapists of both orientations were found to place more of a focus on patients' self-observations, self-evaluations, expectations, and general thoughts, emotions, and behaviors during the significant portions of the session. Cognitive-behavioral therapists were more likely to compare or contrast the patient's functioning with others, to encourage between-session activities, to focus more on other people, and to focus attention on the patient's future. Psychodynamic-interpersonal therapists were more likely to highlight a patient's emotional reactions, to make a reference to their experience, and to highlight instances of more general themes in the patient's life. Many similarities were found between the two orientations during clinically significant portions of the session. These included a greater focus on the patients' ability to observe themselves in an objective way, their evaluation of their self-worth and expectations, their thoughts in general, their emotions, and aspects of their generalized aspects of their functioning. In general, Goldfried et al. concluded that master therapists are generally more similar than different, blending interventions that usually are associated with one specific orientation.

Another set of interesting studies on the psychotherapy process was produced by the Berkeley Psychotherapy Research Group, headed by Enrico Jones. Jones (1985, 2000) developed an interesting assessment tool to assess intervention strategies used by therapists in their sessions. This measure is the Psychotherapy Process Q-Set, which contains 100 items that describe therapist, patient, and therapist–patient activities that occur in the psychotherapy hour. Raters listen to an entire psychotherapy session and then place all 100 items into one of nine categories. The categories are ranked from "most characteristic" to "least characteristic," and a fixed number of items go into each category. This structure forces the ratings into a normal distribution and requires the rater to think carefully and critically about each item prior to placing it into a category. Many studies have supported the validity of the measure to assess change processes (Jones, Hall, & Parke, 1991).

Jones and Pulos (1993) were interested in the processes actually utilized in session by cognitive-behavioral and psychodynamic therapists. Since many studies have failed to find differences across types of psychotherapies, Jones and Pulos were interested in whether actual differences in technique and process existed. Using the archival transcripts of 32 patients in either brief psychodynamic or cognitive-behavioral treatment, they obtained Q-set ratings assigned by expert raters. Although therapeutic outcome was comparable across groups, there were differences in the therapy processes. Psychodynamic treatment was most characterized by the following:

- An emphasis on patients' current or recent life situation
- Interpersonal relationships
- Therapists identifying a recurring theme in patients' experience
- Therapists clarifying or rephrasing patients' communication
- Patients initiating important content for discussion
- A focus on patients' self-image and how feelings and perceptions are linked to the past
- Therapists emphasizing patients' feelings for them to experience them more deeply
- Patients feeling depressed
- Therapists conveying a sense of acceptance

Cognitive-behavioral treatment was most characterized by the following:

- Therapists exerting control over the interaction
- Therapists behaving like a teacher
- A focus on cognitive themes
- An emphasis on patients' current or recent life situation
- A discussion of what patients could do outside of the session
- A focus on patients' self-image
- Therapists explaining a rationale for the technique, adopting a supportive stance, and clarifying or rephrasing a patient's communication

Jones and Pulos (1993) also found 57 significant differences on other item ratings, suggesting that there are many differences between cognitive-behavioral and psychodynamic treatment. A factor analysis of the 100 items yielded four broad factors: psychodynamic technique, cognitive-behavioral technique, patient resistance, and patient negative affect. Factor scores were then correlated with many of the outcome measures, with very many interesting results. The psychodynamic technique factor was favorably correlated with four of the five positive outcomes in the cognitive-behavioral group and one of the four outcome measures in the psychodynamic group. The cognitive-behavioral factor was only correlated with one favorable outcome in the psychodynamic group and not any in the cognitive-behavioral group. The patient resistance factor was associated with a negative outcome in all five outcome measures in the cognitive-behavioral group and in two of the four outcome measures in the psychodynamic therapy group. Jones and Pulos concluded that many of the psychodynamic suppositions about psychotherapy process underlie favorable outcomes and that a sizeable portion of the favorable outcome in cognitive-behavioral therapy was associated with patients' ability to attend to their affect and to develop insight into their problems, which Jones and Pulos characterized as a metacognitive process.

In another study, Ablon and Jones (1998) were interested in how well prototypes of psychodynamic and cognitive-behavioral psychotherapy sessions were related to what clinicians actually did. They had 11 psychodynamic and 10 cognitive-behavioral clinicians use the Psychotherapy Process Q-Set (Jones, 1985, 2000) to create ideal prototypes of what sessions should look like. The top 10 items that characterized psychodynamic therapy were as follows: Discussion of the patient's dreams or fantasies, therapist neutrality and attention toward the patient's use of defenses, the therapist making connections between the therapeutic relationship and other relationships, the therapist being empathically attuned and interpreting warded off wishes, feelings, or ideas, and the therapist conveying a sense of acceptance along with the patient achieving a new level of insight. Cognitive-behavioral prototypes consisted of the following top 10 items: discussions of what the patient is to do outside of the session; a focus on cognitive themes and the patient's treatment goals; the therapist encouraging the patient to try out new ways of behaving with others and actively exerting control over the therapist-patient interactions; the therapist adopting a supportive stance, the dialogue being specifically focused; the therapist asking for more information or elaboration; and the patient's current or recent life situation being examined.

Once the prototypes were developed, they were then compared with 68 brief psychodynamic and 32 cognitive-behavioral archival psychotherapy sessions in which outcome measures of psychiatric symptoms were obtained. In the study, 30 of the psychodynamic patients were treated for a wide range of psychiatric symptoms, whereas the other 38 were treated at a different clinic with a manualized version of brief therapy for posttraumatic stress disorder (PTSD). The cognitive-behavioral therapy group was treated for unipolar depression. The psychodynamic prototype was favorably associated with three of the six outcome measures in one of the psychodynamic groups and five of the six outcome measures in the cognitive-behavioral group. The cognitive-behavioral prototype was favorably associated with one rating of improvement in the one of the psychodynamic groups and one outcome measure in the cognitive-behavioral. There were no correlations between outcome and intervention (psychodynamic or cognitive-behavioral) in the PTSD group. These results suggested that psychodynamic clinicians tended to incorporate more cognitive-behavioral techniques (and not resemble the prototype created by expert judges), whereas cognitive-behavioral clinicians tended to intervene in ways similar to what expert judges described; however, favorable outcome was much more strongly associated with psychodynamic interventions than cognitive-behavioral interventions. Ablon and Jones (1998) pointed out that, in another study with this same sample, cognitive-behavioral interventions that focus on the impact of the distorted cognitions on patients were actually negatively associated with a favorable outcome (Castonguay, Goldfried, Wiser, Raue, & Hayes, 1996). This appeared to be associated with problems in the therapeutic alliance, and by adhering strictly to the manual's emphasis on looking at the negative impact of the cognitions, the relationship suffered, which ultimately produced a negative outcome. As for the absence of results in the PTSD group, Ablon and Jones noted that the PTSD group was known to have benefited by treatment by scores on the outcome measures. Consequently, the lack of findings may reflect a lack of sensitivity to detecting meaningful process variables in the Psychotherapy Process Q-Set. In sum, Ablon and Jones concluded that clinicians do not tend to adhere to prototypes in their work with patients.[1]

Because of the evolving interest in mechanisms of therapeutic action in psychoanalysis and related therapies, Ablon and Jones

(2005) decided to look at process variables in these types of treatments to see if they could provide empirical support for hypotheses about therapeutic mechanisms. They obtained an experienced, expert panel of psychoanalysts and asked them to develop a prototype of an ideal psychoanalytic therapy hour, which appeared very similar to the analytic prototype in Ablon and Jones (1998). This prototype was then compared with judges' ratings of psychotherapy processes in three different treatments: psychoanalysis, long-term psychoanalytic psychotherapy, and brief psychodynamic therapy. The judges' ratings correlated with the prototype as one might expect: The highest correlation was between psychoanalysis and the prototype ($r = .58$); the next highest was between psychoanalytic therapy and the prototype ($r = .45$); and the lowest correlation was between brief psychodynamic therapy and the prototype ($r = .37$).

Ablon and Jones (2005) also reported two case studies of patients who had undergone psychoanalysis and for whom multiple years of treatment data were available. Over seventy sessions were rated, and a prototype for each analysis was created. Not only did the ratings differ for each analysis, but the factor structure of the ratings varied, too. For the first patient, three broad factors emerged that consisted of patient self-exploration/analyst acceptance, analyst's activity, and a series of items related to a unique set of transactions of transference–countertransference between the patient and analyst over the patient's sexual thoughts and feelings. The second patient's ratings also clustered into three factors: positive transference/countertransference, analyst's authoritative responses, and eroticized transference. Ablon and Jones noted that these findings have important implications about the nature of what is therapeutically effective. Specifically, it is the repetitive, interactional nature of patient and therapist that creates certain kinds of therapy processes, and these processes are unique to each patient–therapist dyad. Ablon and Jones believed that their findings bridge the gap between insight and interpersonal relationship mechanisms of therapeutic action. Insight is derived from a relationship, and relationship dynamics are necessary for insight to be offered by the analyst. Such ideas cut across various models of therapeutic action in psychoanalytic theory and provide a broader context by which the process may be understood.

In a more recent paper, Ablon, Levy, and Katzenstein (2006) evaluated the therapeutic activities of 17 psychodynamic clinicians who were treating patients with panic disorder. Though their aims were many, a major focus of the study was to identify which prototypical treatment processes best characterize psychodynamic treatment and which prototypical processes are most predictive of positive outcome. On all outcome measures, patients fared much better at the end of treatment than at the beginning of treatment. Sessions were scored on the Psychotherapy Process Q-Set during the 12th session, and ratings were compared with psychodynamic, cognitive-behavioral, and interpersonal psychotherapy prototypes derived from past studies (Ablon & Jones, 1998, 2002). Results indicated that therapy processes conformed most with cognitive-behavioral prototypes (r = .50), followed by psychodynamic (r = .35) and interpersonal prototypes (r = .32). In terms of content, effective treatment was associated with helping patients recognize, experience, and express negative emotions, sexual desires, and fears about their dependency and separation in the context of a caring, empathic therapy relationship. A favorable outcome was associated with two of three outcome measures when evaluating sessions for their prototypically interpersonal interventions and with one outcome measure when evaluating sessions for their prototypically psychodynamic interventions. The cognitive-behavioral therapy prototype was not associated with any of the three outcome measures. Taken as a whole, these findings suggest that psychodynamic clinicians tend to employ a multitude of interventions and that those specific to interpersonal and psychodynamic treatment are more associated with favorable outcomes. As Ablon et al. suggest, to better understand what kind of interventions are actually being employed in treatment, the "resolving power of the (psychotherapy) microscope must be turned higher" (p. 228).

Summary

This chapter discussed psychoanalytic and psychodynamic theories about the mechanisms of therapeutic action and corresponding research that has addressed this issue. It is clear that the psychotherapy relationship is highly important in producing a good outcome but that what psychodynamic clinicians actually do in treatment may not always appear to be psychodynamic. Results from Ablon and Jones (2005) demonstrate that prototypes of psychoanalytic treatment are clearly most associated with psychoanalysis. But in today's world of managed care, empirically supported treatments

(ESTs), brief treatments, and limited finances and available time, psychoanalytic and psychodynamic clinicians have effectively learned how to integrate ideas from various schools of therapy to work within these constraints. As Westen et al (2004) pointed out, brief, manualized ESTs have many limitations, and clinicians hoping to build their work on this kind of approach are setting themselves up for significant challenges. By looking more closely at the psychotherapy processes, Ablon, Jones, and colleagues (1993, 1998, 2005, 2006) demonstrated that there is clear empirical support for the effectiveness of psychoanalytic and psychodynamic interventions, more so than those that are more characteristically cognitive-behavioral. These interventions are characterized by elements of the therapeutic alliance, by therapists' attitude toward their patients, and by directing attention to psychoanalytically important components of mental functioning (e.g., fantasies, wishes, defenses, and relationship history). As psychoanalytic and psychodynamic therapy moves into the 21st century, it is clear that there is much to be retained from the theories of therapeutic action as well as things to be better understood and refined. Perhaps the current status of psychoanalytic and psychodynamic therapy research is best captured by a phrase from an old television commercial: "It's not your father's Oldsmobile anymore."

Note

1. Similar findings on clinicians' use of blended interventions have been found in studies with interpersonal psychotherapy and cognitive-behavioral therapy (Ablon & Jones, 1999, 2002).

8

Cognitive Neuroscience

Clinical psychology and psychiatry abandoned psychoanalytic and psychodynamic ideas some time ago as the major paradigm by which cases are conceptualized and treated. This occurred as biological psychiatry and pharmacotherapy advances suggested that a biologically informed treatment had much potential to alleviate psychiatric symptoms and disorders. This is regrettable in that Sigmund Freud himself viewed psychoanalysis as a scientific endeavor that someday would account for mental processes via an understanding of the neurological mechanisms and underpinnings of conscious and unconscious processes, dreams, wishes, instinctual impulses, and the like (Freud, 1895/1953, 1900/1953, 1940/1964). Included in Freud's work in this domain are drawings and neural maps to account for repression and the separation of the conscious and unconscious mind. The interested reader is directed toward Solms (2002) for a more detailed history of Freud's neuroscience writings.

In what follows, I present a selected review of studies and papers on the cognitive and neuroscientific underpinnings of psychoanalytic theory. This work has flourished in recent times, including the development of the multidisciplinary International Neuro-Psychoanalysis Society and its related journal, *Neuro-Psychoanalysis*. As an exemplar of the growing influence of this field, Shevrin (2006, p. 493) wrote:

> This widespread interest in investigating unconscious processes is perhaps one of the most remarkable developments in psychology currently underway. It is tantamount to a paradigm shift away from the previous behaviorist view according to which mental processes as such, whether conscious or unconscious, had no scientific standing. The behaviorist position has almost completely been replaced with a cognitive science view that is fully concerned with mental processes and their unconscious as well as conscious character, at least as concerns perception and memory.

For psychoanalytic theory to thrive and reenter the mainstream of clinical psychology and psychiatry (see chapter 2 in this volume and Bornstein, 2001, 2005, 2006), it is of considerable importance to recognize how findings from cognitive neuroscience research converge and support many of Freud's basic ideas. Now more than 100 years old, psychoanalytic ideas can be tested and examined at a level not possible before. Many individuals have addressed this subject with great rigor and detail that space does not allow for here (Bucci, 1997; Horowitz, 1998; Shevrin, Bond, Brakel, Hertel, & Williams, 1996; Shevrin & Dickman, 1980; Westen, 1992, 1999; Westen & Gabbard, 2002a, 2002b). However, a listing of specific areas in which cognitive neuroscience and psychoanalysis should be integrated and inform each other was provided by Kandel (1999):

- The nature of unconscious mental processes
- The nature of psychological causality
- Psychological causality and psychopathology
- Early experience and predisposition to mental illness
- Levels of consciousness and the prefrontal cortex
- Sexual orientation
- Psychotherapy and structural changes in the brain
- Psychopharmacology as an adjunct to psychoanalysis

This chapter discusses how cognitive science and psychoanalytic theory are mutually influencing each other and are providing renewed vigor and support for psychoanalytic ideas as well as necessary empirical refinement. It is particularly in the interface of memory and mental processing of information and the concept of the unconscious where some of the most interesting integration is occurring.

Basic Concepts in Cognitive Science

Research in cognitive science has evolved rapidly. Early models of memory suggested that information was initially held in a sensory register, was placed into short-term memory, and then entered long-term memory under certain conditions of rehearsal and salience (Atkinson & Shiffrin, 1968). This model arose in parallel with the advent of the information processing age and computers. In this sense, the mind was seen as a computer that is able to take in and process information, to hold it in a buffer, and to recall it either more immediately or more distally from when the information was processed, known respectively as short-term and long-term memory. However, this model did not account for certain kinds of processes and phenomena, such as being influenced by information despite no awareness of sensory registration (described below).

In modern times, it is the consensus of most cognitive researchers that the mind has multiple information processing and memory systems (Roediger & Geraci, 2003; Roediger & McDermott, 1993; Schacter & Tulving, 1994; Squire, 1986, 1992). Information and experience is processed and stored throughout multiple neural networks, and much information is processed at the same time, unlike prior models that articulated more serially oriented processes. *Explicit* processes are readily accessible and are seen in *semantic*, or declarative, memory and in *episodic* memory. We know where we live; we can describe ourselves to others or recall the humorous jokes told by a friend at dinner last night. Patients report various symptoms, such as being so sad that they have not left their home for two days. They also recount, sometimes in great detail, episodes in which others discounted what they had to say or ignored them. This type of memory is believed to be related to functioning of the hippocampus and medial temporal lobes.

Implicit processes include those that occur without conscious knowledge. On example is *procedural* information, such as how to drive an automobile, or appearing "calm and polite" in situations in which one feels angry. This type of memory is believed to be related to functioning in the dorsolateral prefrontal cortex and basal ganglia, though much of this activity is centered in the right orbitofrontal cortex during the first three years of life (Kandel, 1999, as cited in Schore, 2000). Implicit processes also include the formation of associative networks of information, which are components of *associative* memory. For example, some theorists (e.g., Fonagy, 1999b; Levin, 1997; Shevrin, 2002) believe that object relations are stored in procedural memory and that they are reactivated in the relationship with the therapist (i.e., the transference) as well as throughout the course of treatment. Understanding and identifying the many ways these associative networks are formed are part of the therapeutic process that sets out to change maladaptive patterns of relating to others.

The distinction between explicit and implicit processes in psychodynamic assessment and treatment is quite important. Simply stated, what patients say and report about themselves reflects explicit, semantic, and episodic memory and information. Their overt symptoms and difficulties in living are related to the implicit processes that are occurring outside of awareness. The resulting behavioral and symptomatic manifestations are a compromise evolving from these multiple processes (Westen & Gabbard, 2002a). In psychological assessment, the explicit–implicit distinction in assessment methodology is well recognized for the utility that such measures offer toward the assessment of personality (Bornstein, 2002a, 2007; Ganellen, 1996; Huprich, 2006; McClelland, Koestener, & Weinberger, 1989; Meyer et al., 2001).[1] Other interesting studies on the association between implicit, performance-based measures (e.g., the Rorschach Inkblot Method and the Thematic Aperception Test) and resulting psychological symptoms and behaviors may be found in Huprich (2006) and Jenkins (2007).

One of the most influential developments in cognitive psychology is the *connectionist*, or parallel distributed processing, model of perception, memory, and thinking (Kunda & Thagard, 1996; Olds, 1994; Rumelhart, McClelland, & the PDP Research Group, 1986; Smith, 1998). Westen and Gabbard summarized the principles of this model as follows:

1. Processing occurs in parallel: That is, most processing occurs outside of awareness and at multiple levels of awareness, such as phonetically, semantically, or syntactically. Thus, as seen in many of the earlier examples in this book, word sounds, meanings, and sentence structures are processed simultaneously and a meaning or understanding is efficiently and automatically provided to processed material.
2. Representations are distributed: That is, particular representations are not located in a particular part of the brain. There is no one location, for instance, of the representation of "father" or "mother."
3. Knowledge lies in the connections among nodes in a network: The nodes influence each other and include excitatory or inhibitory mechanisms. Thus, when understanding complex psychological experiences that bring patients to therapy,

it is not surprising that their descriptions or accounts of their difficulties allow certain material to be discussed and other material to be suppressed. Also, as patients are allowed to discuss whatever they wish, it may be the case that seemingly unrelated ideas come to mind that are identified later as having much importance or meaning to the difficulties just having been discussed.

4. Nodes of stimulation provide a specific kind of information that is used collectively with other input in determining what to make of the information: For instance, seeing teeth and a mouth moving could be part of the perception of smiling, talking, or opening the mouth to eat or drink. To know what this perception represents requires the individual to recognize other stimuli that occur at the same time, such as the presence of food, or the activity of other facial features (e.g., eyebrow position or the "look" in someone's eyes).
5. Frequently used networks create attractor states; that is, they are more easily fired than others: Thus, when individuals have had a history of being unfairly criticized, they are more likely to interpret ambiguous information with a level of sensitivity and concern than other individuals who have not had the same experience. Similar processes occur, for instance, with those who are depressed, anxious, or suspicious.
6. Perception, memory, and cognition involve processes of parallel constraint satisfaction: That is, the brain simultaneously processes features of a stimulus and draws the best conclusion it can from the information that is provided, such that as more information is provided, there is more material from which to interpret and understand experience.

These principles of connectionist models of memory and information processing provide psychodynamic clinicians the empirical support for what they have observed for decades in their clinical work. Dynamic, parallel systems of processing generate a limited amount of conscious awareness. Readily activated nodes of representation that quickly become excited also evoke the inhibition of other nodes of representation and thereby provide a seen/known and unseen/unknown mind. Phenomena such as repression, resistance, transference, and insightfulness are easily understood when one considers the way the brain processes information and accesses it. These are discussed in the following section.

Unconscious Processes: Integrating Cognitive Neuroscience and Psychodynamic Theory

In many ways, evidence for the existence of mental processes that are outside of immediate conscious awareness is apparent in everyday life. Consider these examples:

1. An individual cannot remember the name of someone important, only to recall it hours or days later at a time and place when knowing the name is not needed.
2. Despite one's intentions to offer some control over the process, dreaming appears to occur at its own timing and pace.
3. On September 11, 2001, and the days following, many people watched countless hours of news reports about the terrorist attacks on the United States. Although deeply disturbed by the contents, many individuals could not stop watching such upsetting video footage, saying that it was as if something in them drew them to reports in spite of their conscious awareness of sadness, disbelief, and outrage.
4. Many patients seeking psychotherapy are unable to stop unwanted behaviors or interpersonal problems, despite conscious awareness of their harmfulness. These problems range from relatively simple (e.g., drinking too much alcohol) to relatively complex (e.g., placing oneself in situations in which one is often taken advantage of or obsessing about one's body image if certain kinds of food are consumed).

Other examples are evident, too, in simple exercises that can be easily performed. For instance, consider when three lines are drawn in the shape of a triangle and the ends of each line do not touch, leaving a small gap between them. Depending on the space between the lines, the image may be perceived as a triangle, a triangle with missing edges, three lines that are coming together like a triangle, or just three lines at different angles. When considering perceptual phenomena such as this (i.e., a demonstration of the gestalt principle of closure), it is evident that the mind does the following:

- Takes in sensory information
- Determines what the information is
- Assembles the information in such a way that a percept or concept is formed
- The percept or concept is "seen" and understood

All of this happens quickly, with no awareness of how the process occurs, yet meaning and understanding are formed.

Evidence for the existence of unconscious processes is widely known in cognitive psychology. In a seminal paper in the *American Psychologist*, Shevrin and Dickman (1980) demonstrated how conclusions from studies of selective attention, cortical evoked potentials, and subliminal perception provide support for the concept of an unconscious mind and posit that "no psychological model that seeks to explain how human beings know, learn, or behave can ignore the concept of unconscious psychological processes" (p. 432). They noted that the initial stage for processing all stimuli occurs outside of consciousness and that it affects what is known consciously. This early stage is different in how it operates from conscious cognition, and conscious cognition necessarily occurs after considerable preconscious processing. Years later, their conclusions and ideas appear to be no less true.

In the following section, I offer a brief, heterogeneous, selective review of some studies that support these ideas. These studies come from research on subliminal perception, perceptual illusions, and selective attention and dichotic listening, as well as clinical case studies, including evaluations of dream content. I also note how the classical Freudian view of the unconscious differs from those of cognitive psychology and offer ideas of how and why the two concepts should be integrated and mutually informative, particularly in terms of their relationship to the practice of psychodynamic psychotherapy.

Selected Empirical and Case Studies Demonstrating Unconscious Processes

In studies of subliminal perception, which began in 1950s, the processing of unperceivable stimuli and its effect on behavior has provided interesting results about the unconscious mind. Shevrin and Fisher (1967) subliminally presented participants with a picture of a pen and a knee just prior to falling asleep. When they awoke from rapid eye movement (REM; dream-stage) sleep, participants' associations to their dreams were of a pen or knee or included less rational kinds of associations (a finding that had been well demonstrated in past sleep studies). These included words that sound like pen or knee, such as *pennant*, *hen*, or *neither*. In contrast, those who awoke during nonREM sleep, which had been associated with few dreams or dreams that were more rational, had associations such as *penny* (*pen* + *knee*) or related words, such as *nickel* and *dime*. Shevrin (2006) noted that this study demonstrated that two levels of unconscious processing—irrational and rational—were occurring. He added that once inhibitions (e.g., defenses) weaken—in this case, being awakened from sleep—more rational processes are overtaken by irrational ones. Interestingly, the more irrational process observed in this study produced content similar to what was found in severe types of psychopathology: repetition and clanging. In a follow-up study with the same methodology, Shevrin (1973) presented individuals the same stimuli, this time while they were fully awake and more proximal to entering the sleep state. Again, they found a similar pattern of results in which the type of associations produced varied depending on when participants were awakened.

Some even more interesting results were described by Shevrin and colleagues (Shevrin, 1988; Shevrin, Bond, Brakel, Hertel, & Williams, 1996; Shevrin et al., 1992), who sought to demonstrate that unconscious and conscious processes operate differently. In these studies patients were selected who had either pathological phobic reactions or extended grief. Patients were assessed via interview, and four psychoanalysts listened to the interviews. By way of consensus, the psychoanalyst researchers derived a conceptualization of the core conflicts for each patient; then they selected patients' words that they believed captured patients' conscious experience of the symptoms and words that represented the unconscious conflict. These words along with unrelated words were then presented both subliminally and supraliminally to the patients, who were asked to classify them as belonging together. Using event-related potentials to detect patients' ability to classify or respond to words in similar ways, the researchers found that words representing unconscious conflicts were correctly classified *only when* presented subliminally and that the reverse was true for supraliminally presented words; they were correctly classified *only when* presented supraliminally. Shevrin (1996) concluded, "… When [these studies are] taken in combination, [they] show that unconscious psychological causes affect consciousness in a qualitatively different way … and that the unconscious conflict has an existence independent of the psychoanalyst's inferences from conscious manifestations, an *independence* supported by the brain correlates" (p. 591, italics in original). Shevrin also has published reviews of research showing an association between subliminal perception and dreaming (Shevrin, 1986) and subliminal perception and repression (Shevrin, 1990).

In a more recent meta-analysis of more than 100 studies of subliminal perception, Weinberger and Hardaway (1990) found that psychodynamic material presented subliminally had a noticeable and predictable effect on behavior, suggesting very clearly that unconscious processes affect overt behavior. For instance, studies by Silverman and colleagues (Silverman, 1983, 1986; Silverman, Bronstein, & Mendelsohn, 1976; Silverman, Kwawer, Wolitzky, & Coron, 1973; Silverman, Lachman, & Milich, 1982; Silverman, Ross, Adler, & Lustig, 1978) found that subliminally presented messages of Oedipal content (e.g., "Beating dad is okay") to male participants yielded more competitiveness in a subsequent dart-throwing game than non-Oedipal messages.

Bradley and colleagues (Bradley, Mogg, & Millar, 1996; Bradley, Mogg, and Williams, 1994, 1995) performed a series of studies in which words related to depression (e.g., *misery, grief, despair*) are subliminally presented to individuals who fall into three groups: those meeting *Diagnostic and Statistical Manual of Mental Disorders* (*DSM*) criteria for major depression, those with subclinical levels of depression, and those operating as controls. They consistently found that on implicit memory tests, depressed and subclinically depressed individuals correctly identify words related to depression more often than those who are not depressed. Although their findings have not been consistently replicated for patients with anxiety, studies with depressive patients suggest that a level of processing occurs below conscious awareness that increases individuals' awareness of and identification of depressive material. Clinically, it would suggest that to effectively treat and manage depression, addressing issues related to unconscious sensitivity to depressive material is highly important. Given the relatively high relapse rates for depression and other disorders that are treated with methods focusing on more conscious awareness—via cognitive and behavioral therapies (Westen & Morrison, 2001)—it seems that attention to unconscious processes has the potential to effectively address some depressive disorders.

Eagle (1987) provided support for the notion of unconscious processing in studies of perceptual illusions and dichotic listening, a type of selective attention task. For instance, in the Ames room experiment (Ittleson & Kilpatrick, 1951), the ceiling and floor were not parallel, and two individuals stood either toward the front or back of the room. This led perceivers to believe that the people were very different in size, despite the fact they were not. In the dichotic listening task (Lewis, 1970), individuals heard two different messages in each ear but were trained to attend to just one message. When asked to repeat what was heard in the trained ear, individuals had less of a reaction time in producing the words when words in the other ear were semantically similar. That is, there was a facilitative effect on performance when a semantically similar word was processed (unconsciously) in the "unattended" ear.

Studies of patients who have experienced brain injuries provide interesting clinical observations that support the presence of unconscious processes. Milner, Corkin, and Teuber (1968) reported the famous case of a patient known as H.M., who had undergone surgery on his medial temporal lobes to control very severe seizures. Just below this part of the cortex lies the hippocampus, which is considered an important anatomical locus for learning new information and storing it in working and long-term memory. Because of the damage done to the medial temporal lobes by this procedure, H.M. failed to remember anything that was new to him past the surgery. H.M. could remember information if he rehearsed it, although it was quickly lost if he was interrupted.

One interesting consequence of this procedure was that H.M. appeared not to have lost the affective components of certain experiences. For instance, H.M. had the occasion to visit his mother, who was hospitalized. After leaving the hospital, he had no recollection of visiting her, although he had the idea that something may be wrong with her. H.M. experienced other events like this, demonstrating very nicely that implicit learning was occurring for affectively charged situations and that the unconscious effects of this learning could be identified in everyday life.

More recent studies of unconscious affective processing have suggested that there are at least two neural pathways that process affective information (LeDoux, 1989, 1995, as cited in Westen, 1999). One of these pathways originates in the thalamus and transmits sensory information to other brain regions, whereby emotional meaning is attached to the information. The other pathway, also originating in the thalamus, sends the sensory information to the cortex, where higher levels of emotional processing and emotional meaning are executed.

Mark Solms has reported some exciting work on the effects of unconscious processes on commonly observed clinical syndromes (e.g., Solms, 2000a, 2000b, 2001, 2002, 2004). He has taken a very active role in recent times in integrating neuroscience and psychoanalysis, which has created a relatively new interdisciplinary field of study known as *neuro-psychoanalysis*.[2] He provides an interesting set of case studies (Solms, 2000a) on patients who have experienced a stroke in the right temporal lobe in the region, in which the middle cerebral artery exists. In these case studies, he integrates psychoanalytic theory and treatment into the neurological understanding of the deficits patients are experiencing. The following section presents one of his cases as an exemplar of how psychoanalytic theory adds to the understanding of symptoms seen in such patients.

Right hemisphere syndrome is a neurological disorder consisting of three major symptoms: anosognosia, neglect, and spatial perception and cognition deficits. Anosognosia is the indifference or outright denial of an illness, which in this case was the loss of use of the patient's left arm and side. Neglect occurs when patients ignore their paralyzed limb and side. Patients often feel disgust when they are compelled to attend to the left side of the body, sometimes experiencing a sense of revulsion. The spatial and cognitive deficits observed consist of defective facial recognition, imperception of facial emotion, environmental disorientation, and various kinds of apraxia (the inability to complete an activity involving muscle movement). There are various theories about the emotional deficits in patients with right hemisphere syndrome. One theory suggests that the stroke affects attentional arousal that is mediated through activity in the right perisylvian region of the temporal lobe, which leads to anosognosia and neglect. Another theory has focused on the fact that the left hemisphere is more involved with positive emotional processing and the right with more negative emotional processing. Because the right hemisphere is damaged, anosognosia and neglect occur because there is little to no processing of negative effect in the right hemisphere. A final theory states that it is the right hemisphere that is dominant for the perceptual representation of bodily states, which include more somatic or visceral perceptions. When this part of the brain is compromised, the brain can only rely on past somatosensory representations of bodily states, which provide the patient with the impression that there is no deficit or problem.

Solms (2000a) described Mr. C., a 59-year-old engineer who experienced right hemisphere syndrome after complications from a mild stroke. He had only part of his visual field remaining and would not attempt to compensate for it (i.e., neglect), and he ignored sensory stimulation that occurred on the left side of his body (anosodiaphoria). He ignored and minimized his paralyzed left arm, referring to it as being "like a dead piece of meat, but now it's just a little bit lame and lazy" (p. 71). Other deficits existed due to right parietal damage.

Mr. C. was "aloof, imperious, and egocentric" (Solms, 2000a, p. 72). He seemed unconcerned about others and would sit blankly at times staring into space. However, on occasion he would burst into tears or look as if this were the case. These periods were brief yet stood in contrast to the emotional coldness that he often presented with. During one physical therapy session, Mr. C. was making very little progress in learning how to walk. The physiotherapist reported to the treating psychologist that Mr. C. seemed "indifferent to the errors he was making, and he simply ignored her when she pointed them out to him" (p. 74). In a session the next day, Mr. C. told the psychologist that the physiotherapist indicated that he had been making mistakes, sounding as if he were confessing something. He then said that another therapist had asked him to do some activities with blocks but that he could not do it. At this point the therapist replied to Mr. C.:

> ... it was difficult for him to acknowledge the problems his stroke had left him with, but it seemed that he was now more able to see them. Mr. C. carried on ... [saying] his physiotherapy was "okay" but that his arm had not progressed to the degree that he required. Then, at this point, he suddenly withdrew from conversing ... and began to exercise his left hand and arm with the right one. [The therapist] commented that it seemed as if he could not bear the wait, and wanted his arm to be completely better immediately .... [He replied] "I just don't want my left arm to get weak from non-use." [The therapist then replied] perhaps it was too painful for him to acknowledge what he was on the verge of recognizing a moment earlier—namely that his arm really was completely paralyzed—and that the question of whether it would recover or not was largely beyond his control. This comment provoked an instantaneous crumpling of his face and a burst of painful emotion accompanied by pre-tearfulness. [Turning to his therapist] he said in desperation "but look at my arm [pointing to his left arm]—what am I going to do if it doesn't recover? (Pp. 74–75)

Solms (2000a) noted that this case demonstrates how unconscious material that was too painful to acknowledge was accessed through careful interpretations. More so, the case example controverts the theory that these patients lack negative emotions or have no awareness of their bodies and their deficits. In Mr. C's case, it is clear that implicit processes were at work and that the emotional response originated out of the complex, associative networks that were formed by this patient's unconscious processing of the painful loss of his bodily integrity.

Transference phenomena, too, can be better understood in light of recent findings in cognitive psychology. To understand transference phenomena, Westen and Gabbard (2002b, pp. 103–104) highlighted important ideas in recent studies of cognitive processing:

1. Most representations consist of memory traces that are multimodal, which include semantic, sensory, and emotional components.
2. Representations of self and other exist as potentials for activation. Because these are potentials, they are subject to modification, which will interact with new knowledge, further developing the self and other representations.
3. Memory networks consist of semantic, episodic, and procedural knowledge, along with differing affects and motives.
4. Unconscious procedures to manage emotions are defenses and may be triggered outside of awareness. Co-occurring motives and affects also may be activated, such that the individual may not be aware of either one or the defense being used.
5. Conscious representations are some of many representations that get activated. Consciousness is a serial processing system, whereas multiple parallel processes get activated that are not available to consciousness.

As can be seen in these principles, Westen and Gabbard (2002b) suggested that transference phenomena represent a dynamic, ongoing process that occurs at the conscious and unconscious level. Because multiple cognitive events occur at one time, transference phenomena can be highly complex phenomena and can represent one of many possible reactions to the therapist, as well as other meaningful individuals in the patient's life. In fact, multiple transferences can occur. For instance, a patient may feel particularly challenged by his work and may experience some feedback from his female supervisor about his recent difficulties with his job. Suppose the patient's mother took great strides to help him whenever he felt frustrated in his schoolwork or activities, such that he came to unconsciously expect her to provide assistance during challenging times. At work the patient may have experienced the supervisor's comments as an invitation for help and assistance. Should no help be forthcoming, the patient would become irritated and disappointed with such a difficult supervisor. Likewise, suppose that this patient's father was unavailable to help him. He may have come to view male authorities as uncaring and disinterested in his plight. Thus, in his present treatment, the patient may find himself feeling scared and anxious toward his male therapist when talking about his recent disappointment with the supervisor. An exploration of his interaction with his supervisor may elicit anxiety in the patient toward his therapist, whom he experiences as a disinterested and uncaring male. Likewise, he may feel very frustrated toward the therapist who is not willing to tell him how to manage his interactions with his supervisor, reflecting a maternal transference to the therapist who unconsciously should be offering help and assistance quickly and without much effort on the patient's part.

Differences between the Psychoanalytic and Cognitive Unconscious and Their Reconciliation

As interesting as the research summaries just presented are, it is important to note that Freud's idea of the unconscious and cognitive psychology's understanding of the unconscious are different in important ways. First, many have noted that Freud's idea of the unconscious was limited to impulses and wishes that operated under irrational processes related to drive gratification, which stands in contrast to unconscious operations described in cognitive psychology (Bucci, 1997, 2000; Eagle, 1987; Epstein, 1980, 1994; Shevrin, 1992). The Freudian interpretation is no longer fully supported, as affects, representations, and thoughts all have been demonstrated to exist in the unconscious (Blatt, 1974; Bucci, 2000; Eagle, 1987; Greenberg & Mitchell, 1983; Sandler & Rosenblatt, 1962; Sandler & Sandler, 1994; Westen, 1999). More so, it has been suggested that the unconscious is not irrational but operates on its own rules that are better described as "arational" (Brakel, 2002). Related to the first concern is the idea that a purely Freudian view of the unconscious mind would make little evolutionary sense, given the maladaptation of primary process thinking (Epstein, 1980, 1994). Although secondary process (reality-based) thinking and the functions of the ego adaptively serve the person, cognitive psychology recognizes the adaptive, effortless advantages offered by its rendition of the unconscious. Third, psychodynamic theories of the unconscious emphasize repression and retrievability of unconscious material, whereas cognitive psychology has focused more on processes, which are not seen as readily retrievable. Fourth, the concept of the dynamic unconscious found in psychoanalytic theory differs from the automated mechanics of unconscious processing that is understood in cognitive psychology (Shevrin, 1992). Fifth, traditional Freudian theory has suggested that what is repressed and subsequently consciously experienced is identical to the wish or impulse as it originally occurred. However, more contemporary psychoanalytic theory and cognitive psychology recognize that much of what is recalled is a construction from past experience (Eagle, 1987; Loftus, 1991, 2003; Roediger, 1996; Roediger & McDermott, 2000), as can be clearly evidenced in false memory research and in research of optical illusions, in which a constructed perception is made that varies from the original stimulus features (e.g., the triangle example previously described).

Besides these issues, other important matters arise when considering how to integrate bodies of research. First, there is the subject of language. To what extent can constructs from these psychoanalytic theory account for or overlap with constructs in cognitive neuroscience, and how are these similarities to be accounted for? This leads to a second issue: There is a tendency to explain one set of findings in the context of one theory over the other, perhaps with the intention of replacing one theory with the other (Westen & Gabbard, 2002a). This can lead to various dangers, including a premature conclusion that one theory fully explains the topic, theoretical rigidity at the expense of theoretical integration, and discounting evidence that stands to the contrary (Reiser, 1996). Third, with specific respect to psychoanalytic theory and cognitive science, one may believe that treatment will be hindered by focus on one model over the other. For instance, Westen and Gabbard (2002a, p. 59) speculated, "Psychoanalytic theory will rapidly become an anachronism if theorists imagine that reclining on a couch (as in psychoanalysis) generates useful data but reclining on a table during neuroimaging procedures does not." Likewise, "We can learn a great deal by looking for the neuropsychological correlates of psychologically meaningful processes, but if our fantasy is to reduce mind to brain, we are likely to reduce only our knowledge in the effort .... Discovering neural correlates of mental processes does not obviate the need to understand them psychologically or interpret their meaning" (ibid.). Solms (2004, p. 337) echoed this sentiment: "Modern neuropsychology has demonstrated that ... simple mental functions have widely distributed physical correlates, and simple physical structures participate in a wide variety of mental functions. For this reason, mental functions can never be found inside neuroanatomical structures; they exist, as it were, between them."

Although these problems are real, it is certainly the case that human knowledge is limited and that theories once held as fundamentally true have been amenable to modification. Discovery of knowledge and applying it to understand and improve human functioning is at the heart of all scientific and clinical endeavors. Integration of findings and theories allows for an expanded, more complete description of human functioning. So, for psychoanalytic theory and cognitive neuroscience to "speak to" and inform each other, it is important to understand the phenomena that each discipline is studying and how these phenomena are defined. At least three efforts have been undertaken to account for these differences, leading to the articulation of different theories of integration:

- A dual-track approach (Reiser, 1984, 1990, 1996)
- Multiple code theory (Bucci, 1997, 2000)
- The nature of attentional processes (Shevrin, 1992)

The dual-track approach (Reiser, 1996) is the most straightforward in the way it suggests that different domains of research should be integrated. Reiser (1984, 1990, 1996) suggested that to avoid interpretive problems that result when integrating biological and psychoanalytic theories of mind, it is important to first separately track the data that pertain to the same phenomena in question in both fields. Next, one should derive functional principles that seem to occur in each domain or research and should evaluate principles that have been derived uniquely by one model of the other, looking for areas of similarity. When patterns of similarity occur, there is convergence of the principles derived from each domain of study. By employing this approach, Reiser (1996) suggested that a clearer picture of the mental processes can be understood. "For example, ascending excitation originating in the pons can induce a dreaming state of the brain (rapid eye movement [REM] sleep), but not a dream experience (higher level, different domain" (Reiser, 1996, p. 612).

Bucci (1997, 2000) described the *multiple code theory* as a way emotional information is processed. Her model integrated the understanding of explicit and implicit cognitive processes with the duality of primary and secondary thought, such that conscious and unconscious emotional processes may be joined together. She noted that humans represent and processes information in three ways: via subsymbolic processes, via symbolic imagery, and via symbolic verbal codes. Subsymbolic processes are implicit and operate in sensory, motoric, and somatic modalities. They are not represented in higher, abstract levels of awareness but occur without explicit intention and may seem as if one has no control over them. These representations are based on parallel distributed processing systems that are composed of multiple neural pathways. Symbolic processing involves the processing of discrete entities with the properties of reference and generativity. This means that individuals understand the representation as something outside of themselves and may be combined in ways to create new or more complex representations. Words and images are all part of symbolic processing.

Bucci (1997, 2000) suggested that human information processing is connected via a referential process, in which elements of each code interact with each other to form memory traces or memory schema. Young children begin with their representation of the mother in subsymbolic ways; however, quickly in development a visual representation is symbolized as mother, and soon the word *mother* comes to be represented in memory. Bucci (2001, p. 217) defined emotions as "memory schemas built up through repetitions of interactions with significant other people, from the beginning of life. The emotion schemas are represented as prototypic events that share a common subsymbolic core of sensory, visceral, somatic, and motoric experience. They incorporate our expectations of others and of ourselves: how others will act toward us in particular circumstances, how we are likely to act and react, and how we are likely to feel." Bucci and colleagues (Bucci, 1993, 1995, 1997; Bucci & Miller, 1993) identified language and behavior that is associated with each stage, thus operationalizing important processes that occur in emotional processes. Bucci (2001, p. 221) suggested that this paradigm can be used for research on psychotherapy and other narrative material so that "we can make inferences from the observable events of the treatment processes occurring within the speaker's (patient's) mind."

Finally, Shevrin (1992) provided some ideas that may prove valuable in the process of integrating these two domains. He compared the psychoanalytic and cognitive view of the unconscious, saying that the ideas may be like identical or fraternal twins who have been reared apart. He noted that recent studies demonstrate that "twins reared apart somehow manage to marry people by the same names and show other remarkable parallels in life courses" (p. 324). In predicting how these two psychological twins may come to find common life courses, Shevrin proposed that a focus on attention and effortful versus noneffortful processing may be useful in elucidating the way by which information is processed without conscious awareness. He suggested that studies showing unconscious processing of material and its effect on behavior have the most promise in unifying the two fields, such that they may speak of similar processes. This would bridge the gap between the psychoanalytic unconscious, which focuses on conflict, affect, and motive, and the cognitive unconscious, which focuses on purely cognitive processes: "We need only to apply our imaginations and good will" (p. 325).

Summary

The integration of psychoanalytic and psychodynamic theory with research in cognitive psychology and neuroscience is an exciting venture. More than ever, psychoanalytic and psychodynamic ideas are entering the empirical spotlight with increasing recognition and appreciation for what they offer. The implications of these findings are significant when it comes to how clinicians conceptualize and treat patients. It is no longer enough to attend just to conscious processes and believe that our patients and their problems can be fully understood by simply what they are aware of. Memory networks are complicated but can be understood through the associative process that is central to psychoanalytic and psychodynamic treatment. The representation of others and experiences is unique for each person, though a grounding in psychoanalytic and psychodynamic ideas of the unconscious and how its processes work makes this idiographic network knowable. Hence, the ideas of the unconscious being made conscious are being realized not only in the treatment room but also in cognitive psychology and neuroscience. With the field evolving this way, the general practice of psychotherapy may find itself returning to the principles of psychoanalytic and psychodynamic theory, which could be unsettling for those who are opposed to such ideas. That is often the case when fundamental realities of human experience are first (or, in this case, finally) recognized.

Notes

1. An interesting example is found in the literature on explicit and implicit assessment of interpersonal dependency, which was reported in the previous chapter. However, it bears repetition. Using an implicit measure, the Rorschach Oral Dependency Scale (ROD; Masling, Rabie, & Blondheim, 1967) and an explicit measure, the Interpersonal Dependency Inventory (IDI; Hirschfeld et al., 1977), Bornstein (1998) identified four groups of individuals: High Dependency (HD; high scores on both the IDI and ROD), Unacknowledged Dependency (UD; high ROD and low IDI), Dependent Self-Presentation (DSP; high IDI and low ROD), and Low Dependency (LD; low scores on both the IDI and ROD). Bornstein then assigned individuals in each of these categories to one of two experimental groups. In one group, individuals were told that they were in a study of problem solving, while the other was told that they were in a study of dependency and help seeking. As predicted, study instructions interacted with dependency status to predict trait-relevant behavior. Specifically, the UD group engaged in help seeking at rates similar to the HD group when they believed they were involved in a problem-solving task; however, the UD group did not show high rates of help seeking when they believed they were in a study of dependency. In contrast, the DSP group engaged in moderate amounts of help seeking when they believed they were in a problem-solving task; however, when told they were in a study of dependency, the DSP group engaged in help-seeking behavior at a rate similar to that of the HD group.
2. There are many individuals who have made significant contributions on the integration of cognitive neuroscience and psychoanalysis. Some of these occurred prior to the development of neuro-psychoanalysis as a field of study. The interested reader is directed to some of the representative works of Fred Levin and colleagues (Levin, 1991, 1993, 1998, 2006; Levin & Vuckovich, 1983) and Jaak Panksepp and colleagues (Davis, Panksepp, & Normansell, 2003; Panksepp, 1999a, 1999b, 2001, 2005). A Web site devoted to the field of neuro-psychoanalysis may be found at http://www.neuro-psa.org.uk/npsa/.

Section III

Therapeutic Process

9

Diagnosis and Assessment

Modern-day psychiatric diagnosis can trace its roots back to Hippocrates, who identified personality types based on the composition of the bodily humors (i.e., fluids). Obviously, the field has evolved quite a ways from its very earliest nomenclature, yet it remains the case that the major objective throughout the evolution of psychiatric diagnosis has been to create the most accurate description of a complex collection of cognitive, emotional, social, motivational, and behavioral symptoms that characterize a psychiatric disorder. Early efforts to do this were presented by Kretschmer (1925) and Kraepelin (1921), as were later notable taxonomies reported by Fenichel (1945), Laughlin (1956), Schneider (1958), Shapiro (1965), and Kernberg (1970). Notable was the influence of psychoanalytic theory on the development of the American Psychiatric Association's *Diagnostic and Statistical Manual of Mental Disorders* (*DSM*) system. However, as the *DSM* system evolved, there was increasing pressure to move away from its psychoanalytic origins to a more "atheoretical" system. This was precisely the intention when the *DSM*, 3rd ed. (*DSM-III*) (American Psychiatric Association, 1980) was published. A multiaxial system of diagnosis was offered, and psychiatric disorders were to be placed on either Axis I or II. The former was for clinical syndromes and problems, most of which were acute in nature, whereas the latter was reserved for personality disorders and mental retardation. However, many were unhappy with this change.

A good example of this is the creation in the *DSM-III* (American Psychiatric Association, 1980) of the diagnostic category dysthymic disorder (DD), which was to be placed on Axis I. DD was believed to be a pathological disease state, based on the findings of Akiskal, Bitar, Puzantian, Rosenthal, and Walker (1978) and Klerman, Endicott, and Spitzer (1979), both of whom noted that chronic, low-grade depression (formerly known as *depressive neurosis*) appeared to have a biogenetic underpinning and that many patients with these symptoms could be treated with antidepressant medication. They reasoned that it was appropriate to think of chronic depressions as having a biological basis, which inherently reflects the idea that depression is a pathological, disease state.

This subsequent change in the diagnostic concept of DD invoked substantial criticism. Cooper and Michels (1981) argued that such a change did not reflect an atheoretical orientation but rather made the assumption that all depressions share a biological basis. A similar concern was raised by Frances and Cooper (1981), who noted that characterologically depressed patients are individuals who have the poorest response to medication and that just because some do respond to medication does not imply that the disorder is fundamentally a disease state.

Kernberg (1984) and Goldstein and Anthony (1988) also criticized the approach to chronic depressive disorders taken in the *DSM-III* as it related to the well-known psychoanalytic construct of depressive personality disorder. Kernberg wrote, "It should be noted that clinical descriptions arrived at by means of psychoanalytic exploration, with its eminently phenomenological characteristics, must be differentiated from the etiological, psychopathological, and psychodynamic theories of psychoanalysis. To throw out prevalent clinical syndromes because they were discovered, studied, and described by psychoanalysts is not an expression of atheoretical objectivity but may reveal a theoretical bias against psychoanalysis" (p. 82).

Many other problems have been inherent in the *DSM* system throughout its history. One of these has been the issue of comorbidity (Carson, 1997; Herzig & Licht, 2006). Despite an effort to describe disorders with greater precision and the inclusion of additional disorders with each new *DSM* edition, comorbidity has been the rule rather than the exception (e.g., National Comorbidity Survey and National Comorbidity Survey-Replication). Another problem Carson (1997) observed can be traced back to the introduction of the symptom-based, behavioral descriptions of mental disorders found in the *DSM-III* (American Psychiatric Association, 1980). This edition of the diagnostic manual sought to eliminate the subjective and unreliable diagnostic practices that were occurring at the time. These problems were attributed mainly to psychoanalysts, who were not particularly interested in the research literature and whose diagnoses and conceptualizations varied widely from person to person. With the *DSM-III*, greater precision was desired in the description of the diagnostic categories, which placed an emphasis on the observable and the symptomatic nature of the disorders. In theory, this change was supposed to increase diagnostic reliability. However, Kirk and Kutchins (1992) tested the assumption that diagnostic accuracy and reliability improved with the *DSM-III* and found that the average diagnostic reliability of *DSM-III* disorders was $k = .70$, which is not particularly strong when accounting for change agreements.

A lack of reliability continues to be a problem today. Herzig and Licht (2006) reviewed evidence for the reliability and validity of the most common *DSM* disorders and reported wide ranges of diagnostic agreement across recent studies of mood, anxiety, attention-deficit, oppositional defiant, and conduct disorders in the *DSM*, 4th ed. (*DSM-IV*; American Psychiatric Association, 1994). Ganellen (2007) recently observed how personality disorder assessment continues to be filled with substantial levels of diagnostic unreliability. He and Huprich and Bornstein (2007) suggested that such problems are based, in part, on an excessive reliance on self-report data, whether it comes in the form of a structured or unstructured diagnostic interview or in a paper-and-pencil self-report inventory. Because of these problems in personality disorder assessment, there have been calls for reorganizing the personality disorder diagnostic system to reflect a consensus of findings in factor analytic studies of personality, which suggests that there are broad, biological underpinnings of many personality disorders (e.g., Costa & Widiger, 2002; Widiger, Simonsen, Krueger, Livesley, & Verheul, 2005). These ideas also have been extended into the conceptualization and diagnosis of Axis I disorders (Achenbach, Krukowski, Dumenci, & Ivanova, 2005; Helzer, Kraemer, & Krueger, 2006; Krueger & Markon, 2006a; Krueger & Tackett, 2006; Markon, Krueger, & Watson, 2005). Needless to say, the viability of the *DSM* system continues to remain in question.

Psychodynamic Diagnostic Manual

Because of these many concerns with the *DSM* system, the *Psychodynamic Diagnostic Manual* (*PDM* Task Force, 2006) was created by a joint effort of the American Psychoanalytic Association, the International Psychoanalytic Association, Division 39 (Psychoanalysis) of the American Psychological Association, the American Academy of Psychoanalysis, and the National Membership Committee on Psychoanalysis in Clinical Social Work. It represents a significant advancement in the articulation of psychodynamic diagnosis in that it may be used to structure a common terminology among psychoanalytic and psychodynamic clinicians, along with being a common sourcebook reference, much like the *DSM*. The *PDM* uses several of the diagnostic labels that are currently in use with the *DSM*, 4th ed., text revised (*DSM-IV-TR*; American Psychiatric Association, 2001) and International Classification of Diseases-10 (ICD-10) (WHO, 1990). However, the *PDM* is explicit about what it offers that is not to be found in other diagnostic systems: "Despite the fact that mental health professionals are inevitably dealing with the elusive world of subjectivity, we require a fuller description of the patient's internal life to do justice to understanding his or her distinctive experience. We are hoping that with more elaborated depictions, we can make more progress on understanding naturally occurring patterns" (p. 5).

The *PDM* evaluates patients' functioning on three dimensions:

1. Personality patterns and disorders (P axis)
2. Mental functioning (M axis)
3. Manifest symptoms and concerns (S axis)

All assessment begins with the P axis because there is "accumulating evidence that symptoms or problems cannot be understood, assessed, or treated in the absence of an understanding of the mental life of the person who has the symptoms" (*PDM* Task Force, 2006, p. 8). Indeed, any psychoanalytic or psychodynamic clinician will report the importance of understanding persons' personality structure and organization to plan effective treatment. In the *PDM*, personality is assessed as being in the healthy level (meaning that no personality disorder is present), the neurotic level, or the borderline level. Although psychotic personality structures have been described by some, the *PDM* opted not to include this label as it could be confused with psychotic conditions such as schizophrenia. The *PDM* suggests that healthy personalities and neurotic personality disorders may be treated via conventional psychoanalysis or psychoanalytic/psychodynamic therapy; in contrast, borderline personalities require structure and support as part of the treatment, as is found in supportive psychodynamic psychotherapy. A listing of the *PDM* personality disorders is provided in Table 9.1.

The M axis allows clinicians to assess patients' overall level of psychological functioning. This scale is much more complex than the

TABLE 9.1 *Psychodynamic Diagnostic Manual* Personality Disorders

Code	Diagnosis
P101	Schizoid personality disorders
P102	Paranoid personality disorders
P103	Psychopathic (antisocial) personality disorders
P103.1	Passive/parasitic
P103.2	Aggressive
P104	Narcissistic personality disorders
P104.1	Arrogant/entitled
P104.2	Depressed/depleted
P105	Sadistic and sadomasochistic personality disorders
P105.1	Intermediate manifestation: sadomasochistic personality disorder
P106	Masochistic (self-defeating) personality disorders
P106.1	Moral masochistic
P106.2	Relational masochistic
P107	Depressive personality disorders
P107.1	Introjective
P107.2	Anaclitic
P107.3	Converse manifestation: hypomanic personality disorder
P108	Somatizing personality disorders
P109	Dependent personality disorders
P109.1	Passive aggressive versions
P109.2	Converse manifestation: counterdependent personality disorder
P110	Phobic (avoidant) personality disorders
P110.1	Converse manifestation: counterphobic personality disorder
P111	Anxious personality disorders
P112	Obsessive-compulsive personality disorders
P112.1	Obsessive
P112.2	Compulsive
P113	Hysterical (histrionic) personality disorders
P113.1	Inhibited
P113.2	Demonstrative/flamboyant
P114	Dissociative personality disorders (dissociative identity disorder/multiple personality disorder)
P115	Mixed/other

Source: PDM Task Force, *Psychodynamic diagnostic manual.* Silver Spring, MD: Alliance of Psychoanalytic Organizations, 2006 (with permission).

DSM-IV-TR Global Assessment of Functioning Scale. In this case, nine overall dimensions of functioning are assessed:

1. The capacity for regulation, attention, and learning
2. The capacity for relationships and intimacy
3. The quality of internal experience, which includes the level of self-confidence and self-regard
4. The capacity for affective experience, expression, and communication
5. Defensive patterns and capacities
6. The capacity to form internal representations
7. The capacity for differentiation and integration
8. Self-observing capacities, or psychological mindedness
9. The capacity to construct or use internal standards and ideals (i.e., a person's sense of morality)

Individuals are assessed across all of these dimensions, and a rating is provided. The M axis dimensions are listed in Table 9.2. The *PDM* indicates that "there is a growing body of research demonstrating that it is possible to measure these components of mental functioning" (*PDM* Task Force, 2006, p. 74). A representative sample of empirically based measures of M axis dimensions is presented in Table 9.3.

TABLE 9.2 ***Psychodynamic Diagnostic Manual*** **Assessment of Mental Functioning (M Axis)**

Code	Label
M201	Optimal age- and phase-appropriate mental capacities with expected degree of flexibility and intactness
M202	Reasonable age- and phase-appropriate mental capacities with phase expected degree of flexibility and intactness
M203	Age- and phase-appropriate mental capacities with phase-specific conflicts or transient developmental challenges
M204	Mild constrictions and inflexibility
M204.1	Encapsulated character formations
M204.2	Encapsulated symptom formations
M205	Moderate constrictions and alterations in mental functioning
M206	Major constrictions and alterations of mental functioning
M207	Defects in integration and organization or differentiation of self-representations and object representations
M208	Major defects in basic mental functions

Source: PDM Task Force, *Psychodynamic diagnostic manual.* Silver Spring, MD: Alliance of Psychoanalytic Organizations, 2006 (with permission).

TABLE 9.3 Empirically Supported Psychodynamic Measures of Personality and Psychological Functioning

Measure	Key References
Defense Mechanisms	
American Psychiatric Association: DSM-IV Defensive Functioning Scale Association	American Psychiatric Association (1994)
Cramer Defense Mechanism Manual	Cramer (1991)
Defense Mechanism Rating Scale	Perry (1988, 2001)
Defensive Style Questionnaire	Bond (2004), Bond et al. (1989)
Ego Mechanisms of Defense	Vaillant (1985, 1992, 1994)
Lerner Defense Scale	Lerner (2005)
Ego Functions	
Ego Functions Manual	Shaffer (2001)
Ego Function Assessment	Bellak and Goldsmith (1984)
Object Relations	
Attachment and Object Relations Inventory	Buelow, McClain, and McIntosh (1996)
Bell Object Relations and Reality Testing Inventory Object Relations Inventory	Bell (1995)
Child and Adolescent Object Relations Functioning	Kelly (1996, 1997)
Differentiation-Relatedness Scale of the Object Relations Inventory	Diamond, Blatt, Stayner, and Kaslow (1991)
McGill Object Relations Scale	Dymetryszyn, Bouchard, Bienvenu, de Carufel, and Gaston (1997)
Mutuality of Autonomy Scale	Urist (1977), Urist and Shill (1982)
Object Relations Inventory	Blatt, Chevron, Quinlan, Schaffer, and Wein (1988, 1992)
Percept Genetic Object Relation Test	Nilsson (1993, 1995)
Quality of Object Relations Scale	Azim, Piper, Segal, Nixon, and Duncan (1991)
Rorschach Separation-Individuation Scale	Coonerty, Diamond, Kaslow, and Blatt (1987)
Social Cognition and Object Relations Scale	Westen (1993, 1995)
Personality	
Karolinska Psychodynamic Profile	Weinryb, Rossel, and Asberg (1991)
McGlashan Semistructured Interview	Miller et al. (2003)

(*Continued*)

TABLE 9.3 (Continued)

Measure	Key References
Operationalized Psychodynamic Diagnosis	Dahlbender, Rudolf, and OPD Task Force (2006)
Scales of Psychological Capacities	DeWitt, Hartley, Rosenberg, Zilberg, and Wallerstein (1991)
Shedler-Westen Assessment of Personality–200	Shedler & Westen (2006), Westen & Shedler (1999a, 1999b)
Structured Interview of Personality Organization	Clarkin, Caligor, Stern, and Kernberg (2004)

The S axis is for symptom patterns that compose many of the Axis I disorders seen in the *DSM-IV-TR*. These include disorders of adjustment, anxiety disorders, dissociation, mood, eating, sleep, sexual and gender identity, impulse control, substance abuse and addiction, psychosis, and general medical conditions, along with somatoform and factitious disorders. In addition, *PDM* authors have attempted to provide a greater description of patients' subjective experience of the symptom patterns than what is provided in the *DSM* system. For instance, in describing the inner experience of patients with anorexia or bulimia nervosa, the *PDM* (*PDM* Task Force, 2006, p. 121) describes the following emotional states:

1. Feelings of being starved for care and affection and longings to be protected and cherished.
2. Feelings of failure, weakness, and extreme shame.
3. Feelings of being unworthy and ineffective. For example, "I would feel like I couldn't eat, and then if I did, I would feel guilty, like I did something I wasn't supposed to or took in something I didn't deserve."
4. Feelings of being abandoned by others or feelings that others will withdraw their love.
5. Feelings of anger and aggression, which feel frightening, dangerous and intolerable are denied, muted, or hated. For example, "I'm a bubbly person who never gets angry. It doesn't feel good to get angry and nobody around me feels good when I get angry. They would get hurt and you can't hurt the people you care about."
6. Fears that experiencing one's emotions leads to being out of control. For example, an anorexic woman stated that if she were to talk freely about her feelings, she would find herself "blowing in the wind."

It also is noted that "symptom patterns are not simply disorders in their own right but are, rather, overt expressions of the ways in which individual patients characteristically cope with experience" (*PDM* Task Force, 2006, p. 93). Thus, it is important to understand patients' overall personality structure and general level of functioning to best understand the symptom patterns. For many of the disorders, biological predispositions, cognitive, affective, somatic, and relational patterns are described to foster a comprehensive description of the disorder.

The *PDM* has a separate section devoted to child and adolescent disorders. This section follows the same structure as the adult section:

1. Mental functioning for children and adolescents (MCA axis)
2. Child and adolescent personality patterns and disorders (PCA axis)
3. Child and adolescent symptom patterns: the subjective experience (SCA axis)

In addition, an entire section is devoted to mental and developmental disorders in infancy and early childhood. The final section of the *PDM* is devoted to the historical and research underpinnings of a psychodynamically informed classification system. The research section alone is more than 300 pages, providing considerable empirical backing to support the development of a diagnostic manual such as this.

As interesting as the *PDM* is and the potential it shows, there are many unanswered questions about it. It is not clear yet how viable the *PDM* will become and whether it will actually be implemented in everyday clinical practice. For that matter, it is not clear whether insurance carriers will even recognize the manual. The answer to that question will rest, in part, on the empirical evidence that is produced on the diagnostic categories' reliability and validity. In particular, do clinicians make more accurate diagnoses with *PDM* diagnostic categories than with the *DSM-IV-TR* or ICD-10? Is there compelling evidence for the diagnostic categories' convergent, discriminant, and construct validity? Will comorbidity be reduced with this new manual? And, perhaps most important, will the *PDM* have evidence of incremental validity? That is, will diagnoses resulting from the use of this manual's diagnostic process and nomenclature lead to better accuracy and treatment outcomes than prior manuals? These are questions that will take years, if not decades, to answer. Yet, for what it is worth, the *PDM* is a monumental and necessary addition to the psychoanalytic and psychodynamic nomenclature and shows much promise for what it might offer.

Assessing Patients

Outside of establishing a good therapeutic relationship from the beginning of treatment, there is probably nothing more important than conducting a thorough assessment of patients when they start treatment. All too often I have observed beginning therapists thinking that determining the diagnosis is what is required of good assessment. Regrettably, this is one of the most unfortunate myths (and mistakes) that therapists can make. Assessment is a process in which information is obtained about individuals to make informed decisions about their care. There is a focused, specific purpose to this activity, and like any good approach to patient care assessment, it is a process that does not stop. Evaluating the efficacy of patients' treatment requires ongoing information gathering. Monitoring changes that occur during and between sessions provides useful, here-and-now information about patients' responses to therapists' interventions. Thus, part of any excellent psychoanalytic or psychodynamic treatment is excellent assessment.

The information obtained as part of the assessment comes from many avenues. First and foremost, assessment occurs during times of interaction with patients and is based on what patients say and how they say it. Careful listening, behavioral observations (e.g., movements, shifts, posture, tone of voice, nonverbal activities), and awareness of patients' subjective experience and therapists' subjective experience are *necessary ingredients* to the assessment process. Content and process are both relevant concerns here. For instance, a patient who speaks about his desire to meet a "nice woman who I can settle down with" tells the therapist something about what he desires. When the patient goes on for the next 20 minutes to engage in self-deprecating remarks about ways he has failed to meet a woman and his inadequacies in such actions and sheds a couple of tears while telling of these struggles, the therapist learns something about what the patient finds himself feeling conflicted about, his lack of defensiveness in speaking about this conflict, his representations of himself as inadequate or flawed, his threatened sense of self-esteem and agency, his representation of woman as disappointing, his social skills, and his sense of interpreting situations accurately or in slightly distorted ways. Of course, all of this information is to be considered in the context of the patient's presenting problem. Additional information must be brought forth to come to a preliminary assessment and formulation of the patient's personality structure, ego strengths, object relations, sense of self, mastery of impulses and affect, relational capacity, characteristic defenses, and—subsequently—diagnosis.

Not only is the content itself important, but also the absence of content should be dually noted. Patients who do not shed tears for a meaningful, recent loss or who avoid talking about their sexual life provide important observable information about what they are defending against. Patients who refuse to acknowledge the therapist in socially appropriate ways (e.g., calling the therapist by her first name despite the therapist introducing herself as "Dr. Jones") or to speak about material that is directly inquired can identify important information about emotionally provocative and well-defended content, the transference, or their characteristic management of aggressive feelings (e.g., avoidance or acting out in devaluing ways), just to mention a few things.

The interpersonal dynamics of patients and therapists also are tremendously important pieces of information that add to therapists' assessment activities. In the previous example of the lonely man, the patient responded rather openly and in some detail about his failures in his dating life. Contrast this with the same situation in which the patient shared the same content, but as soon as he found himself becoming tearful, he spoke about being "such a wimp" and went on to discuss his success in his private business for the remainder of the session, even after the therapist attempted to gather other information. The process reveals not only how the patient quickly disconnected his conscious experience of sadness from thoughts that he was a weak and incapable man but also how when such threats to his masculinity arose, he defensively redirected his attention (and his experience with another person) to that of his sense of power, success, and capabilities. The process also may provide some clues into the nature of the transference that will arise, as well as information about how the patient is likely to respond to certain types of interpretations related to his sense of masculinity and efficacy. Consequently, if other signs of vulnerability arise in this patient, the therapist can become more attuned to the patient's difficulties as well as think carefully about the type of therapy and therapeutic interventions the patient is or is not ready for at this point.

Process information also can be very helpful to therapists regarding their countertransference experience of patients. How therapists respond to certain content, interpersonal exchanges, or other therapy material and events all can prove to be fruitful in this way. For instance, Racker (1968) noted that countertransference may not only represent one's own unresolved conflicts but may also be related to a projective identification process. Knowledge of this process can be helpful for assessing patients' defenses, for understanding transference, and for planning a treatment intervention. By definition, countertransference is something therapists recognize as uniquely residing within themselves (even though particular material that arose from another person was a precipitating factor). This, then, requires that therapists be very attuned not only to the content and process as it plays out in the experience of their patients but also to their own inner world and experience. It is only when therapists are aware of and attuned to their subjective experience that they can begin to sort out the countertransference issues and assess how they are related to their patients. Thus, good assessment skills require that therapists have good inner awareness.

Within the context of assessment, it is often recognized that obtaining the report of a significant other or parent (in the case of a child) will yield fruitful information. Such ideas have been advocated in methods designed to obtain as much information as possible from multiple sources and methods of collecting such information (e.g., the Longitudinal Expert and All Data [LEADS] method; Spitzer, 1983). However, in the context of psychoanalytic and psychodynamic therapy, such practice is rarely used. This is not too hard to understand when one thinks of the effect this would have on the transference and the fostering of the therapeutic relationship. In this case, a meaningful person is being introduced into the patient–therapist dyad that has the power to influence the therapist's opinion and ideas of the patient. Unconsciously, this allies the therapist with the significant other at some level, thereby making transference phenomena difficult to interpret. For instance, consider the challenges of responding to a patient who says, "You're just thinking that because that's what you heard from my husband." In this case, the husband may be the object of his wife's paternal transference, as could the therapist. When husband and therapist (and unconsciously the father) have met to discuss the patient, resistances can become strong and complicated to sort out. Nonetheless, some do not consider the interview of a significant other to be particularly problematic. Gabbard (2004) wrote that family members can provide important and useful information patients may have overlooked. Also, therapists may be able to educate family members about psychotherapy and what happens in the context of this type of professional relationship. Finally, Gabbard observed how cultural and social factors may be elucidated in such meetings were previously unknown.

Assessment is not just based on patient self-report and observations of the content and process. Assessment may be performed more formally with psychological testing. In the era of managed care, psychological testing is not practically feasible for some clinicians; however, the wealth of information it can provide is substantial. Meyer et al. (2001) performed a comprehensive review of the literature on psychological testing, which included data from more than 125 meta-analyses on test validity and 800 samples examining assessment with self-report and performance based measures of psychological functioning. Meyer and colleagues provided four general conclusions:

1. Psychological test validity is strong and compelling.
2. Psychological test validity is comparable to medical test validity.
3. Distinct assessment methods provide unique sources of information.
4. Clinicians who rely exclusively on interviews are prone to incomplete understandings.

These latter two points are particularly relevant to the practice of psychodynamic psychotherapy. So often, clinicians rely exclusively on patients' self-reported information, and indeed, the focus of attention is on patients' subjective experience. However, when exclusive reliance on one technique takes precedence over the search for clinical "truth," errors are prone to happen. For instance, confirmation bias can occur, in which clinicians fail to attend to information that disconfirms their previously held assumptions and assessments about their patients.

A good example of how different modes of assessment provide useful information about individuals was presented in the last chapter. Summarized brifely, Robert Bornstein (1998) found that self-report and performence based measures of interpersonal dependency each predicted different kinds of help-seeking behavior in a laboratary setting. More so, manipulating help-seeking instructions in the task affected individuals' behavior, but that behavior was best predicted by a performance based measure, not a self-report measure.

This kind of discrimination between self-reported qualities and real-world behaviors lies behind the implicit and explicit methodologies of personality assessment. *Implicit* measures (or methods) assess an individual's automatic, unconsciously motivated patterns of behavior, whereas *explicit* measures assess a person's self-attributed qualities and motives. McClelland, Koestner, and Weinberger (1989), who first made this distinction, noted that implicit measures are less subject to self-report bias or distortion, given that they assess attributes and motives that originated early in childhood, even prior to verbal skill development. In contrast, self-report measures can be distorted and are notoriously unreliable, as seen in the modest degree of correlation between self ratings of personality traits and those by significant others (Ganellen, 2007; Huprich & Bornstein, 2007; Meyer, 1996; Oltmanns & Turkheimer, 2006). Moderate correlations are also seen when patient ratings are correlated with clinician ratings (Huprich & Ganellen, 2006; Zimmerman, 1994). This is not to suggest that implicit measures—most often associated with performance-based (projective) measures—are free from problems. Many have criticized the validity of performance-based measures (see Hunsley & Bailey, 1999; Viglione & Hilsenroth, 2001; Wood, Nezworski, Garb, & Lilienfeld, 2001, for a discussion of this issue). Yet in the context of psychodynamic psychotherapy, it should therefore be recognized that what patients report and what they actually do should not be expected to directly correspond, and, depending on the nature of the psychopathology, the self-report may be highly biased to the point of being unreliable. Thus, psychological testing offers some useful information that may not be captured in the context of the patient–therapist relationship.

Therefore, within the context of patient interviews and observations, observation of therapists' experience of the patient, collateral interviews, and psychological testing, therapists must engage in assessing the major domains of functioning of their patients so that effective treatment can be undertaken. These domains of functioning are similar to the M axis of the *PDM* (see earlier), although I have added a few domains that I believe are just as important. These domains consist of the following:

- Biological and temperamental factors
- Life situation
- Personality organization
- Defenses
- Ego functioning (including affect and impulse regulation, communicative and expressive abilities, cognitive capacities, and reality testing)
- Object representations
- Self-representations, including one's self-esteem and sense of agency
- Capacity for insight or reflective functioning
- Sociocultural factors

The following sections discuss these areas separately.

Biological and Temperament Factors

More and more it is becoming apparent that much of personality and predispositions to psychopathology are inherited (Caspi & Moffitt, 2006; Krueger & Markon, 2006b; Plomin & Caspi, 1999; Rutter, Moffitt, & Caspi, 2006). This knowledge has much potential to identify variables that are risk factors for psychopathology, with estimates of up to 50% or more of the variance in personality traits being accounted for by the inherited factor. A multitude of medical illnesses also are known to have effects on psychological well-being (e.g., hypothyroidism and its association with depression). Patients, too, sustain illnesses or injuries that can permanently change their sense of self and psychological experience, such as the loss of a limb, a serious burn, or a head injury that alters personality and mental functioning. In all of these examples, there is an immutable relationship between biology and predispositions to psychological well-being. Subsequently, there is a need for some patients to learn to accept (and in many cases, grieve) what has been lost and to come to a new sense of understanding themselves and their sense of agency and meaning. In other cases, however, it is *not* the case that biology and genetic predispositions by default prohibit one from achieving greater psychological well-being. For instance, one patient said she felt doomed to a life of great anxiety, given how pervasively impaired her mother was by chronic agoraphobia and social phobia. It was very relieving to her to learn that no psychological research had established a causative link between her biological predisposition to these two disorders and her subsequent development of them. Knowledge of her predisposition improved her ability to look inward, to identify potential signs of anxiety (conscious or unconscious), and to make her concerns more consciously available and mastered. Huprich and Bornstein (2007) made a similar point when discussing biological twins' vulnerability to psychopathology. With reference to a study by Tellegen et al. (1988), Huprich and Bornstein wrote, "Even in genetically similar individuals raised in the same environment, a substantial amount of variability in self-reports is affected by their unique psychological understanding of themselves and their experiences" (p. 8). In other words, it is individuals' internal, subject experience that plays a substantial role in how they understand themselves.

Life Situation

Patients enter treatment with a wide variety of events going on in their life. They are single, married, divorced, separating, cohabitating, or recently widowed. They have meaningful, high-paying jobs, jobs that could be lost, or multiple jobs or may even be changing jobs. Many patients have children, while others hope to have children. Some live in nice homes in high socioeconomic status neighborhoods. Others rent a home or apartment, are in a dangerous neighborhood, or have no home. Many patients have been subject to unfair or abusive treatment by family, friends, or society at large. Some patients may support elderly parents or find they need help from someone else to support themselves. In short, patients come with a whole host of challenges to their daily living.

Knowledge of these stressors is particularly important in the assessment process for several reasons. How patients cope with and defend against stressful or upsetting life events is particularly useful in gauging their overall level of functioning. In my own work, I have been amazed by the resiliency of some patients who have substantial trauma, abusive family members, low income, or chronic stressors from family or within the work environment. These patients may meet *DSM* criteria for posttraumatic stress disorder (PTSD) or borderline personality disorder, yet, with all that is happening in their lives, to diagnose them with these disorders may inadvertently short-circuit the recognition of their incredible defenses and ego strengths. Knowledge of patients' life situations also can foster the therapeutic relationship by the therapist developing an increased sense of empathy and understanding that may not have been there. For instance, I once saw a patient who was inconsistent in his attendance to psychotherapy sessions. Though this could have been interpreted as a form of resistance, it was actually the case that his work schedule was inconsistent, such that he could not always get to a bus at its scheduled time. As transportation by bus was his only means of transportation and work factors were beyond his control, it was certainly not the case that this patient's inconsistency was a clear-cut manifestation of resistance. Finally, life situations are important to assess to have a sense of what kinds of changes are reasonable to expect with patients. A socially anxious patient who seeks to develop more friends and greater relationship satisfaction may have ample resources to meet others (e.g., an automobile, Internet access for dating services, money to pay for social activities); another socially anxious patient may not.

Personality Organization

Evaluating persons' level of personality organization is one of the most fundamental elements of the assessment process. Knowledge of personality structure and pathology substantially affects the type of treatment that one provides. The *PDM* recognizes various categories of personality organization. There are *healthy* personalities, who have an absence of a personality disorder. Such individuals tend to have flexibility in how they cope with problems and accommodate well to stress. Although they may have a particular trait (e.g., introversion), this does not mean their personality is impaired to such an extent that it warrants a diagnosis. *Neurotic-level* personalities are those who tend to function relatively well at work and in relationships but who have some degree of rigidity in their ability to cope with upsetting material. Their problems often are circumscribed to a particular area (e.g., gender and sexuality for the hysterical personality). Neurotic personalities usually have some degree of insight into their problems and form a therapeutic alliance relatively well. The *PDM* lists depressive, depressive-masochistic, hysterical, and obsessive-compulsive personalities in this domain. In the context of *DSM-IV-TR,* Cluster C personality disorders are most like this group. *Borderline-level* personalities tend to have more pervasive problems. They have unstable or very troubled relationships, difficulties in establishing intimacy, extended periods of anxiety or depression, and poor levels of coping or defending against upsetting material. The *PDM* states that splitting and projective identification are the most commonly observed defenses. A host of personality disorders fall into this category: paranoid, psychopathic, narcissistic, sadistic, sadomasochistic, hypomanic, somatizing, and dissociative. The *PDM* notes that schizoid and dependent personalities may present anywhere on the continuum of neurotic to borderline. It adds that narcissistic personalities can also function at the neurotic level, although they more often are found at the borderline level.

Patients are assessed for their level of personality functioning based on a wide range of variables, including predominant or preoccupying themes, relationship patterns (including self and other representations), defenses, ego functioning, and capacity for insight. Thus, within the context of assessing personality, other domains of psychological functioning are simultaneously assessed. In notable contrast to the *DSM* system, the *PDM* (and a psychoanalytic/psychodynamic approach in general) values the importance of assessing personality in the context of assessing persons' difficulties. Personality is not divorced from symptoms and diagnosis; as such, many view psychoanalytic and psychodynamic approaches favorably because of the comprehensiveness with which a patient may be understood.[1]

Defenses

When assessing defenses, it is important to consider two components of the defense: its maturity and its habitual use. By maturity, one is considering the psychological sophistication of the defense. *Immature defenses*, by definition, are ones that are commonly observed earlier in development, prior to the ego's maturing to the point of using more adaptive mechanisms. They involve greater blurring of the distinction between self and the outer world (McWilliams, 1994, 1999) and are commonly utilized by patients with more severe personality disorders or psychopathology (i.e., borderline level of functioning). Immature defenses include denial, projection, projective identification, and splitting. *Mature* defenses are those that involve the ego to a greater extent and involve keeping drive content or other upsetting material from consciously being experienced (Kernberg,

1984). Self–other boundaries are not often blurred in the mature defenses, and as a general principle patients who use more mature defenses tend to function better (although this does not mean that they do not experience psychopathology). Mature defenses include rationalization, intellectualization, sublimation, reaction formation, and isolation of affect.

Defenses also need to be assessed for the regularity by which they are used. Those defenses that are part of a person's personality are called *habitual or characterological* defenses, whereas those that are used in a certain situation are called *reactive* defenses. This distinction may be attributed to Reich (1933/1972), who was one of the first to describe character types and the "character armor" that was prototypical for the type. For example, an individual with an obsessive compulsive personality will very often use intellectualization and rationalization as a defense; however, when faced with the prospect of a job loss, the same person may project feelings of hostility onto his employer and believe he is being unfairly singled out when many others perform more poorly than he does. For most patients entering therapy, they are in the midst of a significant crisis or challenge for which their characteristic ways of coping have broken down (Weiner, 1998). Not only have their characterological defenses failed, but they also likely may have employed more reactive defenses as a way to cope with their difficulties. Therapists need to be attuned to the situational stressors that bring patients into treatment and how their defensive pattern manifests itself from the beginning of treatment into later stages when the stressor has been managed and the person is feeling "more like my typical self." It is very easy for patients (and beginning therapists) to assume once the crisis has passed and they have regained a sense of mastery that was threatened (via the use of their characterological defenses) that no further attention is needed toward their ways of coping with upsetting material. Such assumptions are misleading and inappropriate for most psychoanalytically or psychodynamically oriented psychotherapies, in which insight and structural change is desired.

Ego Functioning

Many psychological abilities fall under the domain of ego functioning. From a biological framework, these activities are related to the workings of the frontal and prefrontal cortex, amygdala, and limbic system. Typically, I categorize ego functions in the broad dimensions of affect and impulse regulation, communicative and expressive abilities, cognitive capacities, and reality testing.

Affect and impulse regulation is invariably connected to the presenting problems of the patient. Patients present with all kinds of troubling emotions that are not well understood or tolerated. Sometimes, affect regulation is not at all determined by what patients say. Avoidance of, acting out, or engaging in specific behaviors are signs that some particular affect is likely intolerable. Other times, affect and impulse control problems are obvious, such as the emotional lability or promiscuous sexual activity found in more severe personality disorders. When assessing this broad dimension, it is useful to determine what kinds of resources and outlets (i.e., subliminatory channels) are available to persons. For instance, the absence of friends or romantic relationships suggests difficulties in seeking out others who can be supportive and helpful in managing one's inner world of affect and impulse.

Communicative and expressive abilities refer to patients' capacity to recognize and express their inner thoughts, feelings, affects, wishes, desires, hopes, and fears to themselves and others. Some patients present clinically as individuals who have great difficulty finding words to express their inner state, a phenomenon known as alexithymia. Others may present as having the ability to verbally express themselves to the therapist but not to meaningful others, suggesting a focused kind of problem with expressive ability. In more severe cases, some may have great difficulty assembling their inner experience into a coherent, purposeful narrative, such as is often found in patients with psychotic experiences. Also included in this dimension is the person's ability to recognize, listen to, and understand the inner thoughts, feelings, affects, wishes, desires, hopes, and fears of other people. Patients who are narcissistic or particularly self-absorbed by their difficulties may show little capacity to attend to others. This may be seen in patients who do not respond to questions asked by the therapist or who respond to a different topic or issue than what was presented by the therapist.

Object Representations

Knowing how others are understood and experienced in the mental life of patients helps therapists tremendously in being empathically attuned to patients. In seeking to discover this part of patients' inner life, therapists also will come to understand how they are represented, which helps immensely in assessing the transference that is likely to unfold. Broadly speaking, object representations vary in complexity and affective quality. At the most poorly developed level of complexity, others cannot be well separated from patients' own experience. There is a psychological fusion of self and other experience, which subsequently hinders reality testing and the capacity to fundamentally relate to others. Moving to a more advanced level, individuals may be represented in ways that are associated with how they gratify or frustrate patients. This level of representation is narcissistic and often relatively simple, since others are viewed only by way of what they provide, not who they are. At more advanced levels of representation, others are seen as separate beings with their own thoughts and feelings. With growing psychological representation, others are viewed as having a mixture of both positive and negative qualities; their experience makes them unique beings that are unlike anyone else in the world. Yet they are not considered unapproachable or incapable of being related to because of their uniqueness; rather, the shared experience of humanity allows patients to approach and experience others and to have reasonable expectations of favorable interrelatedness. An even higher level is seen in patients' capacity to establish a long-term, loving relationship with another person in which intimacy, pleasure, and happiness can be mutually experienced.

At the affective level, psychological maturity and sophistication is associated with affect and emotions toward others that are complex yet positive. At the most immature level, others are seen as hostile and having significant power to harm or control patients. There is a pervasive and powerful negative association to others, making it extremely hard for individuals to enter into any kind of relationship with other persons without considerable concern. If the cognitive complexity is very immature, patients may fear that others will invade them, with the goal of controlling or destroying. This kind of affect is seen in highly paranoid and psychotic individuals. Another less mature way of affectively experiencing others is via a naïve, childish curiosity. Here, there is a disavowal of the potential that others may have motives or desires contrary to the patients', which consequently could be hurtful or harmful. Such representations are seen in unsuspecting children, but they on occasion may be found in patients who continue to be exploited but yet cannot recognize or understand the cause. Not far removed from these experiences are representations that have both idealized and devalued orientations toward others. Others are viewed in an overly favorable or unfavorable light, such that real elements of their personality that are contrary to the representation's emotional valence are overlooked. As emotional and affective complexity grows, others are seen as having both the potential to be gratifying and frustrating. Having various needs and desires, others are experienced in ways that are generally positive. With disappointments or frustrations in a relationship, others are experienced temporarily in a negative light, with a more generalized understanding that the problem can be resolved and that the relationship can be experienced in a more generally favorable and benign way.

Object representations may be ascertained through a number of channels. The way patients treat their therapist when first meeting, including during patients' initial contact, reveals much about the implicit way others are generally experienced. Patients' current relationships and relationship histories also provide a sense of their interest in and representation of others. Those with many short-lived relationships likely have a more need-gratifying and unrealistic expectation of others than do patients who have had a few steady, long-term relationships. The absence of relationships, particularly sexual or more intimate, also provides some clues about potential fears or anxieties that are experienced about these kinds of relationships.

Self-Representations, Esteem, and Agency

It is virtually impossible to assess object representations without learning something about self-representation. How the self is experienced and understood is very important to comprehend in the context of patients' readiness and interest in psychotherapy, as well as their orientation toward assuming responsibility for the treatment process. Overly dependent and needy individuals see themselves as inadequate or incapable of acting in self-enhancing or self-promoting ways. Those who view their needs and desires with contempt, or who disavow them, are likely to view the therapy relationship, like other relationships, as inherently problematic when the focus is turned on them. By contrast, those who view some of their wants, needs, desires, emotions, and goals with excessive attention may be protecting themselves from feelings of powerlessness or unacceptability. Thus, therapy may initially seem highly attractive and necessary, but when upsetting feelings arise they may quickly and effectively move away with defensive prowess and skill that makes it hard for the therapist to intervene.

Like object representations, self-representations exist at various levels of complexity and self-regard. Very primitive and maldadaptive representations are those in which the self is unknown or rapidly changes. At the next level, the self is represented as being highly fragile, vulnerable, and in need of much protection. Need gratification is the central focus of one's experience of the self. Consequently, persons may seem highly narcissistic or fragile. The extent to which persons' sense of self has developed is directly related to how pathological they may appear. For instance, without having others there for protection and basic need fulfillment, individuals may feel like they will disintegrate or fall apart. Here, others are necessary to provide the psychological scaffolding that allows them to exist in their own mind. At slightly higher levels, dependency needs prevail, and individuals actively seek out others for advice and direction, something commonly observed in dependent personality disorder. At a slightly higher level, they disavow their neediness or desires, such that individual efforts and desires are of supreme importance in their mental life. In this case, persons may appear highly independent or aloof and have an exaggerated sense of esteem or agency, beyond what is reasonable. More mature levels of self-representation are composed of representations of oneself as a separate, but related, being who is interested in relatedness. The self is viewed favorably and as capable. Agency and action are seen to reside within the self, and by acting on one's agency one is able to attain satisfaction and gratification. At the same time, others are viewed favorably in their ability to help the person have his or her needs and desires met. Relationships are desired because they enrich one's life, not because they are a means to an end.

Insight and Reflective Functioning

Having the capacity to step outside of one's immediate experience and to think about oneself from the perspective of an observer is a very useful ingredient for most psychoanalytic and psychodynamic therapies. As described by Fonagy and colleagues (Fonagy & Target, 1996, 1997; Fonagy, Gergely, Jurist, & Target, 2002), *mentalization,* or *reflective capacity,* is the ability of patients to conceive of and to understand their mental states and that of others as an understandable causative mechanism of behavior and experience. Mentalization is necessary for the development of a fully developed sense of self and is acquired in the context of early attachments, specifically primary object relationships. It is typically the case that the more severe a persons' psychopathology, the more poorly developed is his/her reflective capacity (mentalization). When patients show very little awareness or recognition of their mental states or inner life, this should be a sign to therapists that more expressive interventions may not be appropriate or well received at this time and that supportive interventions are indicated. The range of interventions would involve reflection and attention by the therapist to signs of patients' mental state and their psychological symptoms. In more extreme cases of limited mentalization, patients may initially respond better to didactic interventions that teach them about the relationship of the inner life to behaviors (such as is found in cognitive therapy) or to behavioral strategies that are targeted to increase the behavioral repertoires necessary to help patients reduce their suffering. By way of contrast, patients with greater levels of mentalization are more likely to come in with some ideas about what is going on in their minds or in the behaviors of others that could be contributing to their difficulties. It is not the case that patients have to have highly well-developed mentalization capacities for psychoanalytic and psychodynamic interventions to be successful, particularly with interventions targeted toward current life situations. However, an indicator of patients' abilities to improve with psychoanalytic or psychodynamic treatment is related to mentalization.

A related concept that is important to assess early in treatment is patients' ability to have some *insight.* Insight is patients' ability to use mentalization skills in a constructive way to obtain a new understanding of their problems and difficulties that had not been consciously realized before. Sometimes, therapists may provide a relatively benign interpretive comment early in treatment to assess patients' readiness, willingness, and capacity for insight (Weiner, 1998). Although such interventions must be very carefully timed and crafted, they may allow therapists to get a sense of how likely patients will engage in obtaining new levels of understanding. In fact, it is often the case that simply summarizing for patients what they have said in ways that draw an association between two important ideas will provide an opportunity to assess how insightful they are. For example, consider Ms. Murdock described in Chapter 1. She described her two husbands as being very different. Her first husband was someone who needed excessive support and reassurance when he was criticized, whereas her second husband worked hard to present himself as very "macho" and likeable to others. I made the observation to her that it sounded like both of her husbands found themselves feeling threatened and anxious when others did not respond to them as they would have liked. This comment provided her with some insight about these two "very different" husbands. Soon thereafter, it became clear that both husbands had rather narcissistic personalities, which provided material for us to work through as to what it was about these men that she found attractive.

Sociocultural Factors

More attention to the effect of patients' social environment and culture is needed in the psychoanalytic and psychodynamic literature (Foster, Moskowitz, & Javier, 1996). Part of this problem originates in the fact that sociocultural factors may be understood in multiple ways. One way I like to think of this dimension is to consider the social and cultural elements in my patients that are different from my own—including age, gender, gender identity, racial, cultural, regional, religious/spiritual, political, and physical differences. In thinking about how patients are different from us, I believe therapists are in a better position to really understand patients' inner world and the factors that have shaped who they are and why they are presenting to us at this time for help. It is always the case that understanding and determining patients' subjective experiences and truths is part of the assessment process and that from our understanding of their life experience, therapists can contemplate appropriate interventions. Sometimes, this is not apparent up front.

Foster (1996) provided a good example of these issues. She described working with a patient named Manash, a 29-year-old political refugee from a country in the Middle East. His family was in a caste that was "semi-religious" and "dedicated to public and community service" (p. 12). Manash sought out treatment about 1 year after being in the United States, feeling very depressed and as if his life had lost its meaning. Given some changes that had occurred in his country, it was unlikely he could return there, where he had been hoping to enter a profession of public service. He had always seen himself in this role, which had been part of his family and caste values. Foster wrote, "As Manash eventually came to show me, the ideal of mental health in his world was not the socially autonomous, externally oriented, self-actualized individual, but rather a person centered in spiritual consciousness, the confluence of will and fate, and the emotional bonding of family and group kinship wherein one's sense of self is deeply involved, throughout life, with others" (p. 13). She used this case to illustrate that, unlike Western and European emphases on separation and independence of individuals from their family, Manash's culture taught him that his sense of self was very much related to his belonging to a community. Thinking ethnocentrically, it could have been easy to think of Manash's problems as a manifestation of psychopathology involving a poor sense of differentiation of himself from others. However, Foster suggested that such thinking would have been misguided, given that Manash's sense of self was firmly established in the context of his family and culture. Her illustration demonstrates the importance of understanding patients' subjective experience in the context of their social and cultural development prior to implementing treatment that may be insensitive to the social and cultural components of persons' psyche.

Summary

This chapter reviewed issues important in the context of diagnosis and assessment from a psychoanalytic and psychodynamic perspective. With the advent of the *PDM*, therapists now have a tool by which to communicate in a common language about their assessments and diagnoses of their patients. It also offers a much needed guide in a world that is driven by atheoretical and symptom-based descriptions of patients as is found in the *DSM-IV-TR*. In the context of assessment, the *PDM* provides an extensive listing of domains of psychological functioning that are to be assessed in the process of coming to understand a patient.

In addition, psychological testing provides a wealth of information to the clinician that is not likely to be reported by patients or to be learned about them until several weeks or months into treatment. Already, many psychoanalytically and psychodynamically based measures have strong empirical support. Despite the challenges that exist to using these instruments, they are an often underrepresented class of assessment tools at clinicians' disposal.

Finally, to make good decisions about how to proceed with treatment, it is necessary to assess patients' psychological well-being and ways of functioning. This can be done by evaluating biological and temperamental factors, life situation, personality organization, defenses, ego functioning (e.g., affect and impulse regulation, communicative and expressive abilities, cognitive capacities, and reality testing), object representations, self-representations (e.g., one's self-esteem and sense of agency), capacity for insight or reflective functioning, and sociocultural factors. With careful review of this information, treatment can be well planned and evaluated throughout its course.

Note

1. In fact, there have been some encouraging signs that assessing personality will take on a more central role in the evolution of psychopathology research and diagnostic systems (Bornstein, 2006; Westen, Gabbard, & Blagov, 2006).

10

Case Study

This chapter presents the case of Eric, who was diagnosed with depressive personality disorder (DPD). As will be seen in Eric's presenting problems and conflicts, elements of masochism, narcissism, and sexual orientation confusion were prominent parts of the distress that he experienced. His sexual conflicts appeared to be related to unresolved issues surrounding his gender identity, which likely stemmed from his earlier experiences of loss, disappointment, and self-recrimination. His case provides an excellent example of the interrelatedness of psychosexual developmental themes and how they help the clinician understand the patient's difficulties.

Introduction

The construct of DPD has a long history in the psychoanalytic tradition (Huprich, 1998). Freud (1917a) and Abraham (1924) explained the earliest model of a depressive personality structure as the result of early object loss. This loss may be tangible, such as the death of a parent, or intangible, such as the lack of support and understanding from parents or caregivers (Jacobson, 1964; Mendelson, 1967). Later models of DPD emphasized the role of the superego, which drives individuals toward perfectionism as a way to avoid being rejected or disappointing to others. Consequently, the superego is extremely harsh and punitive (Berliner, 1966; Jacobson, 1964; Kernberg, 1970, 1984; Laughlin, 1956; Mendelson, 1967), which predisposes persons to a sense of pessimism and negativity. Berliner (1958, 1966) and Kernberg (1984) noted that the depressive personality has masochistic features, which arise from a chronic conflict over the desire for positive attachments to others and the resulting frustration that occurs when the desire is not met. Since the pursuit of love and suffering coincide, individuals become self-defeating and masochistic when pursuing meaningful relationships. Kernberg (1984) added that depressive-masochistic patients may appear more pathological than those with greater disruptions in their object relations.

In 1994, the American Psychiatric Association suggested that DPD be considered for inclusion in the *Diagnostic and Statistical Manual of Mental Disorders* (*DSM*) system. The *DSM*, 4th ed. (*DSM-IV*) (American Psychiatric Association, 1994) and the *DSM*, 4th ed., text revised (*DSM-IV-TR)* (APA, 2001) descriptions of this disorder are similar to those just given and has been met with support. Despite mixed opinions as to whether DPD is a personality or mood disorder, it is now agreed that DPD could be a viable diagnostic category (Huprich, 2008; Laptook, Klein, & Dougherty, 2006; Ryder, Schuller, & Bagby, 2006). From the perspective of clinical utility and ecological validity, a recent survey of psychologists and psychiatrists suggested that DPD is the most common personality disorder they observe in their clinical practice (Westen & Shedler, 1999a).

The Case of Eric

Eric was a Caucasian 22-year-old and the only child of relatively older parents (both of whom were in their 40s when Eric was born). He initially sought treatment because of unremitting feelings of depression and disappointment with relationships. His case was transferred from a therapist who left the clinic where she treated Eric. Her work with Eric was conducted from a cognitive perspective. It was tedious and reportedly not effective. She noted that Eric avoided discussion of his early childhood experiences and familial relationships and tended to intellectualize his experience to the point that his affect was isolated and repressed.

Another source of distress for Eric was his ongoing confusion about his sexual orientation. He interchangeably described himself as heterosexual, homosexual, and bisexual. Eric reported one prior heterosexual relationship, which was very involved. He stated that he was in love with this woman, but when he revealed his bisexuality to her, she immediately broke off the relationship. Eric was devastated by this experience and did not ever expect to meet another woman who understood him as she did. Although he engaged in homosexual fantasy, pornography, and phone sex, Eric had not had a homosexual relationship.

As part of his treatment, Eric consulted a psychiatrist and took prescription antidepressants throughout the course of his therapy. However, he did not notice much of a change in his chronic depressive orientation while taking the medication. At the time of treatment, Eric worked two part-time jobs and lived at home with his parents. In the past, he had pursued his undergraduate degree in the arts but became disenchanted when he was asked to leave his course of study because of not meeting performance criteria for continued enrollment.

Throughout therapy, Eric described himself as overly serious, something I observed as well in our interactions. He provided an example of this in one of his early sessions, in which he said he was "too loyal" at work. By this, he meant that he had felt very obliged to repay an interpersonally difficult, former employer who had covered medical expenses for him after sustaining a minor injury on the job. Eric explained that he felt guilty for having a desire to leave this job, given what medical expense his employer had (appropriately) incurred. As another example, Eric noted in his current job that he once followed a customer out of the store after accidentally overcharging a customer a few dollars. He reported that he did not fear the consequences of his mistake from the customer or employer; rather, he "could not accept the fact that I made the mistake."

Eric's serious nature was captured in his tendency to be very intellectualized and having strong expectations of himself. He often indicated that he felt as if he was "working from a script" in therapy so that he would appear to be an ideal patient. He also avoided appearing weak in front of me as well as in front of his former girlfriend so we would not think negatively about him. Even at our final therapy session, Eric was self-denigrating, describing himself as "an insensitive jerk" for not having any stronger feelings about our separation.

Eric's rigid interpersonal behavior was associated with an emotional life that could frequently be described as pessimistic, constrained, and dysphoric. He rarely smiled in therapy and often minimized his emotional reactions, which were depressive. A few sessions after beginning therapy, Eric described himself in a more spontaneous and open manner; however, he quickly minimized and disavowed this change in his behavior when I observed that he seemed to feel more comfortable in session. He attributed this change to having "drunk too much coffee" and "not having enough sleep the night before." Similarly, Eric would chastise himself for having homosexual feelings. He once reported feeling "like a giddy schoolgirl" when having sexual feelings toward another male, yet this excitement was quickly criticized and shut off from awareness because of the belief that he was "losing perspective." Not surprisingly, Eric's religious beliefs led him toward self-derogatory comments about his "sinful" lifestyle. Even after feeling as if he had experienced a spiritual renewal, Eric quickly became pessimistic and despondent when issues about his sexuality were explored in depth. Eric's pessimism and dysphoria extended into his interpersonal relationships as well. For example, upon encountering his ex-girlfriend one day and discussing reestablishing their relationship, Eric said that he had to "put a rein on his optimism" for fear of being hurt again.

The most pervasive themes throughout the course of therapy appeared to be loss, disappointment, and anger. Eric reported that, as a child, his parents seldom attended his activities at school. He noted that his father often criticized him over "silly things," including his handwriting. Rarely did Eric express his frustration with his father, although when he did, it was expressed in strong ways. For instance, Eric became irate with his father when he picked him up from work one day. His father reportedly began asking about the details of the day, which Eric found highly annoying. As such, he struck his fist against the side of the car and jumped out. A bystander observed this event and inquired about the incident, at which time Eric returned to the car and cried all the way home.

Although treatment was characterized by Eric's defensiveness of his emotional vulnerability, during the 32nd session, Eric stated for the first time that he wanted his parents to love him and accept him as he is. When his desires for love and affection from his parents were explored further, Eric became defensive and angry, but not at them. He said he did not want to speak "too negatively" about his parents, nor did he want to be a "parent hater," as many seemed to be once entering therapy. It seemed clear in this session that Eric's sense of vulnerability was being exposed and that his defense of his parents was highly important to minimize his anger toward them, as well as the pain he might feel by acknowledging such extreme disappointment with them. In the following session, Eric defended his parents again yet was critical of them. He recalled that at age 13, his parents made the comment that he was "smarter" than they were. Eric felt that this was an inappropriate comment for parents to say, yet he noted times when he frequently had to correct them because of making factual errors. Eric described these events as irritating, like a "constant chattering" in the back of his mind; however, there also was a sense of satisfaction he felt by being acknowledged by his parents for his intellectual abilities.

As our sessions progressed and the focus became on Eric's disappointment with his parents, an important theme that emerged was the notable absence of support he felt from them. Eric recounted somewhat painfully how his parents never once attended any of his extracurricular activities associated with school (e.g., orchestra). Their absence from these events was most striking and deeply disappointing. In one session, Eric spoke about wanting to share with his parents his homosexual interests and hoped that they would accept him for having such interests and desires. In speculating about his parents' reactions to this side of himself, Eric thought that his father would likely ask many questions and blame himself for Eric's problem. This thought was irritating to Eric, as this type of behavior (i.e., critical questioning) happened often with his father. Eric predicted that his mother would become tearful at this disclosure and isolate herself in the bedroom, which was her characteristic way of managing upsetting feelings. In Eric's friendships and his relationship with me, Eric reported working hard not to disappoint us, lest we reject him. He noted that by sharing his complex emotions or his conflicts over his sexual orientation, we may view him as being "needy," which was a "selfish and dirty" condition. He went on to say that by expressing his needs, he was certain that he was an "imposition" to those listening to him. Yet it was clear that underneath these conscious concerns was a deep desire to be cared for and accepted.

Eric's sexual history was gradually revealed throughout the course of therapy. He noted that in kindergarten, he preferred to play with girls in his class and their dolls. He recalled an interest in female clothes, which included trying on some of his mother's clothing. He revealed later that, in the past, he had put on female clothes, which he found somewhat sexually arousing. Eric reported that he was "over this phase" and did not have any sexual interest in them anymore.

Around the age of 8 or 9, Eric engaged in "sexual exploration" with a female friend. His free association to this episode was, "This is the sort of thing Mommy wouldn't like," anticipating feelings of guilt and disappointment should his parents learn of this event.

More so, his shame about acting in this way was very difficult to tolerate while telling it.

In the next session, Eric described two dreams. In the first, he was the assistant to a famous actress, who was president of the United States. In the second, he was dating his female cousin, who tried to fix him up with other men. In the dream, his cousin apparently knew of Eric's homosexual interests. Eric's associations to the dreams were that women had an "enviable amount of power." He observed that when he had cross-dressed he felt much of this power. However, he said he frequently felt angry about this degree of power and thought that he understood why men, at times, became enraged with women. Interestingly, these dreams were preceded days earlier by Eric's interactions with a female coworker who had made some sexually explicit comments to him. Eric was confused by this. His discussion of this exchange was described at only a superficial level, in which he described this woman as "overly pierced" (which was a reference to her extensive body piercing). Unconsciously, Eric's confusion toward this woman may have represented repressed feelings of anger and hostility toward his own mother, who seemed to have an ability to exert her power over her family, in particular by being emotionally unavailable and locking herself in a bedroom. It also exemplified Eric's representation of males as being powerless to the point that women are the ones to whom he should look for learning how to become and feel powerful. Perhaps identifying with women may have provided him with the power he needed to interact in assertive and confident ways with other men, something he did not experience at this point in his life. All these ideas seemed plausible and worth considering as the therapy proceeded.

How Eric communicated and expressed his sexual conflicts toward me was interesting. Early in the course of therapy, Eric spoke of being aware of monitoring what he said about his sexuality so that he would appear as the "good client" and would not receive my disapproval. In trying to understand his fears about this, he provided highly intellectualized reasons, and his concerns about my approval still remained even after my reassurance that it was perfectly fine to speak about his sexual conflicts and orientation. Thus, his transference toward me reflected very early fears of being rejected and disapproved of by a father figure. During the 20th session, Eric's anxieties seemed to decrease enough such that he felt confident enough to inquire about my sexual orientation. When exploring the rationale behind this inquiry, Eric again identified strong fears that I would reject him because I might not understand his homosexual interests; however, he also had fears that if I were homosexual, his reactions to this would be overwhelming, which included a fantasy that we would become intimately involved. He was relieved when I shared my heterosexual orientation and even more so by my accepting and validating attitude toward his fears, along with my clarifying that we could work together to better understand his sexual conflicts without his impulses' "getting the best of him."

Eric's transference to me was expressed in other ways, as I was not the only male figure with whom fears were associated. Once at work, Eric reported a situation in which his manager irritated other employees. Eric described his role as that of a "peacemaker." If he did not assume this role, Eric feared that there would be a "bloody revolution," in which everyone was fired. Yet, when carrying out this role, Eric saw himself as having power to "destroy" the manager by revealing to the manager's supervisor how irritable the manager was. This led to considerable distress over the actions he had taken. In contrast to his past fears of rejection from paternal figures, these fears had more of an Oedipal tone, in that he had fantasies of destroying a father figure who interfered with his relationship with his coworkers (who were mostly female). Situations such as these made me wonder about the Oedipal fears that Eric experienced in our relationship.

During the 28th and 29th sessions, pre-Oedipal and Oedipal conflicts were quite clear when he discussed his ambivalence toward his father. Eric described a situation earlier in his adult life when he became worried about having to take care of his father after his father experienced serious health problems. Eric thought that his father's illness was "self-imposed" due to his poor diet. This irritated Eric while also eliciting some fear about his father's death. He speculated that it would be better if his father "would just die" instead of lingering on in poor health in extended nursing care. This speculation was associated with Eric's then having an increased sense of freedom in being able to express his sexuality. His subsequent associations about his father's death were about feeling "cut off" from his family if he ever shared his sexual orientation concerns with them. Subsequently, Eric was not certain how to resolve these feelings and felt trapped in his ambivalent feelings toward his father.

In the next session, Eric said he had discontinued drinking coffee since we met last, as he wanted to be less dependent on the caffeine.

However, a few days prior to the session, he resumed coffee drinking after an encounter with an "irritating customer" at work. When asked about any association between his desire to stop drinking coffee and last week's session, Eric had little to say. As the session continued, it seemed as if Eric was withholding something he wished to say. When I observed this to him, Eric expressed some irritation. But it did pave the way for him to speak about having many recent homosexual oral-sex fantasies while at the same time fearing rejection and disapproval for being "a faggot." It was clear to me at this point that the last session was powerful for Eric in that our discussion about his father's mortality and his reaction led to many associations about being in a loving, dependent relationship with a man and what such desires could mean.

In subsequent sessions, Eric spoke more of his father. He noted some times when he was provocative toward his father. He parenthetically commented that it was no fun to push him "if he does not act back." Surprised by this statement, Eric became self-critical of his aggressive feelings toward his father. He went on to have self-recriminations about his aggression and sexuality and his perceived lack of control over these elements of his personality. I suggested we look further at his conflicted feelings of desire and anger toward his father and how these might be related to the homosexual feelings he was having and his subsequent self-recrimination. Eric found the issues too threatening and had little to say about it, and they did not come up much again in our sessions.

Besides the prevalence of pre-Oedipal and Oedipal issues, there were strong masochistic themes in Eric's relational history. As stated earlier, during a heterosexual relationship, Eric shared his bisexual interests with his girlfriend, which subsequently ended their relationship. Eric thought this behavior may have been done intentionally but could not understand why he might have done this. He also described an event in which he wore a piece of jewelry suggestive of his homosexual orientation. Upon finding himself attracted to a flirtatious woman, he thought his jewelry "stuck out" and that the woman would not be interested in him sexually. As such, he failed to pursue this relationship further. On other occasions, Eric commented that he tried to present himself to others as being odd or bizarre. In doing so, he felt he could keep others away before getting hurt by them, thus perpetuating the perception of himself as being distant or unavailable.

Termination was indicative of the severity of Eric's preoccupation with issues of loss and disappointment. Upon informing Eric of my upcoming departure (due to my work ending at that clinic), Eric spoke at length about the need to gain better control over his sexuality. He reported feeling as if he was in a never-ending desert and wishing he had a companion to be there with him. Interestingly, he did not view me as a companion; rather, his former girlfriend was the only individual who appeared to have met this requirement. It struck me that acknowledging his desire to continue to work with me was way too frightening to admit, when in fact he had shared more with me about his feelings of loss, disappointment, fear of criticism and rejection, and sexual conflicts than any other person in his life. (In an ironic parenthetical statement, Eric observed that he was suddenly feeling hungry, which seemed suggestive of dependency needs that were being felt at the moment).

As termination approached, Eric described his ongoing "melancholy" as a "mystery wound." He hesitated to share these feelings with others (including a new therapist), though, because if others really knew him, they might use his weakness against him. A few sessions before our farewell, Eric speculated about what our experience of separation would be like. He said he feared he would have an emotional outburst and "end up on the floor crying." I reflected his fears about having inconsolable grief and sadness. After some thought and exploration, Eric agreed. He went on to speak about being "put down" at work recently for having angry feelings toward some disappointments with his coworkers. He quickly added that his parents acted the same way when he would feel sad or hurt. In hearing this, I speculated that his transference was speaking about his own fears of being criticized by me were he to express his anger and disappointment toward me for our relationship's ending. In the next-to-last session, Eric's intellectualization defenses were back intact, as he commented that switching therapists was "a bother, but not a big bother." He added later that he is "put off" by those who appear to have their emotions "in order and well understood."

Eric missed the first scheduled termination session. He apologized for the missed session, noting that he had been more absent-minded lately. He commented it was "a shame today is a split transition session," referring to the fact that he was going to meet his new therapist. Eric expressed some irritation about the transition to a new therapist but attributed a lot of his irritation to some recent events at work. Near the end of the session, he speculated about becoming overly dependent on medication.

Discussion

There are many interesting and fascinating elements to this case. Not all of them can be sufficiently addressed here; however, I highlight what I believe to be some of the most salient elements of the therapy related to my conceptualization and our therapeutic relationship. In my discussion, I speak in broad theoretical terms that incorporate ideas from psychoanalytic and psychodynamic approaches, with a particular emphasis on object relations and the interpersonal nature of our therapeutic relationship. I also address what I believe to be the mechanisms responsible for Eric's improvement and where additional work could have been done.

Eric was a self-critical, pessimistic young man who failed to see positive outcomes to life's experiences or interpersonal relationships, which has been commonly observed in psychoanalytic and psychodynamic descriptions of DPD (Bemporad, 1976; Berliner, 1966; Kahn, 1975; Jacobson, 1964; Kernberg 1970, 1984; Laughlin, 1956; Mendelson, 1967) as well as more contemporary descriptions (American Psychiatric Association, 1994). His self-criticism and derogatory remarks are consistent with the observations of many psychoanalytic theorists that the depressive personality has an excessively punitive superego. His early experiences of disappointment and frustration with his emotionally bland and unattuned parents did not allow Eric to establish a sense of identity and healthy self-regard, nor did these experiences allow him much opportunity to reconcile the inevitable ambivalence that is felt and must be dealt with when parents (to whom one is necessarily attached as a child) fail to meet every need of the child and foster the child's ability to overcome such disappointments. In fact, what Eric appeared to internalize about his inner world and desires was that he was to repress and avoid them for fear of what or how they may overtake him. More so, when he did attempt to master these experiences, it appeared as if he punished himself for natural expressions of desire and need. Consequently, when issues related to the phallic period of development emerged, his ambivalent feelings toward both his mother and father naturally led him to experience much confusion about his sexuality, particularly his sexual orientation. His excessive guilt, often filled with religious indignation, did not provide him with the opportunity to sort out these conflicted feelings so that he could know himself as a sexual person and what type of sexual partner he desired. Thus, when considering the psychosexual and developmental trajectory that Eric followed, it is possible to understand Eric's personality and subsequent conflicts. The following sections address these conflicts and problems more specifically by considering their evolution at each psychosexual, or developmental, stage.

Early Loss and Dependency

The idea that that early experiences of loss create an "infantile prototype" of depression that makes the individual vulnerable to later disappointments and letdowns by others has been understood since the time of Sigmund Freud (Abraham, 1924, 1927). Eric's experiences of loss may indeed have been such an "infantile prototype." His "mystery wound" and subsequent associations of hunger and irritation near termination appear to be a reactivation of a preverbal level of disappointment and frustration with his poorly attuned parents. Not only did Eric experience difficulty in describing his experience of sadness and anger in separating from me, he remained well guarded from further exploring these feelings, as observed by his passive avoidance of the initial termination session. This level of detachment functionally appeared to sustain his poorly established and relatively fragile sense of self, which had always been that of a chronic sufferer, and to protect him from very disappointing feelings.

An interesting dynamic representing this theme occurred when I explored Eric's expression of wanting love and affection from his parents. His immediate response to the exploration was his affirmation not to become a "parent hater." However, in defending his parents and minimizing his disappointments and letdowns, Eric's feelings of anger were clearly identifiable: His parents' recriminations were like "constant chattering" in the back of his mind, a likely projection of Eric's aggression toward his disappointing parents. In this sense, he had multiple self and other representations that were difficult to reconcile. He saw himself as someone who had longings and desires for his primary love relationships. These longings created a strong sense of attachment, which were associated with dependency needs. These dependency needs, which were not met adequately, led to a slightly different representation of himself—one of being damaged, depleted, and inherently unlovable and as one who deserved punishment for these needs. His parents were mostly represented as depriving and deficient. This interacted with other representations of his parents as being highly powerful and minimally able to meet his basic needs. (Even at the time of treatment, he lived with them and was dependent on them for basic needs of living and daily life).

Another theme of loss arose when Eric spoke about a time his father almost died from a serious illness. Eric's first wish during this illness was that his father would "just die." This wish was clearly associated with Eric's very angry feelings toward his father and the sense of power he had over Eric's expression of his sexuality, yet as he spoke about his desire for independence from his father's influence, Eric also feared that he would eventually be separated from his mother and extended family when he finally revealed his homosexual interests. As such, Eric suppressed his underlying aggression and disappointment toward his already disappointing father, probably so that no further negative affect would emerge and that he could retain his fragile, but long-desired, connectedness to his parents. Once again, this dynamic appeared to preserve his fragile sense of self by tenuously placating the narcissistic needs provided by his family. It also preserved substantial levels of ambivalence that could not be resolved.

Issues of loss and grief are particularly salient in the formation of gender identity. Fast (1984) and Butler (1995) highlighted how children early on must give up same-sex attachments and gender-inconsistent traits to establish their gender identity in cultures where stereotyped gender roles exist (such as in Western cultures). Butler suggested that children will unconsciously identify with the lost, same-sex parent and subsequently will project the renounced gender traits onto the opposite sex for such traits and desires to be acceptable. In this case, Eric unconsciously desired a positive, caring, same-sex attachment with his father; however, it was very difficult for him to establish a positive attachment to a male figure, given the representation he had of male relationships as experienced in his father. That is, it was very difficult to acknowledge or be aware of the desire for a positive male attachment when he could not draw on many real-world experiences of a close relationship with his father.

Consequently, Eric found himself fantasizing often about being with men in a loving and caring way.

As alluded to earlier, the termination session with Eric was highly suggestive of his feelings of anger and disappointment toward caring objects (i.e., myself). Not only did he miss the first termination session, he also described the session as a "split transition" session. This peculiar phrase impressed upon me of the subjective reality of termination for Eric—there were feelings of disappointment and anger toward me, an individual who also was caring and accepting of him. But now, Eric had little capacity to integrate his emotional reactions of loss toward me (a frustrating object) with awareness of the support of I had been able to provide him throughout therapy (a gratifying object).

Self-Regulation

Eric most certainly demonstrated behavior consistent with very high interpersonal standards and values. His rigidity was evident when, early in the course of therapy, he spoke of working by a script with the hope of being an "ideal psychotherapy patient," which would attain my full acceptance. Despite his relatively high degree of distress, Eric could not allow himself to appear needy or weak. As such, his "selfish and dirty" feelings were associated with a loss of control, which was forbidden. If Eric were to express such feelings, he expected he would be losing the very thing he longed for. At times, when Eric became aware of these longings, his neediness became associated with anger. For example, Eric became irritated when he was asked about a prior session in which he spoke of his need to be loved by his parents. Eric could not integrate the idea that he had desires for love from his parents that have all too often been associated with disappointment. Later in the session, Eric revealed fantasies he had been having about oral sex and how in those fantasies, he was in control of the situation and had the potential to inflict harm. Abraham (1927) reported similar associations in his work with characterologically depressed patients. He wrote that oral sex fantasies are precursors to fantasies of destroying the depriving, but desired, object. In Eric's case, this fantasy emerged after awareness of his need for parental love, and it was (noncoincidentally) preceded by his resuming coffee consumption after he previously denied his need for oral-dependent relationships.

Eric's rigid standards were evident in other ways. His desire to repay his employer for covering the costs of medical treatment from an injury sustained at work and his following a customer out of his place of an employment to please his conscience are good examples of these kinds of standards. These situations also exemplify Eric's need not to appear imperfect or damaged, which seem to have arisen from his inner concerns about being rejected for appearing imperfect or damaged. Laughlin (1956) stated that the depressive personality's denial of neediness and his unspoken rage toward love objects are expressed through a reaction formation, or overcompensation. He wrote that the patient's rigidity and need to be perfect reinforces "control over his more concealed (unconscious) resentment of authority and actual hostility" (p. 405). Such hostility is described in modern conceptualizations of the depressive personality (American Psychiatric Association, 1994) and is supported in the research literature (Bagby, Schuller, Marshall, & Ryder, 2004; Huprich, 2000, 2003, 2005; Huprich, Porcerelli, Kamoo, Binienda, & Karana, 2007; Markowitz et al., 2005). In Eric's case, this seemed quite true.

Kernberg (1984) characterized the depressive character structure as a depressive-masochistic personality. He described these patients as having "high level character pathology," adding that the depressive-masochistic personality "has well-integrated ego identity, shows nonspecific manifestations of ego strength (good anxiety tolerance and impulse control), and has an excessively guilt-ridden but well-integrated moral conscience. [He] is able to establish well-differentiated object relations in depth" (p. 82). Both Kernberg (1984) and Laughlin (1956) wrote that the harsh superego and concealed aggression toward loved and needed objects are the sources of masochistic tendencies. In Eric's case, this again seemed quite true. By adapting such rigid standards and denying his neediness, Eric developed a style of life consisting of frequent disappointment and unhappiness. Unfortunately, this ongoing dynamic maintained Eric's sense of suffering and psychological inaccessibility throughout the course of therapy. This made ongoing therapy with Eric difficult, something Kernberg (1984) noted about working with patients who have a depressive-masochistic personality.

Certain masochistic and self-defeating tendencies were apparent in Eric's transference throughout therapy. His constant disavowal to me of feeling needy or weak yet persistently remaining dysphoric and pessimistic maintained his chronic expectation that men could not be accepting and supportive. His "commitment" to his misery suggested unconscious investment in this position as a means of protecting himself from feelings of deep vulnerability. In the course of therapy, Eric engaged in other, seemingly evident, self-defeating behavior. For example, he desired to have others see him as bizarre or "different." In heterosexual relationships, he inadvertently sabotaged positive outcomes, such as intentionally sharing his bisexuality with his girlfriend and wearing homosexually suggestive jewelry when speaking with potential girlfriends.

Sexual Identity Development

Eric's case clearly exemplifies the incomplete development of Eric's sexual identity and orientation as the result of issues in the pre-Oedipal and Oedipal time periods. Pre-Oedipal problems were evident in many of Eric's verbalizations about his awareness of his sexual desires, particularly when speaking with parental male figures. Eric not only feared that he would be alienated from his father if he knew about his sexual orientation, but he also feared his (and my) reactions to his homosexual tendencies, suggesting a strong negative transference to me as a rejecting father figure. For instance, in the session where Eric asked about my sexual orientation, Eric later revealed that he had fears that either I would reject or overwhelm him with what I would say about my sexuality. At work, Eric's Oedipal fantasies of destroying or being destroyed by his father were evident. When he was forced to play the role of the peacekeeper between other employees and his boss, Eric thought there would be a "bloody revolution" if he did not pacify the situation, yet he also acknowledged a perception of power over his boss in that he could "destroy" his boss's reputation by revealing intimate details about the boss. In other words, his fantasies of injury and destruction were once again directed toward another male authority figure.

Eric's relationship with his mother also seemed to play a role in his sexual identity development. Although she was not discussed much, Eric's mother seems to have had "an enviable amount of power" over him. Her characterological withdrawal from emotionally charged or upsetting situations seems to have left Eric with a sense that women are unavailable for comfort or help him in times of trouble. When this kind of unavailability was experienced as a child, it created in

Eric a sense that his mother had significant power to meet his emotional needs or to leave him alone and helpless. As Eric spoke about his current relationships with women, he found himself intimidated and fearful of them, particularly since they could leave him, triggering all kinds of thoughts about being unacceptable and inadequate and ultimately a feeling of helplessness.

There was also a masochistic element to Eric's sexuality and how he experienced sexual feelings. Like Freud (1924), Kernberg (1987) posited that unconscious sexual conflicts are related to masochistic behaviors. Specifically, "self-punitive behaviors [are] a reflection of unconscious prohibitions against Oedipal impulses" (p. 1009). He added that sexual satisfaction occurs only in the context of some symbolic suffering. This can be seen in the episode where Eric shared his bisexuality with his former girlfriend. In this case, he was dating a woman whom he cared about. Because he was in a relationship that he had longed for, it may have been that expressing his sexual desires for her stirred up too much anxiety about having a desire for a woman. Because the anxiety was too much, he felt the need unconsciously to share these ideas with her so that he could relieve the anxiety over his desire for her in a way that allowed the desire to be experienced more safely. However, sharing his bisexual desires was self-defeating and ultimately contributed to their breakup. Eric's masochistic experience of sexuality also was often seen in his discussions of his sexuality with me. Eric regularly criticized himself for his homosexual ideas and expected that at any point I could chastise him for such feelings.

In line with the ideas of Butler (1995), Fast (1984), and Tyson (1982), Hansell (1998) noted that male sexual identity development is, in part, a product of giving up one's conscious "homoerotic" longings for the same-sex parent. These longings include behaviors such as hugging, holding, touching, and general expressions of care by the father. It is also necessary for the young boy to renounce his feminine qualities. Giving up these longings and qualities are strongly encouraged in a heterosexual culture, in which sexual stereotypes play a strong influence on what a "man" or "woman" should be like. Thus, the young boy increases his identification with his father, to whom he has ambivalent feelings because of the repressed and disavowed homoerotic feelings. Hansell (1998) suggested that in the concrete mind of the young child, homoerotic and feminine qualities are completely divorced from male qualities. This is certainly evident in latency-aged boys who strongly detest being anything like a girl. It is during adolescence that "feminine" qualities that were disavowed and consciously unwanted in males can become gratified through adolescent boys' identification with girls. It is also the case that homoerotic longings become more sublimated, such as through participation in team sports, or "hanging out with the guys."

These ideas seem to apply to Eric's sexual identity development and corresponding anxiety and self-criticism. Eric's experiences with his parents left him very hungry for affection, care, and support. His father was highly critical and emotionally unattuned to him, whereas his mother was emotionally unstable and inconsistently available for his emotional support. In these conditions, there were few experiences to draw on for a representation of a loving and caring relationship, and it was very dangerous to acknowledge one's desires for parents such as these. Consequently, fears about men's criticism and women's unavailability (and power over his emotional life) left him confused about his inner representation of his gender identity, not to mention the kind of person he wanted as a sexual partner. Since Eric's first therapist was a female, it was not surprising that Eric had difficulty establishing a relationship with her and feeling safe enough to discuss his sexual conflicts. When he was transferred to me, he unconsciously faced another set of challenges: Would I criticize him for his sexual conflicts? And would I understand and accept his sexually conflicted sense of himself?

Eric's fears about my accepting him defended him from deeper, positive, and more basic longings and feelings toward me. His question about my sexual orientation really was a question about whether he could share more basic longings and desires with me. When he was assured he could talk with me about these things without being judged and criticized, he experienced some degree of relief, leading him to speak in later sessions more openly about his sexuality. Indeed, his level of positive attachment to me was very strong (albeit more deeply in his unconscious), as evidenced by his fears of having deep sadness and emotional distress in our final session. In fact, missing the originally scheduled termination session was a way he could avoid facing losing his relationship with me.

Eric's questioning me about my sexual orientation deserves further comment. Here was a situation in which there was the opportunity for self-disclosure. As a general rule, if a patient asks me a personal question that impresses me in the context of our working together and at that moment is reasonable and of clinical interest, I will self-disclose very judiciously. In this case, I indicated that my orientation was heterosexual, but I immediately followed it up with the question of learning more about his interest in my sexuality. It is very often the case that personal questions like these relate to patients' manifest and latent ideas and fantasies about their therapists. Eric feared my judgment and his excitement toward me in learning about my sexual orientation. By bringing these fears to conscious awareness, Eric had the opportunity to recognize the power of his fears in suppressing his capacity to become happier and more self-accepting. He learned that talking about his sexuality does not have to be filled with shame or the anticipation of judgment from another person. For some patients, self-disclosure such as this would have been inappropriate, such as a patient who had made overt sexual advances toward me or whom I believe would have had manipulative intentions with the information I provided. Or, had Eric asked me this question in the first session with very little context to understand his anxieties about his sexual conflicts, I would have not self-disclosed. Yet in this case at this moment, my self-disclosure proved therapeutic in bringing many unconscious fears and fantasies to the forefront of our work and to Eric's capacity to think and learn about himself in new ways.

Unfortunately, our work together had to end, and Eric moved forward somewhat in overcoming his anxieties about his sexual orientation and generalized pessimism about being criticized and rejected by others. Ideally, Eric and I could have worked together indefinitely, more than one time per week, so that we could have evaluated and examined his transference to me and better understand what and whom he genuinely wanted in a sexual partner. In retrospect, I wish I had been more attentive to his desires for love, particularly as it played out in his positive transference to me, as I think this might have fostered greater self-acceptance of his desires for both men and women. I cannot speculate whether Eric's sexual orientation was primarily heterosexual or homosexual. However, I do believe he would have achieved more clarity with greater time in treatment, and I hope that he was able to come to some resolution of these very troubling and distressing feelings.

My countertransference also provided me with some therapeutically useful information. I found Eric to be likable and looked forward to our sessions together; hence, I found myself interested and attuned to the many things he had to say. As our sessions progressed,

I found Eric to be somewhat frustrating, given his strong identification with his suffering and conflict. Eric had much difficulty seeing things differently, which spoke to the power of his masochistic tendencies for defining his sense of self. I suspect others, too, had similar reactions. Although Eric seemed likable enough, as one got to know him, it was clear that he was a chronically unhappy person who had intense internal conflict. Eric's interest in my sexual orientation elicited some anxiety. This was the first patient who had ever asked me such a personal question, and as a relatively new therapist I had little experience to draw on. In some ways, it felt a bit intrusive, yet I also experienced the question as one that came from a genuinely conflicted person who so much wanted to relate with another human being in anything but a superficial way. It also brought to my attention the irrational fantasies I had about sharing my sexual orientation with another male who may have a sexual interest in me. Facing these fantasies and irrational worries directly allowed me to become better attuned to my own inner experience, Eric's inner experience, and my capacity to speak with him about highly conflicted parts of himself with greater empathy, candor, and confidence that we could engage in this content. This case certainly confirmed my belief in the necessity of therapists being highly attuned to their inner world and of facing their inner conflicts directly and confirmed how self-examination fosters one's ability to work even more effectively with another person in his own self-examination and discovery.

Conclusions

My work with Eric lasted more than 1 year and involved 47 appointments. During that time, some progress was made in increasing Eric's awareness of his feelings of disappointment and aggression, which before then, were strongly disavowed. A psychodynamically oriented conceptualization of this case provided me with advantages that could not be found in the *DSM-IV* (1994) description. The dynamic approach provided an internally consistent, plausible explanation about Eric's personality development and his intrapersonal and interpersonal difficulties both in and out of the therapy session. This model allowed me to see how the unconscious "faulty metabolism" of his aggression (Kernberg, 1984) and masochism were reenacted in relationships and how the superego maintained Eric's chronic suffering and misery. By understanding these dynamics and being aware of their occurrences, I was much better equipped to treat Eric, more so than if I had focused on cognitive, behavioral, or trait-like elements that remained far removed from the motivational and affective elements of Eric's difficulties. Eric's former therapist was unsuccessful in utilizing a cognitive approach due to Eric's frequent intellectualization of his experiences. When such elements of affective exploration were pursued, they were seen to be dynamically complex and puzzling. As stated earlier, I believe this was a result of the maternal transference Eric experienced with this therapist.

There were many elements of Eric's treatment that I believe contributed to his progress. First and foremost, Eric's experience of a new relationship with me seemed to provide him with the experience base on which to evaluate his inner world and how it affected his relationship with others. This idea is based on the understanding that therapists are able to both participate in and to rise above patients' experiences of their lives and to offer a new level of understanding through interpretation. Patients receive the help of their therapist because there is an inherent tendency in them to achieve greater psychological health (e.g., Shane, 1995, as cited in Hansell, 1997). This is not to say that the "new relationship" was fully integrated. Hansell (1997) noted how resistance to change is a hallmark of neurotic conflict and that getting patients with psychological blinders on to see things outside of the standard range of psychic vision is a significant challenge, even in the most intensive of treatments (i.e., psychoanalysis). Hansell noted, however, that Weiss and Sampson (1986) believed that therapists who respond to their patients in emotionally responsive ways and in ways that are inconsistent with patients' expectations are therapeutic in and of themselves. More so, he suggested that when therapists immerse themselves into the world of their patients and knowingly respond in ways that are based on unconscious influences in both the patient and the therapist, therapeutic progress seems to be allowed to occur. Certainly, research on the robust and powerful effects of the therapeutic alliance and positive therapeutic outcomes across different models of therapy supports this idea (e.g., Norcross, 2002a).

I also believe that the standard therapeutic interventions of psychoanalytic and psychodynamic treatment contributed to Eric's progress. Examining Eric's attachment to his suffering and negativity ultimately challenged his sense of himself as weak and powerless over his feelings. It also unconsciously challenged him to consider abandoning his fantasies of ever receiving the kind of love from his parents he had hoped for, as well as the power he attributed to them, and to begin looking to others for more healthy and fulfilling types of love and support. Examining the defensive processes that maintained these dynamics (e.g., intellectualization, rationalization, projection, repression), helping Eric recognize and accept himself as one who needed love and not feel self-critical for having such feelings, and changing his representations of what others think of him all were significant components of my interventions with him.

Collectively, I believe all these interventions and components to Eric's treatment were helpful and therapeutic. I wonder still what's become of Eric. My hope and strongly held belief is that our work together made a difference in reducing his suffering and improving his life satisfaction in some small way. This is the intangible element of our clinical work that, when fully internalized, provides deep meaning, satisfaction, and gratification to the life's work we have chosen.

References

Ablon, J. S. & Jones, E. E. (1998). How expert clinicians' prototypes of an ideal treatment correlate with outcome in psychodynamic and cognitive-behavioral therapy. *Psychotherapy Research, 8,* 71–83.

Ablon, J. S. & Jones, E. E. (1999). Psychotherapy process in the National Institute of Mental Health treatment of depression collaborative research program. *Journal of Consulting and Clinical Psychology, 67,* 64–75.

Ablon, J. S. & Jones, E. E. (2002). Validity of controlled clinical trials of psychotherapy: Findings from the NIMH collaborative study of depression. *American Journal of Psychiatry, 159,* 775–782.

Ablon, J. S. & Jones, E. E. (2005). On analytic process. *Journal of the American Psychoanalytic Association, 53,* 541–568.

Ablon, J. S., Levy, R. A., & Katzenstein, T. (2006). Beyond brand names of psychotherapy: Identifying empirically supported change processes. *Psychotherapy: Theory, Research, Practice, Training, 43,* 216–231.

Abraham, K. (1921/1953). Contributions to the theory of the anal character. In *Selected Papers of Karl Abraham*, pp. 370–392. New York: Basic Books.

Abraham, K. (1924/1953). The influence of oral eroticism on character formation. In *Selected Papers of Karl Abraham*, pp. 393–406. New York: Basic Books.

Abraham, K. (1924). The influence of oral eroticism on character formation. In *Selected papers on psychoanalysis.* London: Hogarth Press.

Abraham, K. (1927). Psychoanalytic studies on character formation. In *Selected papers on psychoanalysis.* London: Hogarth Press.

Achenbach, T. M., Krukowski, R. A., Dumenci, L., & Ivanova, M. Y. (2005). Assessment of adult psychopathology: Meta-analyses and implications of cross-informant correlations. *Psychological Bulletin, 131,* 361–382.

Ackerman, S. J. & Hilsenroth, M. J. (2003). A review of therapist characteristics and techniques positively impacting the therapeutic alliance. *Clinical Psychology Review, 23,* 1–33.

Adler, G. (1985). *Borderline psychopathology and its treatment.* New York: Jason Aronson.

Ainsworth, M. D. S., Blehar, M. C., Waters, E., & Wall, S. (1978). *Patterns of attachment: Psychological study of the Strange Situation.* Hillsdale, NJ: Erlbaum.

Akiskal, H. S., Bitar, A. H., Puzantian, V. R., Rosenthal, T. L., & Walker, P. W. (1978). The nosological status of neurotic depression: A prospective 3-4 year follow-up examination in the light of the primary-secondary and the unipolar-bipolar dichotomies. *Archives of General Psychiatry, 35,* 756–766.

Alexander, F. (1956). *Psychoanalysis and psychotherapy.* New York: Norton.

American Psychiatric Association (1980). *Diagnostic and statistical manual of mental disorders* (3rd ed.). Washington, DC: Author.

American Psychiatric Association (1987). *Diagnostic and statistical manual of mental disorders* (3rd ed., revised). Washington, DC: Author.

American Psychiatric Association (1994). *Diagnostic and statistical manual of mental disorders* (4th ed.). Washington, DC: Author.

American Psychiatric Association (2001). *Diagnostic and statistical manual of mental* disorders (4th ed., text revision). Washington, DC: Author.

Andersen, S. M. & Baum, A. (1994). Transference in interpersonal relations: Inferences and affect based on significant other representations. *Journal of Personality, 62,* 459–497.

Andersen, S. M. & Cole, S. W. (1990). "Do I know you?": The role of significant others in general social perception. *Journal of Personality and Social Psychology, 59,* 384–399.

Anderson, E. M. & Lambert, M. J. (1995). Short-term dynamically oriented psychotherapy: A review and meta-analysis. *Clinical Psychology Review, 15,* 503–514.

Anthony, M. M., Ledley, D. R., & Heimberg R. G. (2005). *Improving outcomes and preventing relapse in cognitive-behavioral therapy.* New York: Guilford.

Arlow, J. (1969). Unconscious fantasy and disturbances of conscious experience. *Psychoanalytic Quarterly, 38,* 1–27.

Arlow, J. & Brenner, C. (1964). *Psychoanalytic concepts and the structural theory.* New York: International Universities Press.

Atkinson, R. C. & Shiffrin, R. N. (1968). Human memory: A proposed system and its control processes. In K. W. Spence & J. T. Spence (Eds.), *The psychology of learning and motivation* (Vol. 2). New York: Academic Press.

Atwood, G. E. & Stolorow, R. D. (1984). *Structures of subjectivity: Explorations in psychoanalytic phenomenology.* Hillsdale, NJ: Analytic Press.

Azim, H. F., Piper, W. E., Segal, P. M., Nixon, G. W. H., & Duncan, S. (1991). The Quality of Object Relations Scale. *Bulletin of the Menninger Clinic, 55,* 323–343.

Bacal, H. A. (1985). Optimal responsiveness and the therapeutic process. In A. Goldberg (Ed.), *Progress in Self Psychology*, Vol. 1, pp. 202–227. New York: Guilford.

Bacal, H. A. & Newman, K. M. (1990). *Theories of object relations: Bridges to self psychology.* New York: Columbia University Press.

Baddeley, A. (1992, January 31). Working memory. *Science, 255,* 556–559.

Bagby, R. M., Schuller, D. R., Marshall, M. B., & Ryder, A. G. (2004). Depressive personality disorder: Rates of comorbidity and personality disorders and relations to the five factor model of personality. *Journal of Personality Disorders, 18,* 542–554.

Balint, M. (1968). *The basic fault.* London: Tavistock.

Barber, J. P. & Crits-Christoph, P. (1993). Advances in measures of psychodynamic formulations. *Journal of Consulting and Clinical Psychology, 61,* 574–585.

Barber, J. P., Morse, J. Q., Krakauer, I. D., Chittams, J., & Crits-Christoph, P. (1997). Change in obsessive compulsive and avoidant personality disorders following time limited supportive expressive therapy. *Psychotherapy, 34,* 133–143.

Barlow, D. H., Levitt, J. T., & Bufka, L. F. (1999). The dissemination of empirically supported treatments: A view to the future. *Behavior Research and Therapy, 37* (Supplement 1), 147–162.

Bartholomew, K. & Horowitz, L. M. (1991). Attachment styles among young adults: A test of a model. *Journal of Personality and Social Psychology, 61,* 226–244.

Bartholomew, K., Kwong, M. J., & Hart, S. D. (2001). Attachment. In W. J. Livesley (Ed.), *Handbook of personality disorders*, pp. 197–227. New York: Guilford.

Baumann, B. D., Hilsenroth, M. J., Ackerman, S. J., Baity, M. R., Smily, C. L., Smith, S. R. et al. (2001). The capacity for dynamic process scale: An examination of reliability, validity, and relation to therapeutic alliance. *Psychotherapy Research, 11,* 275–294.

Beck, A. T. (1976). *Cognitive therapy and the emotional disorders.* New York: International Universities Press.

Beck, A. T., Freeman, A., Davis, D. D., & Associates (2004). *Cognitive therapy of personality disorders* (2nd ed.). New York: Guilford Press.

Bell, M. D. (1995). *Bell Object Relations and Reality Testing Inventory.* Los Angeles, CA: Western Psychological Services.

Bellak, L. & Goldsmith, L. A. (Eds.). (1984). *The broad scope of ego function assessment.* New York: Wiley.

Bemporad, J. R. (1976). Psychotherapy of the depressive character. *Journal of the American Academy of Psychoanalysis, 4,* 347–372.

Benjamin, J. (1988). *The bonds of love: Psychoanalysis, feminism, and the problem of domination.* New York: Pantheon.

Benjamin, J. (1992). Discussion of Judith Jordan's "The relational self." *Contemporary Psychotherapy Review, 7,* 82–96.

Benjamin, J. (1995). *Like subjects, love objects.* New Haven, CT: Yale University Press.

Bergin, A. E. & Lambert, M. J. (1978). The evaluation of outcomes in psychotherapy. In S. L. Garfield & A. E. Bergin (Eds.), *Handbook of psychotherapy and behavior change* (2nd ed.), pp. 139–189. New York: Wiley.

Berliner, B. (1958). The role of object relations in moral masochism. *Psychoanalytic Quarterly, 27,* 38–56.

Berliner, B. (1966). Psychodynamics of the depressive character. *Psychodynamic Forum, 1,* 244–251.

Beutler, L. E. & Harwood, T. M. (2002). What is and can be attributed to the therapeutic relationship? *Journal of Contemporary Psychotherapy, 32,* 25–33.

Binder, J. L., Strupp, H. H., & Rock, D. L. (1992). A proposal for improving the psychoanalytic theory of technique. In J. W. Barron, M. N. Eagle, & D. L. Wolitsky (Eds.), Interface of psychoanalysis and psychology, pp. 605–626. Washington, DC: American Psychological Association.

Blatt, S. J. (1974). Levels of object representation in anaclitic and introjective depression. *Psychoanalytic Study of the Child, 29,* 107–157.

Blatt, S. J. (1992). The differential effect of psychotherapy and psychoanalysis with anaclitic and introjective patients: The Menninger psychotherapy research project revisited. *Journal of Personality Assessment, 40,* 691–724.

Blatt, S. J., Auerbach, J. S., Zuroff, D. C., & Shahar, G. (2006). Evaluating efficacy, effectiveness, and mutative factors in psychodynamic psychotherapies. In *PDM* Task Force, *Psychodynamic diagnostic manual,* pp. 537–572. Silver Spring, MD: Alliance of Psychoanalytic Organizations.

Blatt, S. J., Brenneis, C. B., Schimek, J. G., & Glick, M. (1976). Normal development and psychopathological impairment of the concept of the object on the Rorschach. *Journal of Abn ormal Psychology, 85,* 364–373.

Blatt, S. J., Chevron, E. S., Quinlan, D. M., Schaffer, C. E., & Wein, S. (1988). *The assessment of qualitative and structural dimensions of object representations* (Rev. ed.). Unpublished manuscript, Yale University, New Haven, CT.

Blatt, S. J., Chevron, E. S., Quinlan, D. M., Schaffer, C. E., & Wein, S. (1992). *The assessment of qualitative and structural dimensions of object representations.* Unpublished manuscript, Yale University, New Haven, CT.

Blatt, S. J., Chevron, E. S., Quinlan, D. M., & Wein, S. (1981). *The assessment of qualitative and structural dimensions of object representations* (Rev. ed.). Unpublished manuscript, Yale University School of Medicine, New Haven, CT.

Blatt, S. J., D'Affliti, J. P., & Quinlan, D. M. (1976). Experiences of depression in normal young adults. *Journal of Abnormal Psychology, 85,* 383–389.

Blatt, S. J. & Shichman, S. (1983). Two primary configurations of psychopathology. *Psychoanalysis and Contemporary Thought, 6,* 187–254.

Blatt, S. J., Wein, S. J., Chevron, E. S., & Quinlan, D. M. (1979). Parental representations and depression in normal young adults. *Journal of Abnormal Psychology, 88,* 388–397.

Bond, M. (2004). Empirical studies of defense style: Relationships with psychopathology and change. *Harvard Review of Psychiatry, 12,* 263–278.

Bond, M., Perry, J. C., Gautier, M., Goldenberg, M., Oppenheimer, J., & Simand, J. (1989). Validating the self-report of defense styles. *Journal of Personality Disorders, 3,* 101–112.

Bornstein, R. F. (1988). Psychoanalysis in the undergraduate curriculum: The treatment of psychoanalytic theory in abnormal psychology texts. *Psychoanalytic Psychology, 5,* 83–93.

Bornstein, R. F. (1998). Implicit and self-attributed dependency strivings: Differential relationships to laboratory and field measures of help-seeking. *Journal of Personality and Social Psychology, 75,* 779–787.

Bornstein, R. F. (2001). The impending death of psychoanalysis. *Psychoanalytic Psychology, 18,* 2–20.

Bornstein, R. F. (2002a). A process dissociation approach to objective-projective test score interrelationships. *Journal of Personality Assessment, 78,* 47–68.

Bornstein, R. F. (2002b). The impending death of psychoanalysis: From destructive obfuscation to constructive dialogue. *Psychoanalytic Psychology, 19,* 580–590.

Bornstein, R. F. (2005). Reconnecting psychoanalysis to mainstream psychology. *Psychoanalytic Psychology, 22,* 323–340.

Bornstein, R. F. (2006). A Freudian construct lost and reclaimed: The psychodynamics of personality pathology. *Psychoanalytic Psychology, 23,* 339–353.

Bornstein, R. F. (2007). From surface to depth: Diagnosis and assessment in personality pathology. *Clinical Psychology: Science and Practice, 14,* 99–102.

Bornstein, R. F. & Masling, J. M. (1998a). *Empirical perspectives on the psychoanalytic unconscious.* Washington, DC: American Psychological Association.

Bornstein, R. F. & Masling, J. M. (1998b). *Empirical perspectives on the therapeutic hour.* Washington, DC: American Psychological Association.

Bornstein, R. F. & Masling, J. M. (2002). *The psychodynamics of gender and gender role.* Washington, DC: American Psychological Association.

Bower, G. H., & Glass, A. L. (1976). Structural units and the redintegrative power of picture fragments. *Journal of Experimental Psychology: Human Learning and Memory, 2,* 456–466.

Bowlby, J. (1973). *Attachment and loss: Volume. 2. Separation*. New York: Basic Books.

Bowlby, J. (1977). The making and breaking of affectional bonds. *British Journal of Psychiatry, 130,* 201–210.

Bowlby, J. (1980). *Attachment and loss, Volume III: Loss: sadness and depression*. New York: Harper Collins/Basic Books.

Bowlby, J. (1988). *A secure base*. New York: Basic Books.

Bradley, B. P., Mogg, I., & Millar, N. (1996). Implicit memory bias in clinical and non-clinical depression. *Behavior Research and Therapy, 34,* 865–879.

Bradley, B. P., Mogg, I., & Williams, R. (1994). Implicit and explicit memory for emotional information in non-clinical subjects. *Behavior Therapy and Research, 32,* 65–78.

Bradley, B. P., Mogg, I., & Williams, R. (1995). Implicit and explicit memory for emotion-congruent information in depression and anxiety. *Behavior Therapy and Research, 33,* 755–770.

Brakel, L. A. W. (2002). Phantasy and wish: A proper function account for human arational primary process mediated mentation. *Australian Journal of Philosophy, 80,* 1–16.

Brennan, K. A., Clark, C. L., & Shaver, P. R. (1998). Self-report measurement of adult attachment: An integrative overview. In J. A. Simpson & W. S. Rholes (Eds.), *Attachment theory and close relationships*, pp. 46–76. New York: Guilford Press.

Brenner, C. (1973). An elementary textbook of psychoanalysis. New York: International University Press.

Brenner, C. (1982). *The mind in conflict*. New York: International Universities Press.

Bucci, W. (1993). The development of emotional meaning in free association. In J. Gedo & A. Wilson (Eds.), *Hierarchical conceptions in psychoanalysis*, pp. 3–47. New York: Guilford Press.

Bucci, W. (1995). The power of the narrative: A multiple code account. In J. Pennebaker (Ed.), *Emotion, disclosure, and health*, pp. 93–122. Washington, DC: American Psychological Association.

Bucci, W. (1997). *Psychoanalysis and cognitive neuroscience: A multiple code theory*. New York: Guilford.

Bucci, W. (2000). The need for a "psychoanalytic psychology" in the cognitive science field. *Psychoanalytic Psychology, 17,* 203–224.

Bucci, W. & Miller, N. (1993). Primary process analogue: The referential activity (RA) measure. In N. Miller, L. Luborsky, J. Barber, & J. Docherty (Eds.), *Psychodynamic treatment research*, pp. 387–406. New York: Basic Books.

Buelow, G., McClain, M., & McIntosh, I. (1996). A new measure for an important construct: The Attachment and Object Relations Inventory. *Journal of Personality Assessment, 66,* 604–623.

Busch, F. (1994). Some ambiguities in the method of free association and their implications for technique. *Journal of the American Psychoanalytic Association, 42,* 363–384.

Butler, J. (1995). Melancholy gender-refused identification. *Psychoanalytic Dialogues,* 5, 165–180.

Carlson, V., Cicchetti, D., Barnett, D., & Braunwald, K. (1989). Disorganized/disoriented attachment relationships in maltreated infants. *Development & Psychopathology, 25,* 525–531.

Carson, R. C. (1997). Costly compromises: A critique of the Diagnostic and Statistical Manual of Mental Disorders. In S. Fisher & R. P. Greenberg (Eds.), *From placebo to panacea: Putting psychiatric drugs to the test,* pp. 98–114. New York: Wiley.

Caspi, A. & Moffitt, T. E. (2006). Gene-environment interactions in psychiatry: Joining forces with neuroscience. *Nature Reviews Neuroscience, 7,* 583–590.

Castonguay, L. J. & Beutler, L. E. (2006). Principles of therapeutic change: A task force on participants, relationships, and technique factors. *Journal of Clinical Psychology, 62,* 631–638.

Castonguay, L. G., Goldfried, M. R., Wiser, S., Raue, P. J., & Hayes, A. M. (1996). Predicting the effect of cognitive therapy for depression: A study of unique and common factors. *Journal of Consulting and Clinical Psychology, 64,* 497–504.

Chambless, D. L. & Peterman, M. (in press). A meta-analysis of cognitive therapy of generalized anxiety disorder and panic disorder: The second decade. In R. L. Leahy (Ed.), *New advances in cognitive therapy.* New York: Guilford.

Chambless, D. L., Sanderson, W. C., Shoham, V., Bennett Johnson, S., Pope, K. S., Crits-Cristoph, P. et al. (1996). An update on empirically validated therapies. *Clinical Psychologist, 49,* 5–18.

Chasseguet-Smirgel, J. (1988). *Female sexuality.* Ann Arbor: University of Michigan Press.

Clarkin, J., Caligor, E., Stern, B. L., & Kernberg, O. F. (2004). *The structured interview of personality organization.* Unpublished manuscript, Weill Medical College of Cornell University.

Cohen, J. (1988). *Statistical power analysis in the behavioral sciences* (2nd ed.). Hillsdale, NJ: Erlbaum.

Compton, A. (1995). Objects and relationships. In B. E. Moore & B. D. Fine (Eds.), *Psychoanalysis: The major concepts,* pp. 433–449. New Haven, CT: Yale University Press.

Collins, A. M., & Loftus, E. F. (1975). A spreading activation theory of semantic processing. *Psychological Review, 82,* 407–428.

Connolly, M. B., Crits-Christoph, P., Demorest, A., Azarian, K., Muenz, L., & Chittams, J. (1996). Varieties of transference patterns in psychotherapy. *Journal of Consulting and Clinical Psychology, 64,* 1213–1221.

Consumer Reports (1995). Mental health: Does therapy help? November, 734–739.

Coonerty, S., Diamond, D., Kaslow, N., & Blatt, S. J. (1987). *The Rorschach Separation–Individuation Scale.* Unpublished manuscript, Yale University at New Haven, CT.

Cooper, A. M. (1989). Concepts of therapeutic effectiveness in psychoanalysis: A historical review. *Psychoanalytic Inquiry, 9,* 4–25.

Cooper, A. M. & Michels, R. (1981). Book review, *American Psychiatric Association: Diagnostic and Statistical Manual of Mental Disorders,* 3rd ed. *American Journal of Psychiatry, 138,* 128–129.

Costa, P. T., Jr. & Widiger, T. A. (2002). *Personality disorders and the five-factor model of personality* (2nd ed.). Washington, DC: American Psychological Association.

Cramer, P. (1991). *The development of defense mechanisms: Theory, research, and assessment.* New York: Springer-Verlag.

Cramer, P. (2000). Defense mechanisms in psychology today: Further processes for adaptation. *American Psychologist, 55,* 637–646.

Crits-Christoph, P. (1992). The efficacy of brief dynamic psychotherapy: A meta-analysis. *American Journal of Psychiatry, 149,* 151–158.

Crits-Christoph, P. & Luborsky, L. (1990). Changes in CCRT pervasiveness during psychotherapy. In L. Luborsky & P. Crits-Christoph (Eds.), *Understanding transference: The Core Conflictual Relationship Theme method,* pp. 133–146. New York: Basic Books.

Crittenden P. M. (1988). Relationships at risk. In J. Belsky & T. Nezworski (Eds.), *Clinical implications of attachment,* pp. 136–174. Hillsdale, NJ: Erlbaum.

Dahlbender, R., Rudolf, G., & OPD Task Force (2006). Psychic structure and mental functioning: Current research on the reliable measurement and clinical validity of Operationalized Psychodynamic Diagnostics (OPD) System. In Alliance of Psychoanalytic Organizations (Ed.), *Psychodynamic Diagnostic Manual,* pp. 615–662. Silver Spring, MD: Author.

Davanloo, H. (1980). *Short-term dynamic psychotherapy.* New York: Aronson.

Davis, K. L., Panksepp, J., & Normansell, L. (2003). The Affective Neuroscience Personality Scales: Normative data and implications. *Neuro-Psychoanalysis, 5,* 57–70.

DeCasper, A. J., Lecanuet, J. P., Busnel, M. C., & Granier-Deferre, C. (1994). Fetal reactions to recurrent maternal speech. *Infant Behavior and Development, 17,* 159–164.

DeCasper, A. J. & Spence, M. J. (1988). Prenatal maternal speech influences newborns' perception of speech sounds. In S. Chess, A. Thomas, & M. Hertzig (Eds.), *Annual Progress in Child Psychiatry and Child Development,* pp. 5–25. Philadelphia, PA: Brunner/Mazel.

Dewald, P. A. (1996). The psychoanalytic psychotherapies. In E. Nersessian & R. G. Kopff, Jr. (Eds.), *Textbook of psychoanalysis*, pp. 455–483. Washington, DC: American Psychiatric Press.

DeWitt, K. N., Hartley, D. E., Rosenberg, S. E., Zilberg, N. J., & Wallerstein, R. S. (1991). Scales of psychological capacities: Development of an assessment approach. *Psychoanalysis and Contemporary Thought, 14*, 343–361.

Diamond, D., Blatt, S. J., Stayner, D., & Kaslow, N. (1991). *Self-other differentiation of object representation.* Unpublished manuscript. Yale University, New Haven, CT.

Diamond, D., Kaslow, N., Coonerty, S., & Blatt, S. J. (1990). Changes in separation–individuation and intersubjectivity in long-term treatment. *Psychoanalytic Psychology, 7*, 363–397.

Dollard, N. & Miller, N. (1950). *Personality and psychotherapy: An analysis in terms of learning, thinking, and culture.* New York: McGraw Hill.

Dymetryszyn, H., Bouchard, M. A., Bienvenu, J. P., de Carufel, F., & Gaston, L. (1997). Overall maturity of object relations as assessed by the McGill Object Relations Scale. *Bulletin of the Menninger Clinic, 61*, 44–72.

Eagle, M. (1987). The psychoanalytic and cognitive unconscious. In R. Stern (Ed.), *Theories of the unconsciousness and theories of the self*, pp. 155–189. Hillsdale, NJ: Analytic Press.

Eagle, M. N. (2000). A critical evaluation of current conceptions of transference and countertransference. *Psychoanalytic Psychology, 17*, 24–37.

Eissler, K. R. (1953). The effect of the structure on the ego on psychoanalytic technique. *Journal of the American Psychoanalytic Association, 1*, 104–143.

Elise, D. (1997). Primary femininity, bisexuality, and the female ego ideal: A re-examination of female developmental theory. *Psychoanalytic Quarterly, 66*, 489–517.

Elise, D. (1998). Gender repertoire: Body, mind, and bisexuality. *Psychoanalytic Dialogues, 8*, 353–371.

Ellman, S. (2001). Modern revisions of Freud's concept of transference. In D. E. Scharff (Ed.), *The psychoanalytic century: Freud's legacy for the future*, pp. 89–102. New York: Other Press.

Epstein, S. (1973). The self-concept revisited, or a theory of a theory. *American Psychologist, 28*, 404–416.

Epstein, S. (1980). The self-concept: A review and the proposal of an integrated theory of personality. In E. Staub (Ed.), *Personality: Basic issues and current research*, pp. 82–132. Englewood Cliffs, NJ: Prentice Hall.

Epstein, S. (1991). Cognitive-experiential self-theory: An integrative theory of personality. In R. Curtis (Ed.), *The relational self: Convergences in psychoanalysis and social psychology*, pp. 111–137. New York: Guilford Press.

Epstein, S. (1994). Integration of the cognitive and psychodynamic unconscious. *American Psychologist, 49,* 709–724.

Fairbairn, W. R. D. (1952). *An object relations theory of personality.* New York: Basic Books.

Fast, I. (1984). *Gender identity: A differentiation model.* Hillsdale, NJ: Analytic Press.

Fast, I. (1990). Aspects of early gender development: Toward a reformulation. *Psychoanalytic Psychology, 7,* 105–117.

Fenichel, O. (1941). *Problems of psychoanalytic technique.* Albany, NY: Psychoanalytic Quarterly.

Fenichel, O. (1945). *The psychoanalytic theory of neurosis.* New York: Norton.

Fisher, S. & Greenberg, R. P. (1996). *Freud scientifically reappraised: Testing the theories and therapy.* New York: Guilford.

Fonagy, P. (1999a). Memory and therapeutic action. *International Journal of Psychoanalysis, 80,* 215–223.

Fonagy, P. (1999b). Points of contact and divergence between psychoanalytic and attachment theories: Is psychoanalytic theory truly different? *Psychoanalytic Inquiry, 19,* 448–480.

Fonagy, P. (2006). Evidence-based psychodynamic psychotherapies. In *PDM* Task Force, *Psychodynamic diagnostic manual*, pp. 735–818. Silver Spring, MD: Alliance of Psychoanalytic Organizations.

Fonagy, P., Gergely, G., Jurist, E., & Target, M. (2002). *Affect regulation, mentalizaiton and the development of the self.* New York: Other Press.

Fonagy, P., Leigh, T., Steel, M., Steele, H., Kennedy, R., Mattoon, G., et al. (1996). The relation of attachment status, psychiatric classification, and response to psychotherapy. *Journal of Consulting and Clinical Psychology, 64,* 22–31.

Fonagy, P., Stein, H., Allen, J., & Fultz, J. (2003). *The relationship of mentalization and childhood and adolescent adversity to adult functioning.* Paper presented at the Biennial Meeting of the Society for Research in Child Development, Tampa, FL.

Fonagy, P. & Target, M. (1996). Playing with reality: I. Theory of mind and normal development of psychic reality. *International Journal of Psychoanalysis, 77,* 217–233.

Fonagy, P. & Target, M. (1997). Attachment and reflective function: Their role in self-organization. *Development and Psychopathology, 9,* 679–700.

Fonagy, P. & Target, M. (2006). The mentalization-focused approach to self pathology. *Journal of Personality Disorders, 20,* 544–576.

Foster, R. P. (1996). What is a multicultural perspective for psychoanalysis? In R. P. Foster, M. Moskowitz, & R. A. Javier (Eds.), *Reaching across boundaries of culture and class: Widening the scope of psychotherapy,* pp. 3–19. Northvale, NJ: Jason Aronson.

Foster, R. P., Moskowitz, M. & Javier, R. A. (Eds.) (1996). *Reaching across boundaries of culture and class: Widening the scope of psychotherapy.* Northvale, NJ: Jason Aronson.

Frances, A. (1980). The DSM-III personality disorders section: A commentary. *American Journal of Psychiatry, 137,* 1050–1054.

Frances, A. & Cooper, A. M. (1981). Descriptive and dynamic psychiatry: A perspective of DSM-III. *American Journal of Psychiatry, 138,* 1198–1202.

Frank, G. (2000). The status of psychoanalytic theory today. *Psychoanalytic Psychology, 17,* 174–179.

Frayn, D. H. (1992). Assessment factors associated with premature psychotherapy termination. *American Journal of Psychotherapy, 46,* 250–261.

Frederickson, J. (1999). *Psychodynamic psychotherapy.* Philadelphia, PA: Brunner/Mazel.

Freedman, N., Hoffenberg, J. D., Vorus, N., & Frosch, A. (1999). The effectiveness of psychoanalytic psychotherapy: the role of treatment duration, frequency of sessions and the therapeutic relationship. *Journal of Personality Assessment, 47,* 741–772.

Freud, A. (1936). *The ego and mechanisms of defense.* London: Hogarth.

Freud, A. (1936/1966). The ego and mechanisms of defense. In *The Writings of Anna Freud Vol. 2* (Rev. Ed.). New York: International Universities Press.

Freud, A. (1963). The concept of developmental lines. *Psychoanalytic Study of the Child, 18,* 245–265.

Freud, A. (1965). *Normality and pathology of childhood.* New York: International Universities Press.

Freud, S. (1896a). Heredity and the aetiology of the neuroses. *Standard Edition, 3,* 141–156.

Freud, S. (1896b). Further remarks on the neuropsychoses of defence. *Standard Edition, 3,* 157-185.

Freud, S. (1898). Sexuality in the aetiology of the neuroses. *Standard Edition, 3,* 259–285.

Freud, S. (1900). The interpretation of dreams. *Standard Edition, 4,* 5.

Freud, S. (1905). Three essays on the theory of sexuality. *Standard Edition, 7,* 135–243.

Freud, S. (1906). My views on the part played by sexuality in the aetiology of the neuroses. *Standard Edition, 7,* 269–279.

Freud, S. (1908). Character and anal eroticism. *Standard Edition, 9,* 167–175.

Freud, S. (1913). On beginning the treatment. *Standard Edition, 12,* 123–144.

Freud, S. (1915a). Observations on transference love. *Standard Edition, 12,* 159–171.

Freud, S. (1915b). The unconscious. *Standard Edition, 14,* 159–216.

Freud, S. (1916–1917). Introductory lectures on psychoanalysis. *Standard Edition, 15, 16,* 13–496.

Freud, S. (1917a). Mourning and melancholia. *Standard Edition, 14,* 237–258.

Freud, S. (1917b). On transformations of instinct as exemplified in anal eroticism. *Standard Edition, 17,* 125–133.

Freud, S. (1920). Beyond the pleasure principle. *Standard Edition, 18,* 7–64.

Freud, S. (1923a). The ego and id. *Standard Edition, 19,* 12–66.

Freud, S. (1923b). The infantile genital organization of the libido: An interpolation into the theory of sexuality. *Standard Edition, 19,* 139–145.

Freud, S. (1924). *The economic problem of masochism* (Standard Ed., Vol. 19). London: Hogarth Press.

Freud, S. (1931). Libidinal types. *Standard Edition, 21,* 215–220.

Freud, S. (1940). An outline of psychoanalysis. *Standard Edition, 23,* 144–207.

Freud, S. (1953a). Project for a scientific psychology. In J. Strachey (Ed. and Trans.), *The standard edition of the complete psychological works of Sigmund Freud* (Vol. 1), pp. 295–301. London: Hogarth Press. (Original work published 1895)

Freud, S. (1953b). The interpretation of dreams. In J. Strachey (Ed. and Trans.), *The standard edition of the complete psychological works of Sigmund Freud* (Vol. 4), pp. 1–627. London: Hogarth Press. (Original work published 1900)

Freud, S. (1964). Analysis terminable and interminable. In J. Strachey (Ed. and Trans.), *The standard edition of the complete psychological works of Sigmund Freud* (Vol. 23), pp. 216–253. London: Hogarth Press. (Original work published 1940)

Fried, D., Crits-Christoph, P., & Luborsky, L. (1992). The first empirical demonstration of transference in psychotherapy. *Journal of Nervous and Mental Disease, 180,* 326–331.

Gabbard, G. O. (1989). Two subtypes of narcissistic personality disorder. *Bulletin of the Menninger Clinic, 53,* 527–532.

Gabbard, G. O. (1999). *Psychodynamic psychiatry in clinical practice* (3rd ed.). Washington, DC: American Psychiatric Press.

Gabbard, G. O. (2000). *Psychodynamic psychotherapy in clinical practice* (3rd ed.). Washington, DC: American Psychiatric Press.

Gabbard, G. O. (2004). *Long-term psychodynamic psychotherapy.* Washington, DC: American Psychiatric Publishing Incorporated.

Gabbard, G. O. & Westen, D. (2003). Rethinking therapeutic action. *International Journal of Psychoanalysis, 84,* 823–841.

Galletly, C., Clark, C., McFarlane, A., & Weber, D. (2001). Working memory in posttraumatic stress disorder: A even-related potential study. *Journal of Traumatic Stress, 14,* 295–309.

Ganellen, R. J. (1996). *Integrating the Rorschach and the MMPI-2 in personality assessment.* Mahwah, NJ: Erlbaum.

Ganellen, R. J. (2007). Assessing normal and abnormal personality functioning: Strengths and weaknesses of self-report, observer, and performance based methods. *Journal of Personality Assessment, 89,* 30–40.

Gaston, L. (1990). The concept of the alliance and its role in psychotherapy: Theoretical and empirical considerations. *Psychotherapy, 27,* 143–153.

Gelso, C. J., Fassinger, R. E., Gomez, M. J., & Latts, M. G. (1995). Countertransference reactions to lesbian clients: The role of homophobia, counselor gender and countertransference management. *Journal of Counseling Psychology, 42,* 356–364.

George, C., Kaplan, N., & Main, M. (1985). *The adult attachment interview.* Unpublished manuscript. University of California at Berkeley, Department of Psychology.

Giesen-Bloo, J., van Dyck, R., Spinhoven, P., van Tilburg, W., Dirksen, C., van Asselt, T. et al. (2006). Outpatient psychotherapy for borderline personality disorder. *Archives of General Psychiatry, 63,* 649–659.

Gill, M. (1994). *Psychoanalysis in transition: A personal view.* Hillsdale, NJ: Analytic Press.

Gill, M. M. (1963). Topography and systems in psychoanalytic theory. *Psychological Issues, Monograph 10.* New York: International Universities Press.

Goisman, R. M., Rogers, M. P., Steketee, G. S., Warshaw, M. G., Cuneo, P. & Keller, M. B. (1993). Utilization of behavioral methods in a multicenter anxiety disorders study. *Journal of Clinical Psychiatry, 54,* 213–218.

Goisman, R. M., Warshaw, M. G., & Keller, M. B. (1999). Psychosocial treatment prescriptions for generalized anxiety disorder, panic disorder, and social phobia, 1991–1996. *American Journal of Psychiatry, 156,* 1819–1821.

Goldfried, M. R., Castonguay, L. G., Hayes, A. M., Drozde, J. F., & Shapiro, D. A. (1997). A comparative analysis of the therapeutic focus in cognitive-behavioral and psychodynamic-interpersonal sessions. *Journal of Consulting and Clinical Psychology, 65,* 740–748.

Goldfried, M. R., Newman, C. F., & Hayes, A. M. (1989). *The coding system of therapeutic focus.* Unpublished manuscript, State University of New York at Stony Brook.

Goldfried, M. R., Raue, P. J., & Castonguay, L. G. (1998). The therapeutic focus in significant sessions of master therapists: A comparison of cognitive-behavioral and psychodynamic-interpersonal interventions. *Journal of Consulting and Clinical Psychology, 66,* 803–810.

Goldstein, W. N. (1998). *A primer for beginning psychotherapy.* Bristol, PA: Brunnzer/Mazel.

Goldstein, W. N. & Anthony, R. N. (1988). The diagnosis of depression and the DSMs. *American Journal of Psychotherapy, 42,* 180–196.

Greenberg, J. (2001a). The analyst's participation: A new look. *Journal of the American Psychoanalytic Association, 49,* 359–381.

Greenberg, J. (2001b). Thinking, talking, playing: The peculiar goals of psychoanalysis. *Psychoanalytic Quarterly, 70,* 131–148.

Greenberg, J. R. (1986). Theoretical models and the analyst's neutrality. *Contemporary Psychoanalysis, 22,* 87–106.

Greenberg, J. R. & Mitchell, S. A. (1983). *Object relations in psychoanalytic theory.* Cambridge, MA: Harvard University Press.

Greenson, R. R. (1967). *The technique and practice of psychoanalysis.* New York: International Universities Press.

Grinker, R. R., Jr., Werble, B., & Drye, R. C. (1968). *The borderline syndrome: A behavioral study of ego functions.* New York: Basic Books.

Guntrip, H. (1961). *Personality structure and human interaction.* New York: International Universities Press.

Guntrip, H. (1969). *Schizoid phenomena, object relations and the self.* New York: International Universities Press.

Hansell, J. H. (1997). The interactive paradigm and a psychoanalytic paradox. *Psychoanalytic Quarterly, 66,* 470–488.

Hansell, J. H. (1998). Gender anxiety, gender melancholia, gender perversion. *Psychoanalytic Dialogues, 8,* 337–351.

Hardy, G. E., Barkham, M., Shapiro, S. A., Stiles, W. B., Rees, A., & Reynolds, S. (1995). Impact of Cluster C personality disorders on outcomes of contrasting brief psychotherapies for depression. *Journal of Consulting and Clinical Psychology, 63,* 997–1004.

Harlow, H. (1958). The nature of love. *American Journal of Psychology, 13,* 673–686.

Hartmann, H. (1958). *The ego and the problem of adaptation.* New York: International Universities Press.

Hayes, J. A. (1995). Countertransference in group psychotherapy: Waking a sleeping dog. *International Journal of Group Psychotherapy, 45,* 521–535.

Hayes, J. A., McCracken, J. E., McClanahan, M. K., Hill, C. E., Harp, J. S., & Carozzoni, P. (1998). Therapist perspectives on countertransference: Qualitative data in search of a theory. *Journal of Counseling Psychology, 45,* 468–482.

Hayes, J. A., Riker, J. R., & Ingram, K. M. (1997). Countertransference behavior and management in brief counseling: A field study. *Psychotherapy Research, 7,* 145–153.

Hayes, S. C., Follette, V. M., & Linehan, M. M. (2004). *Mindfulness and acceptance: Expanding the cognitive-behavioral tradition.* New York: Guilford Press.

Hayes, S. C. & Strosahl, K. D. (2004). *A practical guide to acceptance and commitment therapy.* New York: Springer-Verlag.

Hazan, C. & Shaver, P. (1987). Romantic love conceptualized as an attachment process. *Journal of Personality and Social Psychology, 52,* 511–521.

Helzer, J. E., Kraemer, H. C., & Krueger, R. F. (2006). The feasibility and need for dimensional psychiatric diagnosis. *Psychological Medicine, 36,* 1671–1680.

Herbert, J. (2003). The science and practice of empirically supported treatments. *Behavior Modification, 27,* 412–430.

Herzig, A. & Licht, J. (2006). Overview of empirical support for the DSM symptom-based approach to diagnostic classification. In Alliance of Psychoanalytic Organizations (Ed.), *Psychodynamic diagnostic manual (PDM),* pp. 663–6901. Silver Spring, MD: Alliance of Psychoanalytic Organizations.

Hirschfeld, R. M. A., Klerman, G. L., Gough, H. G., Barrett, J., Korchin, S. J., & Chodoff, P. (1977). A measure of interpersonal dependency. *Journal of Personality Assessment, 41,* 610–618.

Høglend, P. (1993a). Transference interpretations and long-term change after dynamic psychotherapy of brief to moderate length. *American Journal of Psychotherapy, 47,* 494–507.

Høglend, P. (1993b). Suitability for brief dynamic psychotherapy: Psychodynamic variables as predictors of outcome. *Acta Psychiatrica Scandinavica, 88,* 104–110.

Høglend, P., Amlo, S., Marble, A., Bogwald, K. P., Sørbye, Ø., Sjaastad, M. C. et al. (2006). Analysis of the patient–therapist relationship in dynamic psychotherapy: An experimental study of transference interpretations. *American Journal of Psychiatry, 163,* 1739–1746.

Holmes, J. (2002). All you need is cognitive behaviour therapy? *British Medical Journal, 324* (7332), 288–290; discussion 290–294.

Horowitz, M. (1987). *States of mind: Configurational analysis of individual psychology* (2nd ed.). New York: Plenum.

Horowitz, M. J. (1998). *Cognitive psychodynamics: From conflict to character.* New York: Wiley.

Horowitz, M. J., Gabbard, G. O., Allen, J. G., Frieswyk, S. H., Colson, D. B., Newsom, G. E. et al. (1996). *Borderline personality disorder: Tailoring psychotherapy to the patient.* Washington, DC: American Psychiatric Press.

Horvath, A. O. & Bedi, R. P. (2002). The alliance. In J. C. Norcross (Ed.), *Psychotherapy relationships that work*, pp. 37–69. New York: Oxford.

Horvath, A. O., Gaston, L., & Luborsky, L. (1993). The therapeutic alliance and its measures. In N. E. Miller, L. Luborsky, J. P. Barber, J. P. & Docherty (Eds.), *Psychodynamic treatment research: A handbook for clinical practice*, pp. 247–273. New York: Basic Books.

Horvath, A. O. & Greenberg, L. S. (Eds.) (1994). *The working alliance: Theory, research, practice.* New York: Wiley.

Horvath, A. O. & Luborsky, L. (1993). The role of the therapeutic alliance in psychotherapy. *Journal of Consulting and Clinical Psychology, 61,* 561–573.

Horvath, A. O. & Symonds, B. D. (1991). Relation between working alliance and outcome in psychotherapy: A meta-analysis. *Journal of Counseling Psychology, 38,* 139–149.

Hull, C. L. (1951). *Essentials of behavior.* New Haven, CT: Yale University Press.

Hunsley, J. & Bailey, J. M. (1999). The clinical utility of the Rorschach: Unfulfilled promises and an uncertain future. *Psychological Assessment, 11,* 266–277.

Huprich, S. K. (1998). The depressive personality disorder: Theoretical issues, clinical findings, and future research questions. *Clinical Psychology Review, 18,* 477–500.

Huprich, S. K. (2000). Describing depressive personality analogues and dysthymics on the NEO-Personality Inventory-Revised. *Journal of Clinical Psychology, 56,* 1521-1534.

Huprich, S. K. (2003). Testing facet-level predictions and construct validity of depressive personality disorder. *Journal of Personality Disorders, 17,* 219–232.

Huprich, S. K. (2004a). The evolution of cognitive therapy for personality disorders: Convergence in theories and therapies. A review of *Cognitive Therapy of Personality Disorders* (2nd ed.; A. T. Beck, A. Freeman, D. D. Davis, & Associates). *PsycCritiques, 49* (Supplement 2).

Huprich, S. K. (2004b). Psychodynamic conceptualization and treatment of suicidal patients. *Journal of Contemporary Psychotherapy, 34,* 23–39.

Huprich, S. K. (2005). Differentiating avoidant and depressive personalities. *Journal of Personality Disorders, 19,* 659–673.

Huprich, S. K. (Ed.) (2006). *Rorschach assessment of the personality disorders.* Mahwah, NJ: Erlbaum Publishers.

Huprich, S. K. (2008, in press). What should become of depressive personality disorder in DSM-V? *Harvard Review of Psychiatry.*

Huprich, S. K. & Bornstein, R. F. (2007). An overview of issues related to categorical and dimensional assessment of personality disorders. *Journal of Personality Assessment, 89,* 3–15.

Huprich, S. K. & Ganellen, R. J. (2006). The advantages of using the Rorschach to assess personality disorders. In S. K. Huprich (Ed.), *Rorschach Assessment of the Personality Disorders*, pp. 27–53. Mahwah, NJ: Erlbaum Publishers.

Huprich, S. K. & Greenberg, R. P. (2003). Contemporary advances in the assessment of object relations. *Clinical Psychology Review, 23,* 665–698.

Huprich, S. K. & Keaschuk, R. (2006). Psychodynamic psychotherapy. In F. Andrasik (Ed.), *Comprehensive Handbook of Personality and Psychopathology: Volume II: Adult Psychopathology* (M. Hersen & J. Thomas, Series Editors), pp. 469–486. New York: John Wiley & Sons.

Huprich, S. K., Porcerelli, J., Kamoo, R., Binienda, J., & Karana, D. (2007). Parental representations, object relations and their relationship to depressive personality disorder and dysthymia. *Personality and Individual Differences, 43,* 2171–2181.

Isay, R. A. (1986). The development of sexual identity in homosexual men. *Psychoanalytic Study of the Child, 41,* 467–489.

Ittleson, W. H. & Kilpatrick, F. P. (1951). Experiments in perception. *Scientific American, 185,* 50–55.

Jacobs, T. J. (1987). Countertransference enactments. In E. Slakter (Ed.), *Countertransference*, pp. 165–183. Lanham, MD: Jason Aronson.

Jacobs, T. J. (1991). *The use of the self: Countertransference and communication in the analytic situation.* Madison, CT: International University Press.

Jacobs, T. J. (1993). The inner experience of the analyst: Their contribution to the analytic process. *International Journal of Psychoanalysis, 74,* 7–14.

Jacobson, E. (1964). *The self and the object world.* New York: International Universities Press.

Jenkins, S. R. (2007). *A scoring handbook for the Thematic Apperception Test.* Mahwah, NJ: Erlbaum.

Jones, E. E. (1985). *Manual for the psychotherapy process Q-set.* Unpublished manuscript. University of California, Berkeley.

Jones, E. E. (2000). *Therapeutic action: A guide to psychoanalytic therapy.* Northvale, NJ: Jason Aronson.

Jones, E. E., Hall, S., & Parke, L. A. (1991). The process of change: The Berkeley Psychotherapy Research Group. In L. M. Beutler & M. Crago (Eds.), *Psychotherapy research: An international review of programmatic studies*, pp. 98–107. Washington, DC: American Psychological Association.

Jones, E. E. & Pulos, S. M. (1993). Comparing the process in psychodynamic and cognitive-behavioral therapies. *Journal of Consulting and Clinical Psychology, 61,* 306–316.

Kahn, E. (1975). The depressive character. *Folia Psychiatrica et Neurologica Japonica, 29,* 291–303.

Kandel, E. R. (1999). Biology and the future of psychoanalysis: A new intellectual framework for psychiatry revisited. *American Journal of Psychiatry, 156,* 505–524.

Kantrowitz, J. L. (1986). The role of the patient-analyst match in the outcome of psychoanalysis. *Annual of Psychoanalysis, 14,* 273–297.

Kantrowitz, J. L., Katz, A. L., Greenman, D. K., Morris, H., Paolitto, F., Sashin, J. et al. (1989). The patient-analyst match and the outcome of psychoanalysis: A pilot study. *Journal of the American Psychoanalytic Association, 37,* 893–919.

Kantrowitz, J. L., Katz, A. L., & Paolitto, F. (1990a). Follow-up of psychoanalysis five to ten years after termination: I. Stability of change. *Journal of the American Psychoanalytic Association, 38,* 471–496.

Kantrowitz, J. L., Katz, A. L., & Paolitto, F. (1990b). Follow-up of psychoanalysis five to ten years after termination: II. Development of the self-analytic function. *Journal of the American Psychoanalytic Association, 38,* 637–654.

Kantrowitz, J. L., Katz, A. L., & Paolitto, F. (1990c). Follow-up of psychoanalysis five to ten years after termination: III. The relation between the resolution of the transference and the patient-analyst match. *Journal of the American Psychoanalytic Association, 38,* 655–678.

Kantrowitz, J. L., Katz, A. L. Paolitto, F., Sashin, J., & Solomon, L. (1987a). Changes in the level and quality of object relationships in psychoanalysis: Follow-up of a longitudinal prospective study. *Journal of the American Psychoanalytic Association, 35,* 23–46.

Kantrowitz, J. L., Katz, A. L., Paolitto, F., Sashin, J., & Solomon, L. (1987b). The role of reality testing in psychoanalysis: Follow-up of 22 cases. *Journal of the American Psychoanalytic Association, 35,* 367–385.

Kantrowitz, J. L., Paolitto, F., Sashin, J., Solomon, L., & Katz, A. L. (1986). Affect availability, tolerance, complexity, and modulation in psychoanalysis: Follow-up of a longitudinal prospective study. *Journal of the American Psychoanalytic Association, 34,* 529–559.

Keithly, L. J., Samples, S. J., & Strupp, H. H. (1980). Patient motivation as a predictor of process and outcome in psychotherapy. *Psychotherapy and Psychosomatics, 33,* 87–97.

Kelly, F. D. (1996). *Object relations assessment in younger children.* Springfield, IL: Charles C. Thomas.

Kelly, F. D. (1997). *The assessment of object relations phenomena in adolescents: TAT and Rorschach measures.* Mahwah, NJ: Erlbaum.

Kernberg, O. F. (1970). A psychoanalytic classification of character pathology. *Journal of the American Psychoanalytic Association, 18,* 800–822.

Kernberg, O. F. (1973). Summary and conclusions of "psychotherapy and psychoanalysis, final report of the menninger foundation's psychotherapy research project." *International Journal of Psychiatry, 11,* 62–77.

Kernberg, O. F. (1975). *Borderline conditions and pathological narcissism.* New York: Jason Aronson.

Kernberg, O. F. (1983). Object relations theory and character analysis. *Journal of the American Psychoanalytic Association, 31,* 247–271.

Kernberg, O. F. (1984). *Severe personality disorders.* New Haven, CT: Yale University Press.

Kernberg, O. F. (1987). Clinical dimensions of masochism. *Journal of the American Psychoanalytic Association, 36,* 1005–1029.

Kernberg, O. F. (1991). Sadmomasochism, sexual excitement, and perversion. *Journal of the American Psychoanalytic Association, 39,* 333–362.

Kernberg, O. F. (1993). Convergences and divergences in contemporary psychoanalytic technique. *International Journal of Psychoanalysis, 74,* 659–673.

Kernberg, O. F. (2001). Convergences and divergences in contemporary psychoanalytic technique. *International Journal of Psychoanalysis, 74,* 659–673.

Kirk, S. A. & Kutchins, H. (1992). *The selling of DSM: The rhetoric of science in* psychiatry. New York: Aldine de Gruyter.

Klein, M. (1964). *Contributions to psychoanalysis,* 1921–1945. New York: McGraw Hill.

Klein, M. (1975). *Envy and gratitude and other works,* 1946–1963. New York: Delacorte Press.

Klerman, G. L., Endicott, J., & Spitzer, R. (1979). Neurotic depressions: A systemic analysis of multiple criteria and meanings. *American Journal of Psychiatry, 136,* 57–61.

Knight, R. P. (1945). The relationship of psychoanalysis to psychiatry. *American Journal of Psychiatry, 101,* 777–782.

Kohlberg, L. (1981). *The philosophy of moral development: Moral stages and the idea of justice: Essays on moral development,* Vol. 1. New York: Harper & Row.

Kohlenberg, R. J. & Tsai, M. (1991). *Functional analytic psychotherapy: Creating intense and curative therapeutic relationships.* New York: Plenum.

Kohut, H. & Wolf, E. S. (1978). The disorders of the self and their treatment: An outline. *International Journal of Psychoanalysis, 59,* 413–425.

Kohut, H. (1971). *The analysis of the self.* New York: International Universities Press.

Kohut, H. (1977). *The restoration of the self.* New York: International Universities Press.

Kopta, S. M., Howard, K. E., Lowry, J. L., & Beutler, L. E. (1994). Patterns of symptomatic recovery in time-unlimited psychotherapy. *Journal of Consulting and Clinical Psychology, 62,* 1009–1016.

Kraepelin, E. (1921). *Manic-depressive insanity and paranoia.* Edinburgh: E.S. Livingstone.

Kretschmer, E. (1925). *Physique and character.* New York: Harcourt & Brace.

Krueger, R. F. & Markon, K. E. (2006a). Reinterpreting comorbidity: A model based approach to understanding and classifying psychopathology. *Annual Review of Clinical Psychology, 2,* 111–133.

Krueger, R. F. & Markon, K. E. (2006b). Understanding psychopathology: Melding behavior genetics, personality, and quantitative psychology to develop an empirically based model. *Current Directions in Psychological Science 15,* 113–117.

Krueger, R. F. & Tackett, J. L. (2006). *Personality and psychopathology: Building bridges.* New York: Guilford.

Krupnick, J. L., Sotsky, S. M., Simmens, S., Moyer, J., Elkin, I., Watkins, J. et al. (1996). The role of the therapeutic alliance in psychotherapy and pharmacotherapy outcome: Findings in the National Institute of Mental Health Treatment of Depression Collaborative Research Program. *Journal of Consulting and Clinical Psychology, 64,* 532–539.

Kulish, N. & Holtzman, N. (2008). *A story of her own: The female Oedipus complex reexamined and renamed.* Northvale, NJ: Jason Aronson.

Kunda, Z. & Thagard, P. (1996). Forming impression from stereotypes, traits, and behaviors: A parallel-constraint-satisfaction theory. *Psychological Review, 103,* 284–308.

Lambert, M. J. & Barley, D. E. (2002). Research summary on the therapeutic relationship and psychotherapy outcome. In J. C. Norcross (Ed.), *Psychotherapy relationships that work,* pp. 17–36. New York: Oxford.

Lambert, M. J. & Bergin, A. E. (1994). The effectiveness of psychotherapy. In A. E. Bergin & S. L. Garfield (Eds.), *Handbook of psychotherapy and behavior change* (4th ed.), pp. 143–189. New York: Wiley.

Lambert, M. J. & Ogles, B. M. (2003). The efficacy and effectiveness of psychotherapy. In M. J. Lambert (Ed.), *Handbook of psychotherapy and behavior change* (5th ed.), pp. 157–212. New York: Wiley.

Laptook, R. S., Klein, D. N., & Dougherty, L. R. (2006). Ten-year stability of depressive personality disorder in depressed outpatients. *American Journal of Psychiatry, 162,* 865–871.

Latts, M. G. & Gelso, C. J. (1995). Countertransference behavior and management with survivors of sexual assault. *Psychotherapy, 32,* 405–415.

Laughlin, H. P. (1956). *The neuroses in clinical practice.* Philadelphia: W. B. Saunders.

LeDoux, J. (1989). Cognitive-emotional interactions in the brain. *Cognition and Emotion, 3,* 267–289.

LeDoux, J. (1995). Emotion: Clues from the brain. *Annual Review of Psychology, 46,* 209–235.

Leichsenring, F. (2006). Review of meta-analyses of outcome studies of psychodynamic therapy. In *PDM* Task Force, *Psychodynamic diagnostic manual,* pp. 819–837. Silver Spring, MD: Alliance of Psychoanalytic Organizations.

Leichsenring, F., Hiller, W., Weissberg, M., & Leibing, E. (2006). Cognitive-behavioral therapy and psychodynamic psychotherapy: Techniques, efficacy, and indications. *American Journal of Psychotherapy, 60,* 233–259.

Lerner, M. J., & Miller, D. T. (1978). Just world research and the attribution process: Looking back and ahead. *Psychological Bulletin, 85,* 1030–1051.

Lerner, P. M. (2005). Defense and its assessment: The Lerner Defense Scale. In R. F. Bornstein & J. M. Masling (Eds.), *Scoring the Rorschach: Seven validated systems,* pp. 237–269. Mahwah, NJ: Lawrence Erlbaum Associates.

Levenson, E. A. (1972). *The fallacy of understanding: An inquiry into the changing structure of psychoanalysis.* New York: Basic Books.

Levin, F. M. (1991). *Mapping the mind.* Madison, CT: International Universities Press.

Levin, F. M. (1993). The hierarchical developmental model: Neural control, natural language, and the recurrent organization of the brain. In A. Wilson & J. Gedo (Eds.), *Hierarchical concepts in psychoanalysis: Theory, research, and clinical practice,* pp. 153–169. New York: Guilford Press.

Levin, F. M. (1997). Integrating some mind and brain views of transference: The phenomena. *Journal of the American Psychoanalytic Association, 45,* 1121–1151.

Levin, F. M. (1998). The amygadala, hippocampus, and psychoanalysis. *Psyche: Zeitschrift fur Psychoanalyse und ihre Anwendungen, 52,* 1004–1013.

Levin, F. M. (2006). Recent findings in neuroscience and their relevance to psychoanalysis. *Psychoanalytic Quarterly, 75,* 1227–1244.

Levin, F. M. & Vuckovich, D. M. (1983). Psychoanalysis and the two cerebral hemispheres. *Annual of Psychoanalysis, 11,* 171–197.

Levy, K. N., Meehan, K. B., Kelly, K. M., Reynoso, J. S., Weber, M. Clarkin, J. et al. (2006). Change in attachment patterns and reflective functioning in a randomized control trial of transference-focused psychotherapy for borderline personality disorder. *Journal of Consulting and Clinical Psychology, 74,* 1027–1040.

Lewis, J. L. (1970). Semantic processing of unattended messages during dichotic listening. *Journal of Experimental Psychology, 85,* 225–228.

Lindon, J. A. (1994). Gratification and provision in psychoanalysis: Should we get rid of the "rule of abstinence?" *Psychoanalytic Dialogues, 4,* 549–582.

Linehan, M. M. (1993). *Cognitive-behavioral therapy of borderline personality disorder.* New York: Guilford.

Loewald, H. (1960). On the therapeutic action of psychoanalysis. *International Journal of Psychoanalysis, 41,* 16–33.

Loftus, E. F. (1991). Made in memory: Distortions in recollection after misleading information. In G. H. Bower (Ed.), *The psychology of learning and motivation* (Vol. 27), pp. 187–215. New York: Academic Press.

Loftus, E. F. (2003). Make believe memories. *American Psychologist, 58,* 867–873.

Luborsky, L. (1990). Theory-based research for understanding the process of dynamic psychotherapy. *Journal of Consulting and Clinical Psychology, 58,* 281–287.

Luborsky, L. (1996). Theories of cure in psychoanalytic psychotherapies and the evidence for them. *Psychoanalytic Inquiry, 16,* 257–264.

Luborsky, L. (2001). The meaning of empirically supported treatment research for psychoanalytic and other long-term therapies. *Psychoanalytic Dialogues, 11,* 583–604.

Luborsky, L. & Crits-Cristoph, P. (1990). *Understanding transference: The CCRT method.* New York: Basic Books.

Luborsky, L., Diguer, L., Luborsky, E., McLellan, A. T., Woody, G., & Alexander, L. (1993). Psychological health-sickness (PHS) as a predictor of outcomes in dynamic and other psychotherapies. *Journal of Consulting and Clinical Psychology, 61,* 542–548.

Luborsky, L., Mellon, J., Cohen, K. D., van Ravenswaay, P., Hole, A.V., Childress, A. R. et al. (1985). A verification of Freud's grandest hypothesis: The transference. *Clinical Psychological Review, 5,* 231–246.

Luborsky, L., Rosenthal, R., Diguer, L., Andrusyna, T. P., Levitt, J. T., Seeligman, D. A. et al. (2003). Are some psychotherapies much more effective than others? *Journal of Applied Psychoanalytic Studies, 5,* 455–460.

Luborsky, L., Singer, B., & Luborsky, L. (1975). Comparative studies in psychotherapy. *Archives of General Psychiatry, 32,* 995–1008.

Mahler, M., Pine, F., & Bergman, A. (1975). *The psychological birth of the human infant.* New York: Basic Books.

Main, M., Kaplan, N., & Cassiday, J. (1985). Security in infancy, childhood and adulthood: A move to the level of representation. *Monographs of the Society for Research in Child Development, 50,* 66–104.

Main, M. & Solomon, J. (1986). Discovery of an insecure-disorganized/disoriented attachment pattern: Procedures, findings, and implications for the classification of behavior. In T. Brazelton & M. Yogman (Eds.), *Affective development in infancy,* pp. 95–124. Norwood, NJ: Ablex.

Malan, D. H. (1976). *The frontier of brief psychotherapy.* New York: Plenum.

Marcus, E. R. (1999). Modern ego psychology. *Journal of the American Psychoanalytic Association, 47,* 843–871.

Markon, K. E., Krueger,R. F., & Watson, D. (2005). Delineating the structure of normal and abnormal personality: An integrated hierarchical approach. *Journal of Personality and Social Psychology, 88,* 139–157.

Markowitz, J. C., Skodol, A. E., Petkova, E., Xie, H., Cheng, J., Hellerstein, D. J. et al. (2005). Longitudinal comparison of depressive personality disorder and dysthymic disorder. *Comprehensive Psychiatry, 46,* 239–245.

Masling, J. M. & Bornstein, R. F. (1993). *Psychoanalytic perspectives on psychopathology.* Washington, DC: American Psychological Association.

Masling, J. M. & Bornstein, R. F. (1994). *Empirical perspectives on object relations theory.* Washington, DC: American Psychological Association.

Masling, J. M. & Bornstein, R. F. (1996). *Psychoanalytic perspectives on developmental psychology.* Washington, DC: American Psychological Association.

Masling, J. M., Rabie, L., & Blondheim, S. H. (1967). Obesity, level of aspiration, and Rorschach and TAT measures of oral dependence. *Journal of Consulting Psychology, 31*, 233–239.

McClelland, D. C., Koestner, R., & Weinberger, J. (1989). How do self-attributed and implicit motives differ? *Psychological Review, 96*, 690–702.

McDougall, J. (1995). *The many faces of Eros.* New York: Norton.

McGuire, W. (Ed.) (1974). *The Freud/Jung letters: The correspondence between Sigmund Freud and C. G. Jung* (R. Manheim & R. F. C. Hull, Trans.). Princeton, NJ: Princeton University Press.

McWilliams, N. (1994). *Psychoanalytic diagnosis.* New York: Guilford.

McWilliams, N. (1999). *Psychoanalytic case formulation.* New York: Guilford.

McWilliams, N. (2004). *Psychoanalytic psychotherapy: A practitioner's guide.* New York: Guilford.

Meissner, W. M. (2000). *Freud and psychoanalysis.* South Bend, IN: Notre Dame University Press.

Mendelson, M. (1967). Neurotic depressive reactions. In A. M. Freedman & S. I. Kaplan (Eds.), *Comprehensive textbook of psychiatry*, pp. 928-936. Baltimore, MD: Williams & Wilkins.

Menninger, K. (1958). *Theory of psychoanalytic technique.* New York: Basic Books.

Messer, S. (1986). Behavioral and psychoanalytic perspectives at therapeutic choice points. *American Psychologist, 41*, 1261–1272.

Messer, S. B. & McWilliams, N. (2007). Insight in psychodynamic therapy: Theory and assessment. In L. G. Castonguay & C. E. Hill (Eds.), *Insight in psychotherapy*, pp. 9–30. Washington, DC: American Psychological Association.

Messer, S. B. & Warren, C. S. (1995). *Models of brief psychodynamic therapy.* New York: Guilford.

Meyer, G. J. (1996). The Rorschach and MMPI: Toward a more scientific understanding of cross-method assessment. *Journal of Personality Assessment, 67*, 558–578.

Meyer, G. J., Finn, S. E., Eyde, L. D., Kay, G. G., Moreland, K. L., Dies, R. R. et al. (2001). Psychological testing and psychological assessment: A review of evidence and issues. *American Psychologist, 56*, 128–165.

Michels, R. (1986). Oedipus and insight. *Psychoanalytic Quarterly, 55,* 599–617.

Miller, T. J., McGlashan, T. H., Rosen, J. L., Cadenhead, K., Ventura, J., McFarlane, W. et al. (2003). Prodromal assessment with the structured interview for prodromal syndromes and the scale of prodromal symptoms: Predictive validity, interrater reliability, and training to reliability. *Schizophrenia Bulletin, 29,* 703–715.

Miller, W. R., Taylor, C. A., & West, J. C. (1980). Focused versus broad-spectrum behavior therapy for problem drinkers. *Journal of Consulting and Clinical Psychology, 48,* 590–601.

Mills, J. (2002). Reexamining the psychoanalytic corpse: From scientific psychology to philosophy. *Psychoanalytic Psychology, 19,* 552–558.

Milner, B., Corkin, S., & Teuber, H. L. (1968). Further analysis of the hippocampal amnesic syndrome: Fourteen year follow-up study of H.M. *Neuropsychologia, 6,* 215–234.

Milrod, B., Busch, F., Leon, A. C., Aronson, A., Roiphe, J., Rudden, M. et al. (2001). A pilot open trial of brief psychodynamic psychotherapy for panic disorder. *Journal of Psychotherapy Practice Research, 10,* 239–245.

Milrod, B., Leon, A. C., Busch, F., Rudden, M., Schwalberg, M., Clarkin, J. et al. (2007). A randomized controlled clinical trail of psychoanalytic psychotherapy for panic disorder. *American Journal of Psychiatry, 164,* 265–272.

Mitchell, S. A. & Black, M. J. (1995). *Freud and beyond: A history of modern psychoanalytic thought.* New York: Basic Books.

Morrison, C., Bradley, R., & Westen, D. (2003). The external validity of efficacy trials for depression and anxiety: A naturalistic study. *Psychology and Psychotherapy: Theory, Research, and Practice, 76,* 109–132.

Neisser, U. (1976). *Cognition and reality.* San Francisco: Freeman.

Nelson-Gray, R. O. (2003). Treatment utility of psychological assessment. *Psychological Assessment, 15,* 521–531.

Nilsson, A. (1993). Preliminary scoring schema, interrater and parallel test reliability of the PORT, the Perceptgenetic Object Relations Test. *Psykologi I Tillampning, 11,* 1–37.

Nilsson, A. (1995). Differentiation between patients with schizophrenia and borderline disorders in the Perceptgenetic Object-Relations Test (PORT). *British Journal of Medical Psychology, 68,* 287–309.

Norcross, J. C. (2002a). Empirically supported therapy relationships. In J. C. Norcross (Ed.), *Psychotherapy relationships that work,* pp. 3–16. New York: Oxford.

Norcross, J. C. (2002b). *Psychotherapy relationships that work.* New York: Oxford.

Norcross, J. C., Hedges, M., & Castle, P. H. (2002). Psychologists conducting psychotherapy in 2001: A study of the Division 29 membership. *Psychotherapy: Theory/Research/Practice/Training, 39,* 97–102.

Norman, H. F., Blacker, K. H., Oremland, J. D., & Barrett, W. G. (1976). The fate of the transference neurosis after termination of a satisfactory analysis. *Journal of the American Psychoanalytic Association, 24,* 471–498.

Novick, J. & Novick, K. K. (1996). *Fearful symmetry.* Northvale, NJ: Aronson.

Novick, J. & Novick, K. K. (2001). Two systems of self-regulation. *Journal of Psychoanalytic Social Work, 8,* 95–122.

Novick, J. & Novick, K. K. (2004). The superego and the two-system model. *Psychoanalytic Inquiry, 24,* 232–256.

Novick, K. K. & Novick, J. (1987). The essence of masochism. *Psychoanalytic Study of the Child, 42,* 353–384.

Novick, K. K. & Novick, J. (1998). An application of the concept of the therapeutic alliance to sadomasochistic pathology. *Journal of the American Psychoanalytic Association, 46,* 813–846.

Novick, K. K. & Novick, J. (2003). Two systems of self-regulation and the differential application of psychoanalytic technique. *American Journal of Psychoanalysis, 63,* 1–20.

Olds, D. (1994). Connectionism and psychoanalysis. *Journal of the American Psychoanalytic Association, 42,* 581–611.

Oltmanns, T. F. & Turkheimer, E. (2006). Perceptions of self and others regarding pathological personality traits. In R. F. Krueger & J. L. Tackett (Eds.), *Personality and psychopathology,* pp. 71–111. New York: Guilford.

Oremland, J. D., Blacker, K. H., & Norman, H. F. (1975). Incompleteness in "successful" psychoanalysis: A follow-up study. *Journal of the American Psychoanalytic Association, 23,* 819–844.

Orlinsky, D. & Howard, K. E. (1977). The therapist's experience of psychotherapy. In A. S. Gurman & A. M. Razin (Eds.), *Effective psychotherapy: A handbook of research,* pp. 566–589. New York: Pergamon.

Orlinsky, D. & Howard, K. E. (1980). Gender and psychotherapeutic outcome. In A. M. Brodsky & R. T. Hare-Mustin (Eds.), *Women in psychotherapy,* pp. 3–34. New York: Guilford.

Panksepp, J. (1999a). Drives, affects, id energies, and the neuroscience of emotions: Response to the commentaries by Jaak Panksepp. *Neuro-Psychoanalysis, 1,* 69–89.

Panksepp, J. (1999b). Emotions as viewed by psychoanalysis and neuroscience: An exercise in consilience. *Neuro-Psychoanalysis, 1,* 15–38.

Panksepp, J. (2001). The long-term psychological consequences of infant emotions: Prescriptions for the twenty-first century. *Neuro-Psychoanalysis, 3,* 149–178.

Panksepp, J. (2005). Commentary on "Integrating the Psychoanalytic and Neurobiological Views of Panic Disorder." *Neuro-Psychoanalysis, 7,* 145–150.

Parens, H., Pollock, L., Stern, J., & Kramer, S. (1977). On the girl's entry into the Oedipus Complex. In H. Blum (Ed.), *Female psychology: Contemporary psychoanalytic views*, pp. 79–107. Oxford: International Universities Press.

Perry, J. C. (1988). A prospective study of life stress, defenses, psychotic symptoms, and borderline and antisocial personality disorders and bipolar II type affect. *Journal of Personality Disorders, 2,* 49–51.

Perry, J. C. (2001). A pilot study of defenses in adults with personality disorders entering psychotherapy. *Journal of Nervous and Mental Disease, 189,* 651–660.

Pfeffer, A. Z. (1959). A procedure for evaluating the results of psychoanalysis: A preliminary report. *Journal of the American Psychoanalytic Association, 7,* 418–444.

Pfeffer, A. Z. (1961). Follow-up study of a satisfactory analysis. *Journal of the American Psychoanalytic Association, 9,* 698–718.

Pfeffer, A. Z. (1963). The meaning of the analyst after analysis: A contribution to the theory of therapeutic results. *Journal of the American Psychoanalytic Association, 11,* 229–244.

Piaget, J. (1954). *The construction of reality in the child.* New York: Basic Books.

Piaget, J. (1990). *The child's conception of the world.* New York: Littlefield Adams.

Pine, F. (1990). *Drive, ego, object, self: A synthesis for clinical work.* New York: Basic Books.

Pine, F. (1998). *Diversity and direction in psychoanalytic technique.* New Haven, CT: Yale University Press.

Piper, W. E., Azim, H. F., Joyce, A. S., & McCallum, M. (1991a). Quality of object relations versus interpersonal functioning as predictors of therapeutic alliance and psychotherapy outcome. *Journal of Nervous and Mental Disease, 179,* 432–438.

Piper, W. E., Azim, H. F., Joyce, A. S., & McCallum, M. (1991b). Transference interpretations, therapeutic alliance, and outcome in short-term individual psychotherapy. *Archives of General Psychiatry, 48,* 946–953.

Piper, W. E. & Duncan, S. C. (1999). Object relations theory and short-term dynamic psychotherapy: Findings from the Quality of Object Relations Scale. *Clinical Psychology Review, 19,* 669–685.

Piper, W. E., Joyce, A. S., McCallum, M., & Azim, H. F. (1998). Interpretive and supportive forms of psychotherapy and patient personality variables. *Journal of Consulting and Clinical Psychology, 66,* 558–567.

Piper, W. E., McCallum, M., Joyce, A. S., Azim, H. F., & Ogrodniczuk, J. S. (1999). Follow-up findings for interpretive and supportive forms of psychotherapy and patient personality variables. *Journal of Consulting and Clinical Psychology, 67,* 267–273.

Plomin, R. & Caspi, A. (1999). Behavioral genetics and personality. In L. A. Pervin & O. P. John (Eds.), *Handbook of personality* (2nd ed.), pp. 251–276. New York: Guilford.

Porcerelli, J. H., Dauphin, V. B., Ablon, J. S., Leitman, S., & Bambery, M. (2007). Psychoanalysis with avoidant personality disorder: A systematic case study. *Psychotherapy: Theory/Research/Practice/Training, 44,* 1–13.

Psychodynamic Diagnostic Manual (*PDM*) Task Force (2006). *Psychodynamic diagnostic manual.* Silver Spring, MD: Alliance of Psychoanalytic Organizations.

Pulver, S. E. (1992). Psychic change: Insight or relationship? *International Journal of Psychoanalysis, 73,* 199–208.

Puschner, B., Kraft, S., Kachele, H., & Kordy, H. (2007). Course of improvement over 2 years in psychoanalytic and psychodynamic outpatient psychotherapy. *Psychology and Psychotherapy: Theory, Research, and Practice, 80,* 51–68.

Racker, H. (1968). *Transference and countertransference.* Madison, CT: International Universities Press.

Raine, A., Park, S., Lencz, T., Bihrle, S. Lacasse, L., Widom, C. et al. (2001). Reduced right hemisphere activation in severely abused violent offenders during a working memory task: An fMRI study. *Aggressive Behavior, 27,* 111–129.

Rangell, L. (1974). A psychoanalytic perspective leading currently to the syndrome of the compromise of integrity. *International Journal of Psychoanalysis, 55,* 3–12.

Rangell, L. (1981). Psychoanalysis and dynamic psychotherapy: Similarities and differences twenty-five years later. *Psychoanalytic Quarterly, 50,* 665–693.

Rangell, L. (1982). The self in psychoanalytic theory. *Journal of the American Psychoanalytic Association, 30,* 863–891.

Rangell, L. (1988). The future of psychoanalysis: The scientific crossroads. *Psychoanalytic Quarterly, 59,* 347–369.

Reich, W. (1933). *Character analysis.* New York: Noonday Press.

Reich, W. (1949). *Character analysis.* New York: Farrar, Straus, & Giroux.

Reich, W. (1972). *Character analysis.* New York: Farrar, Straus, & Giroux. (Original manuscript published 1933)

Reiser, M. F. (1984). *Mind, brain, body: Toward a convergence of psychoanalysis and neurobiology.* New York: Basic Books.

Reiser, M. F. (1990). *Memory in mind and brain: What dream imagery reveals.* New York: Basic Books.

Reiser, M. F. (1996). Relationship of psychoanalysis to neuroscience. In E. Nersessian & R. G. Kopff, Jr. (Eds.), *Textbook of psychoanalysis,* pp. 605–633. Washington, DC: American Psychiatric Press.

Robins, R. W., Gosling, S. D., & Craik, K. H. (1999). An empirical analysis of trends in psychology. *American Psychologist, 55,* 117–128.

Roediger, H. L. (1996). Memory illusions. *Journal of Memory and Language, 35,* 76–100.

Roediger, H. L. & Geraci, L. (2003). Implicit memory. In J. W. Guthrie (Ed.), *Encyclopedia of Education* (2nd ed.,Vol. 5), pp. 1596–1600. New York: MacMillan.

Roediger, H. L. & McDermott, K. B. (1993). Implicit memory in normal human subjects. In F. Boller & J. Grafman (Eds.), *Handbook of Neuropsychology* (Vol. 8), pp. 63–131. Amsterdam: Elsevier.

Roediger, H. L. & McDermott, K. B. (2000). Tricks of memory. *Current Directions in Psychological Science, 9,* 123–127.

Rosenberger, E. W. & Hayes, J. A. (2002). Therapist as subject: A review of the empirical countertransference literature. *Journal of Counseling and Development, 80,* 264–270.

Roughton, R. (2002). Rethinking sexuality: What it teaches us about psychoanalysis. *Journal of the American Psychoanalytic Association, 50,* 733–763.

Rumelhart, D. E., McClelland, J. L., & the PDP Research Group (1986). Parallel distributed processing: *Explorations in the microstructure of cognition* (Vol. 1). Cambridge, MA: Massachusetts Institute of Technology Press.

Rutter, M., Moffitt, T. E., & Caspi, A. (2006). Gene-environment interplay and psychopathology: Multiple varieties but real effects. *Journal of Child Psychology and Psychiatry, 47,* 226–261.

Ryder, A. G., Schuller, D. R., & Bagby, R. M. (2006). Depressive personality disorder and dysthymia: Evaluating symptom and syndrome overlap. *Journal of Affective Disorders, 91,* 217–227.

Safran, J. D., Muran, J. C., & Samstag, L. W. (1994) Resolving therapeutic alliance ruptures: A task analytic investigation. In A. O. Horvath & L. S. Greenberg (Eds.), *The working alliance: Theory, research and practice,* pp. 38–50. New York: Wiley.

Sandell, R., Blomberg, J., & Lazar, A. (2002). Time matters: On temporal interactions in long-term follow-up of long-term psychotherapies. *Psychotherapy Research, 12,* 39–58.

Sandell, R., Blomberg, J., Lazar, A., Carlsson, J., Broberg, J., & Schubert, J. (2000). Varieties of long-term outcome among patients in psychoanalysis and long-term psychotherapy: A review of findings in the Stockholm Outcome of Psychoanalysis and Psychotherapy Project (STOPP). *International Journal of Psychoanalysis, 81,* 921–942.

Sandler, J. (1976). Dreams, unconscious fantasies and "identity perception." *International Review of Psychoanalysis, 3,* 43–47.

Sandler, J. & Rosenblatt, B. (1962). The concept of the representational world. *Psychoanalytic Study of the Child, 17,* 128–145.

Sandler, J. & Sandler, A. M. (1984). The past unconscious, the present unconscious and interpretation of the transference. *Psychoanalytic Inquiry, 4,* 367–399.

Sandler, J. & Sandler, A. M. (1988). Reality and the stabilizing function of unconscious fantasy. *Bulletin of the Anna Freud Centre, 9,* 177–192.

Sandler, J. & Sandler, A. M. (1994). The past unconscious and the present unconscious: A contribution to a technical frame of reference. *Psychoanalytic Study of the Child, 49,* 278–292.

Schacter, D. L. (1987). Implicit memory: History and current status. *Journal of Experimental Psychology: Learning, Memory, and Cognition, 13,* 501–518.

Schacter, D. L. & Tulving, E. (Eds.) (1994). *Memory systems.* London: Massachusetts Institute of Technology Press.

Schafer, R. (1968). *Aspects of internalization.* New York: International Universities Press.

Schafer, R. (1976). *A new language for psychoanalysis.* New Haven, CT: Yale University Press.

Schafer, R. (1992). *Retelling a life.* New York: Basic Books.

Schlessinger, N. & Robbins, F. P. (1974). Assessment and follow-up in psychoanalysis. *Journal of the American Psychoanalytic Association, 22,* 542–567.

Schlessinger, N. & Robbins, F. P. (1975). The psychoanalytic process: Recurrent patterns of conflict and changes in ego functions. *Journal of the American Psychoanalytic Association, 23,* 761–782.

Schlessinger, N. & Robbins, F. P. (1983). *A developmental view of the psychoanalytic process: Follow-up studies and their consequences.* New York: International Universities Press.

Schneider, K. (1958). *Psychopathic personalities.* London: Cassell.

Schore, A. N. (1994). *Affect regulation and the origin of the self: The neurobiology of emotional development.* Mahwah, NJ: Erlbaum.

Schore, A. N. (2000). Attachment and the regulation of the right brain. *Attachment & Human Development, 2,* 23–47.

Schore, A. N. (2002). Advances in neuropsychoanalysis, attachment theory, and trauma research: Implications for self psychology. *Psychoanalytic Inquiry, 22,* 433–484.

Seligman, M. E. P. (1995). The effectiveness of psychotherapy: The *Consumer Reports* study. *American Psychologist, 50,* 965–974.

Shaffer, T. W. (2001). *An ego functions model for the organization of test data. Revision 3.1* Fresno, CA: Haverford Press.

Shane, M. (1995). *Resistance from a contemporary developmental perspective.* Oral presentation at the Michigan Psychoanalytic Symposium on Resistance and Analysis and the Clinical Setting: Current Controversies. Ann Arbor, MI.

Shapiro, D. (1965). *Neurotic styles*. New York: Basic Books.

Shapiro, D. (1981). *Autonomy and rigid character*. New York: Basic Books.

Shapiro, D. A., Barkham, M., Stiles, W. B., Hardy, G. E., Rees, A., Reynolds, S. et al. (2003). Time is of the essence: A selective review of the fall and rise of brief therapy research. *Psychology and Psychotherapy, 76,* 211–235.

Shapiro, D. A., Firth-Cozens, J., & Stiles, W. B. (1989). The question of therapists' differential effectiveness: A Sheffield psychotherapy project addendum. *British Journal of Psychiatry, 154,* 383–385.

Shapiro, D. A. & Shapiro, D. (1982). Meta-analysis of comparative therapy outcome studies: A republication and refinement. *Psychological Bulletin, 92,* 581–604.

Shaver, P. R. & Clark, C. L. (1994). The psychodynamics of adult romantic attachment. In J. M. Masling & R. F. Bornstein (Eds.), *Empirical perspectives on object relations theory* (Vol. 5), pp. 105–156. Washington, DC: American Psychological Association.

Shedler, J. & Westen, D. (2004a). Refining personality disorder diagnosis: Integrating science and practice. *American Journal of Psychiatry, 161,* 1350–1365.

Shedler, J. & Westen, D. (2004b). Dimensions of personality pathology: An alternative to the Five-Factor Model. *American Journal of Psychiatry, 161,* 1743–1754.

Shedler, J. & Westen, D. (2006). Personality diagnosis with the Shedler-Westen Assesment Procedure (SWAP): Bridging the gulf between science and practice. In Alliance of Psychoanalytic Organizations (Ed.), *Psychodynamic diagnostic manual (PDM),* pp. 663–690. Silver Spring, MD: Alliance of Psychoanalytic Organizations.

Shevrin, H. (1973). Brain wave correlates of subliminal stimulation, unconscious attention, primary- and secondary-process thinking and repressiveness. *Psychological Issues, 30,* 56–87.

Shevrin, H. (1978). Evoked potential evidence for unconscious mental processes: A review of the literature. In A. S. Prangishvilli, A. E. Sherozia, & F. V. Bassin (Eds.), *The unconscious: Nature, functions, methods of study.* Tbilisi, USSR: Metsnjereba.

Shevrin, H. (1986). Subliminal perception and dreaming. *Journal of Mind and Behavior, 7,* 379–395.

Shevrin, H. (1988). Unconscious conflict: A convergent psychodynamic and electrophysiological approach. In M. J. Horowitz (Ed.), *Psychodynamics and cognition,* pp. 117–167. Chicago, IL: University of Chicago Press.

Shevrin, H. (1990). Subliminal perception and repression. In J. L Singer (Ed.), *Repression and dissociation: Implications for personality theory, psychopathology, and health,* pp. 103–119. Chicago, IL: University of Chicago Press.

Shevrin, H. (1992). The Freudian unconscious and the cognitive unconscious: Identical or fraternal twins. In J. W. Barron, M. N. Eagle, & D. L. Wolitzky (Eds.), *Interface of psychoanalysis and psychology*, pp. 313–326. Washington, DC: American Psychological Association.

Shevrin, H. (1996). Psychoanalytic research: Experimental evidence in support of basic psychoanalytic assumptions. In E. Nersessian & R. G. Kopff, Jr. (Eds.), *Textbook of psychoanalysis*, pp. 575–603. Washington, DC: American Psychiatric Press.

Shevrin, H. (2002). A psychoanalytic view of memory in light of recent cognitive and neuroscience research. *Neuro-Psychoanalysis, 4*, 131–139.

Shevrin, H. (2006). The contribution of cognitive behavioral and neurophysiological frames of reference to a psychodynamic nosology of mental illness. In Alliance of Psychoanalytic Organizations, *Psychodynamic diagnostic manual (PDM)*, pp. 483–509. Silver Spring, MD: Alliance of Psychoanalytic Organizations.

Shevrin, H., Bond, J., Brakel, L., Hertel, R., & Williams, W. J. (1996). *Conscious and unconscious processes: Psychodynamic, cognitive, and neurophysiological convergences*. New York: Guilford.

Shevrin, H. & Dickman, S. (1980). The psychological unconscious: A necessary assumption for all psychological theory? *American Psychologist, 35*, 421–434.

Shevrin, H. & Fisher, C. (1967). Changes in the effects of a waking subliminal stimulus as a functioning of dreaming and non-dreaming sleep. *Journal of Abnormal Psychology, 72*, 362–368.

Shevrin, H., Williams, W. J., Marshall, R. E., Hertel, R. K., Bond, J. A., & Brakel, L. A. W. (1992). Event-related potential indicators of the dynamic unconscious. *Consciousness and Cognition, 1*, 340–366.

Sifneos, P. E. (1978). Motivation for change: A prognostic guide for successful psychotherapy. *Psychotherapy and Psychosomatics, 29*, 293–298.

Sifneos, P. E. (1992). *Short-term anxiety-provoking psychotherapy*. New York: Basic Books.

Silverman, L. S. (1983). The psychodynamic activation method: Overview and comprehensive listing of studies. In J. Masling (Ed.), *Empirical studies of psychoanalytic theories* (Vol. 1), pp. 69–100. Hillsdale, NJ: Erlbaum.

Silverman, D. K. (1986). Some proposed modif dations of psychoanalytic theories of early child development. In J. Masling, (Ed.), *Empirical studies of psychoanalytic theories*, pp. 49–72. Hillsdale, NJ: Erlbaum.

Silverman, L. H., Bronstein, A., & Mendelsohn, E. (1976). The further use of psychodynamic activation method for experimental study of the clinical theory of psychoanalysis: On the specificity of the relationships between symptoms and unconscious conflicts. *Psychotherapy: Theory, Research, and Practice, 13*, 2–16.

Silverman, L. H., Kwawer, J. S., Wolitzky, C., & Coron, M. (1973). An experimental study of aspects of the psychoanalytic theory of male homosexuality. *Journal of Abnormal Psychology, 82*, 178–188.

Silverman, L. H., Lachman, F. M., & Milich, R. H. (1982). *The search for oneness.* New York: International Universities Press.

Silverman, L. H., Ross, D. L., Adler, J. M., & Lustig, D. A. (1978). Simple research paradigm for demonstrating subliminal activation effects: Effects of Oedipal stimuli on dart-throwing accuracy in college males. *Journal of Abnormal Psychology, 87,* 341–347.

Singer, J. A. & Singer, J. L. (1992). Transference in psychotherapy and daily life: Implications of current memory and social cognition research. In J. W. Barron, M. N. Eagle, & D. L. Wolitzky (Eds.), *Interface of psychoanalysis and psychology,* pp. 516–538. Washington, DC: American Psychological Association.

Smith, E. R. (1998). Mental representation and memory. In D. T. Gilbert, S. T. Fiske, & G. Lindzey (Eds.), *Handbook of social psychology,* pp. 391–445. New York: McGraw Hill.

Smith, M. L., Glass, G. V., & Miller, T. I. (1980). *The benefits of psychotherapy.* Baltimore, MD: Johns Hopkins University press.

Socarides, C. W. (2002). *Advances in the psychoanalytic theory and therapy of male homosexuality.* Madison, CT: International Universities Press.

Socarides, C. W. & Volkan, V. D. (1991). *The homosexualities and the therapeutic process.* Madison, CT: International Universities Press.

Solms, M. (2000a). A psychoanalytic contribution to contemporary neuroscience. In G. van de Vijver & F. Geerardyn (Eds.), *The pre-psychoanalytic writings of Sigmund Freud*, pp. 17–35. London: Karnac Books.

Solms, M. (2000b). Preliminaries for an integration of psychoanalysis and neuroscience. *Annals of Psychoanalysis, 28,* 179–200.

Solms, M. (2001). The interpretation of dreams and the neurosciences. *Psychoanalytic History, 3,* 79–91.

Solms, M. (2002). An introduction to the neuroscientific works of Sigmund Freud. In M. Velmans (Ed.), *Investigating phenomenal consciousness: New methodologies and maps.* Advances in Consciousness Research Series (M. Stamenov, Series Ed.), pp. 67–95. Amsterdam: John Benjamins Publishing.

Solms, M. (2004). Is the brain more real than the mind? In A. Casement (Ed.), *Who owns psychoanalysis?,* pp. 323–324. London: Karnac.

Spence, D. P. (1982). *Narrative truth and historical meaning: Meaning and interpretation in psychoanalysis.* New York: Norton.

Spence, D. P. (1992). Interpretation: A critical perspective. In J. W. Barron, M. N. Eagle, & D. L. Wolitzky (Eds.), *Interface of psychoanalysis and psychotherapy,* pp. 558–572. Washington, DC: American Psychological Association.

Spitz, R. A. (1945). Hospitalism: An inquiry into the genesis of psychiatric conditions in early childhood. *Psychoanalytic Study of the Child, 1,* 53–74.

Spitz, R. A. (1946a). Anaclitic depression. *Psychoanalytic Study of the Child, 2,* 313–342.

Spitz, R. A. (1946b). Hospitalism: a follow-up report. *Psychoanalytic Study of the Child, 2,* 113–118.

Spitzer, R. L. (1983). Psychiatric diagnosis: Are clinicians still necessary? *Comprehensive Psychiatry, 24,* 399–411.

Squire, L. (1986). Mechanisms of memory. *Science, 232,* 1612–1619.

Squire, L. (1992). Declarative and nondeclarative memory: Multiple brain systems supporting learning and memory. *Journal of Cognitive Neuroscience, 4,* 232–243.

Sterba, R. (1934). The fate of the ego in analytic therapy. *International Journal of Psychoanalysis, 15,* 115–126.

Stern, D. N., Sander, L. W., Nahum, J. P., Harrison, A. M., Lyons-Ruth, K., Morgan, A. C. et al. (1998). Non-interpretive mechanisms in psychoanalytic psychotherapy. *International Journal of Psychoanalysis, 79,* 903–921.

Stoller, R. (1972). The "bedrock" of masculinity and femininity: Bisexuality. *Archives of General Psychiatry, 26,* 207–212.

Stolorow, R. D., Atwood, G. E., & Brandchaft, B. (1994). *The intersubjective perspective.* Northvale, NJ: Aronson.

Strachey, J. (1934). The nature of the therapeutic action of psycho-analysis. *International Journal of Psychoanalysis, 15,* 127–159.

Stricker, G. & Healey, B. J. (1990). Projective assessment of object relations: A review of the empirical literature. *Psychological Assessment, 2,* 219–230.

Strupp, H. H. & Binder, J. L. (1984). *Psychotherapy in a new key: A guide to time-limited dynamic psychotherapy.* New York: Basic Books.

Sullivan, H. S. (1953). *The interpersonal theory of psychiatry.* New York: Norton.

Sutherland, J. D. (1980). The British object relations theorists: Balint, Winnicott, Fairbairn, Guntrip. *Journal of the American Psychoanalytic Association, 28,* 829–860.

Task Force on Promotion and Dissemination of Psychological Procedures (1995). Training in and dissemination of empirically validated psychological treatments: Report and recommendations. *Clinical Psychologist, 48,* 3–23.

Task Force on Psychological Intervention Guidelines (1995). *Template for developing guidelines: Interventions for mental disorders and psychosocial aspects of physical disorders.* Washington, DC: American Psychological Association.

Tellegen, A., Lykken, D. T., Bouchard, T. J., Jr., Wilcox, K. J., Segal, N., & Rich, S. (1988). Personality similarity in twins reared apart and together. *Journal of Personality and Social Psychology, 54,* 1031–1039.

Thackrey, M., Butler, S. F., & Strupp, H. H. (1993). The Capacity for Dynamic Process Scale (CDPS). In M. L. Canfield & J. E. Canfield (Eds.), *A collection of psychological scales*, pp. 57–63. Bartlesville, OK: Research, Evaluation & Statistics.

Thompson, C. M. (1964). *Interpersonal psychoanalysis.* New York: Basic Books.

Thompson-Brenner, H., Glass, S., & Westen, D. (2003). A multidimensional meta-analysis of psychotherapy for bulimia nervosa. *Clinical Psychology: Science and Practice, 10,* 269–287.

Tomkins, S. S. (1979). Script theory. In H. E. Howe & R. A. Dienstbeir (Eds.), *Nebraska Symposium on Motivation* (Vol. 26, pp. 306–329). Lincoln: University of Nebraska Press.

Treisman, A. M. (1969). Strategies and models of selective attention. *Psychological Review, 76,* 282–299.

Trimboli, F. & Farr, K. L. (2000). A psychoanalytic guide for essential treatment planning. *Psychoanalytic Psychology, 17,* 336–359.

Tulving, E. (1983). *Elements of episodic memory.* Oxford, England: Clarendon Press.

Tyson, P. (1982). A developmental line of gender identity, gender role, and choice of love object. *Journal of the American Psychoanalytic Association, 30,* 61–86.

Urist, J. (1977). The Rorschach test and the assessment of object relations. *Journal of Personality Assessment, 41,* 3–9.

Urist, J. & Shill, M. (1982). Validity of the Rorschach Mutuality of Autonomy Scales: A replication using excerpted responses. *Journal of Personality Assessment, 46,* 450–454.

Vaillant, G. (1985). An empirically derived hierarchy of adaptive mechanisms and its usefulness as a potential diagnostic axis. *Acta Psychiatrica Scandinavia, 71,* 171–180.

Vaillant, G. (1992). The beginning of wisdom is never calling a patient borderline: Or the clinical management of immature defenses in the treatment of individuals with personality disorders. *Journal of Psychotherapy Practice & Research, 1,* 117–134.

Vaillant, G. (1994). Ego mechanisms of defense and personality psychopathology. *Journal of Abnormal Psychology, 103,* 44–50.

Van Wagoner, S., Gelso, C. J., Hayes, J. A., & Diemer, R. (1991). Countertransference and the reputedly excellent therapist. *Psychotherapy, 28,* 411–421.

Viglione, D. J., Jr. & Hilsenroth, M. J. (2001). The Rorschach: Facts, fictions, and future. *Psychological Assessment, 13,* 452–471.

Waelder, R. (1936). The principle of multiple function. *Psychoanalytic Quarterly, 5,* 45–62.

Wachtel, P. (1977). *Psychoanalysis, behavior therapy, and the relational world.* Washington, DC: American Psychological Association Press.

Wachtel, P. (1987). *Action and insight.* New York: Guilford.

Wallerstein, R. S. (1986). *Forty-two lives in treatment: A study of psychoanalysis and psychotherapy.* New York: Guilford.

Wallerstein, R. S. (1988). Psychoanalysis and psychotherapy: Relative roles reconsidered. *Annual of Psychoanalysis, 16,* 129–151.

Wallerstein, R. S. (1989). Psychoanalysis and psychotherapy: An historical perspective. *International Journal of Psychoanalysis, 70,* 563–591.

Wallerstein, R. S. (2001). The generations of psychotherapy research: An overview *Psychoanalytic Psychology, 18,* 243–267.

Wallerstein, R. S. (2002). The growth and transformation of American ego psychology. *Journal of the American Psychoanalytic Association, 50,* 135–169.

Wallerstein, R. S. (2006). Psychoanalytic therapy research: Its history, its present status, and its projected future. In *PDM* Task Force, *Psychodynamic diagnostic manual,* pp. 511–535. Silver Spring, MD: Alliance of Psychoanalytic Organizations.

Wampold, B. E. (2001). *The great psychotherapy debate: Models, methods, and findings.* Mahwah, NJ: Erlbaum.

Wampold, B. E., Mondin, G. W., Moody, M., Stich, F., Benson, K., & Ahn, H. (1997). A meta-analysis of outcome studies comparing bona fide psychotherapies: Empirically, "all must have prizes." *Psychological Bulletin, 122,* 203–215.

Waters, E., Merrick, S., Treboux, D., Crowell, J., & Albersheim, K. (2000). Attachment security in infancy and early adulthood: A twenty-year longitudinal study. *Child Development, 71,* 684–689.

Weinberger, J. & Hardaway, R. (1990). Separating science from myth in subliminal psychodynamic activation. *Clinical Psychology Review, 10,* 727–756.

Weiner, I. B. (1998). *Principles of psychotherapy.* New York: Wiley.

Weinryb, R. M., Rossel, R. J., & Asberg, M. (1991). The Karolinska Psychodynamic Profile: I. Validity and dimensionality. II. Interdisciplinary and cross-cultural reliability. *Acta Psychiatrica Scandinavia, 83,* 64–76.

Weiss, J. & Sampson, H. (1986). *The psychoanalytic process: Theory, clinical observation, and empirical research.* New York: Guilford.

Werner, H. (1948). *Comparative psychology of mental development.* New York: International Universities Press.

Westen, D. (1992). Social cognition and social affect in psychoanalysis and cognitive science: From analysis of regression to regression analysis. In J. W. Barron, M. N. Eagle, & D. L. Wolitzky, (Eds.), *The interface of psychoanalysis and psychology*, pp. 375–388. Washington, DC: American Psychological Association.

Westen, D. (1993). *The Social Cognition and Object Relations Scale: Q-sort for Projective Stories.* Unpublished manuscript, Harvard University Medical School, Cambridge, MA.

Westen, D. (1995). *SCORS-Q for projective stories: Addendum.* Unpublished manuscript, Harvard University Medical School, Cambridge, MA.

Westen, D. (1998). The scientific legacy of Sigmund Freud: Toward a psychodynamically informed psychological science. *Psychological Bulletin, 124,* 333–371.

Westen, D. (1999). The scientific status of unconscious processes: Is Freud really dead? *Journal of the American Psychoanalytic Association, 47,* 1061–1106.

Westen, D. (2000). Integrative psychotherapy: Integrating psychodynamic and cognitive-behavioral theory and technique. In C. R. Synder & R. E. Ingram, (Eds.), *Handbook of psychological change: Psychotherapy processes and practices for the 21st century*, pp. 217–242. Hoboken, NJ: Wiley.

Westen, D. & Gabbard, G. O. (2002a). Developments in cognitive neuroscience: I. Conflict, compromise, and connectionism. *Journal of the American Psychoanalytic Association, 50,* 53–98.

Westen, D. & Gabbard, G. O. (2002b). Developments in cognitive neuroscience: II. Implications for theories of transference. *Journal of the American Psychoanalytic Association, 50,* 99–134.

Westen, D., Gabbard, G. O., & Blagov, P. (2006). Back to the future: Personality structure as a context for psychopathology. In R. F. Krueger & J. L. Tackett (Eds.), *Personality and psychopathology: Building bridges*, pp. 335–384. New York: Guilford.

Westen, D. & Morrison, K. (2001). A multidimensional meta-analysis of treatments for depression, panic, and generalized anxiety disorder: An empirical examination of the status of empirically supported therapies. *Journal of Consulting and Clinical Psychology, 69,* 875–899.

Westen, D., Novotny, C. M., & Thompson-Brenner, H. (2004). The empirical status of empirically supported psychotherapies: Assumptions, findings, and reporting in controlled clinical trials. *Psychological Bulletin, 130,* 633–663.

Westen, D. & Shedler, J. (1999a). Revising and assessing Axis II, Part I: Developing a clinically and empirically valid assessment method. *American Journal of Psychiatry, 156,* 258–272.

Westen, D. & Shedler, J. (1999b). Revising and assessing Axis II, Part II: Toward an empirically based and clinically useful classification of personality disorders. *American Journal of Psychiatry, 156,* 273–285.

Widiger, T. A., Simonsen, E., Krueger, R., Livesley, W. J., & Verheul, R. (2005). Personality disorder research agenda for the DSM-V. *Journal of Personality Disorders, 19,* 315–338.

Williams, E. N., Judge, A. B., Hill, C. E., & Hoffman, M. A. (1997). Experiences of novice therapists in prepracticum: Trainees', clients', and supervisors' perceptions of therapists' personal reactions and management of strategies. *Journal of Counseling Psychology, 44,* 390–399.

Wink, P. (1991). Two faces of narcissism. *Journal of Personality and Social Psychology, 61,* 590–597.

Winnicott, D. W. (1965). *The maturational process and the facilitating environment.* New York: International Universities Press.

Winnicott, D. W. (1971). *Playing and reality.* London: Tavistock.

Wood, J. M., Nezworski, M. T., Garb, H. N., & Lilienfeld, S. (2001). The misperception of psychopathology: Problems with the norms of the Comprehensive System of the Rorschach. *Clinical Psychology: Science and Practice,* 8, 350–373.

World Health Organization (WHO) (1990). *International Classification of Diseases* (10th ed.). Geneva: Author.

Zetzel, E. (1956). Current concepts of transference. *International Journal of Psychoanalysis, 37,* 369–376.

Zimmerman, M. (1994). Diagnosing personality disorders: A review of issues and research methods. *Archives of General Psychiatry, 51,* 225–245.

Index

www.ingramcontent.com/pod-product-compliance
Lightning Source LLC
LaVergne TN
LVHW011119300926
849160LV00008B/438
9780805864014